MAN'S PRESU

An Evolutionary Interpretation
of Psychosomatic Disease

A. T. W. SIMEONS, M.D. was born in London and graduated in medicine (*summa cum laude*) from the University of Heidelberg. After post-graduate studies in Germany and Switzerland he was appointed to a large hospital near Dresden. Later he became engrossed in the study of tropical diseases and joined the School of Tropical Medicine in Hamburg. In 1931 Dr. Simeons went to India and stayed for eighteen years. He discovered the use of injectable atebrin for malaria (for which he was awarded a Red Cross Order of Merit) and also a new method of staining malaria parasites, which is now known as "Simeons' stain." During the War he held several important posts under the Government of India and conducted extensive research on bubonic plague and leprosy control, and a model leper colony which he built has now become an all-India center. It was during these years that his interest in psychosomatic diseases began to grow. In 1949 Dr. Simeons left India and went to Rome, where he now works on psychosomatic disorders at the Salvator Mundi International Hospital. He is the author of several medical books and has contributed to many scientific publications.

MAN'S PRESUMPTUOUS BRAIN was first published in 1961.

MAN'S PRESUMPTUOUS BRAIN

*An Evolutionary Interpretation
of Psychosomatic Disease*

BY A. T. W. SIMEONS, M.D.

With a Foreword by Joost A. M. Meerloo, M.D.

A Dutton  *Paperback*

NEW YORK

E. P. DUTTON

TO MY WIFE

ACKNOWLEDGEMENTS

My thanks are due to Martha Gellhorn for insisting that ideas conceived in the shorthand of medical jargon be presented in a form intelligible to non-medical readers; to her husband T. S. Matthews, who protected me from her unbending literary severity and pointed out a number of weaknesses in earlier drafts.

I wish to thank Dr. Kenneth Oakley, D.S.C., F.B.A., of the British Museum (Natural History), for his invaluable paleo-anthropological advice in writing the first three chapters, his interest and his many important suggestions.

Medical colleagues, too numerous to be thanked individually, have given me an opportunity of discussing my views against their superior specialized knowledge. Many of them were unable to agree with me; yet they all encouraged me to publish my ideas as a basis for further discussion, and for this I am grateful to them.

I am deeply indebted to my psychiatric collaborator Dr. Anna Bisogni, who in years of clinical trials, observations and deductions has helped the ideas here presented to mature and expand.

I finally thank Margaret Lucas for her help in preparing the typescript.

A.T.W.S.

FOREWORD

WHEN AN author sets out to write a book, he has the choice between various ways in which to capture and hold the interest of inquisitive readers. He can follow the straight scientific method, spreading the observable facts thinly and in the end saying more and more about less and less. He can also express himself in the ancient mystic way of saying a few wise aphorisms and virtually nothing about the essence of everything. But a new way of communicating is growing, in which both clarity and universality, wisdom and fact, are tied together. Such an attempt at synthesis has to combine the ripe insight of science with the expressivity of the arts. It has to create a new and broad intelligible language, free of obscure "scientific" jargon. These new forms of writing aim at reaching the minds of those not as yet steeped in detached terminology and thirsting for greater understanding.

That is why books on scientific subjects written for the general public—often abusively labeled "popular"—have to search for the synthesis of the style of specialists and a rather simply-worded universality. An author possessing this rare creative gift can clear up the dim confusion of the old type of compartmentalizing knowledge.

Simeons' book, MAN'S PRESUMPTUOUS BRAIN, should be read in the first place as an example of this new form of integrated science. With impressive originality the author reaches far beyond horizons which were sometimes already better explored by professional friends, but whose sophisticated adventures are hidden beyond reach in forbidding scientific folios.

When I first started Simeons' book I found myself challenging minor details about which I prided myself I knew a bit more than the author. But then I became aware that a general simplicity of expression, combined with a total insight, is more important and infinitely more valuable than a squabble over minor details, and my attitude changed into one of appreciation. The further I read, the more I enjoyed the author's probing of "man's presumptuous brain."

Dr. Simeons is a general practitioner with a deep interest and great involvement in man and mankind. He has gathered vast medical knowledge in travels all over the world. His experiences with surgery and tropical medicine, and especially with the social aspects of the art of healing, have aroused in him a keen zest to study the psychosomatic aspects of man suffering under the burden of his peculiar civilization.

In observing the strange evolution of man, so different from the development of other animals, the author finds the explanation for that mysterious interrelation between body and mind. Psychosomatic disorders arise from the unnecessary and unequal struggle between man's ancient drives and human goals. Something went awry in the evolution of the central management of his reactions. The impact of culture on the brain-body unit made the organism more vulnerable.

This theory is not new. We recognize in it Freud's crusade against repression and frustration and the anatomist Bolk's thoughts about foetalized man. But Simeons has integrated these thoughts and made them more lucid. The author describes how the brain of human animals in the pre-culture period of evolution was well adapted to its environment. It served adequately to master the dangers of the world. But man is born like a monkey foetus, naked and unprotected, with a freakish brain, an overgrown computer, far too advanced for its body. Such a presumptuous brain gradually leads to an overgrown censorship. Man, the helpless baby—but born with strange human means of adaptation: his long youth, his instrumental hands, and his erect inquisitive posture—begins at the dawn of culture to build a new artificial environment which makes many of his animal reflexes nearly obsolete.

In the second part of the book the author explains man's psychosomatic ailments more specifically as a conflict between his brazen brain and his body. Although various assumptions need further testing, the solutions the author suggests are clear. He mentions that man's cerebral cortical habits make him jump to conclusions too readily and that nobody can escape this weird explanation-mania. Behind Simeons' often new speculations we detect a rich clinical experience.

The final part of the book observes man as the pusillanimous creator of artificial defenses. Those who are unfit for rugged wild life and its continuous battle for survival have to learn to assert themselves through a cultural elaboration of their weaknesses. Man's civilization is an artifact, the perfection of an artificial means of escape. Man neglects his midbrain and the direct instinctual functions there localized and manages to adjust the world to his body rather than following the original biological way of adaptation to environment. Under the compulsive stress of traditional cultural habits, man has almost excluded himself from natural selection and biological adjustment.

Yet out of all this adaptive frustration, instinctual lack, and biological weakness comes forth man's creativeness as a secondary elaboration of repression and frustration. The psychologist would say: "Masochism makes man the instrument of learning and creating."

Civilized and technologized, man lives in a new state of emergency: the fear of fear and the dread of disease, substituting for his animal alertness. The antagonism between instinct and intellect, or as expressed in anatomical terms between diencephalic and cortical functions, throws man into a primeval panic. As yet, he has been unable to come to biological terms with his own overgrown brain. When this internal conflict remains unchecked, it may even lead man to psychosomatic suicide: ultimate surrender to the fear that devours him.

Man's brazen and presumptuous brain has grasped too much in too short a time. His brain cortex, as a tool with which to master the world around him intelligently, even becomes an obstacle in the comprehensive understanding of himself. The tool of research is the dilemma of all research!

Can man conquer this dilemma of using his cortex as a bumptious yet limited tool? Can he learn to think with his guts, his heart, his hands, and the wholeness of his body? This is the psychosomatic dilemma Simeons puts before us in a brilliantly written, fascinating book. It is not only a book for lay people but also a must for all those physicians who wish to overcome their scientific presumptuousness.

Joost A. M. Meerloo, M.D.

CONTENTS

DIAGRAMS

PREFACE

THIS BOOK is not a popular rendering of established scientific views or theories. In fact, most of the views expressed are contrary to current medical opinion. Normally a controversy of this kind would be conducted in the rarefied atmosphere of theoretical technicalities long before it reaches the lay reader.

One reason why this book has been written in plain language is that psychosomatic disorders are to a great extent subjective. They cannot as yet be objectively defined in clear-cut technical terms, because we do not know enough about them. The other reason for making the book intelligible to the lay reader is that diagnosis and treatment of these disorders require far more active and intelligent co-operation from the patient than any other form of disease. This co-operation can be forthcoming only if the patient can make for himself some sort of intellectually satisfying picture of what he is suffering from. Whether this picture represents the truth is for the moment beside the point.

The author hopes that his suggestions may contribute to the erection of a theoretical structure into which individual cases can be fitted. He also hopes to build a platform, albeit only a flimsy one, on which a more satisfactory patient-physician relationship and a better mutual understanding of the psychosomatic mechanism can be worked out. If this platform crumbles under the weight of clinical facts, a sturdier one must replace it, but at least a little ground will have been cleared.

From what has been said it is obvious that this book is certainly not a do-it-yourself primer. Only a qualified physician and a psychiatrist working as a team can correctly assess to what extent psychic factors are involved in a given case and only they can safely conduct the treatment of a psychosomatic disorder.

This is a very controversial and highly speculative book intended at most to give some slight bias to modern thought on the psychosomatic mechanism. In science it is usual to speculate in an extremely cautious and tentative manner. It is also customary to add as much substantiating evidence as possible by giving references to the work of others. Such pains are unavoidable when an author sets out to promulgate a new theory or doctrine. The present book has no such ambitions, its aim is only to suggest one of the ways in which a number of isolated clinical facts might be drawn together in a single working-hypothesis. It is meant to be read merely as a possible point of view.

The flow of the text will therefore not be interrupted by frequent footnotes and references. Clinical views will be expressed without the usual hedging and with more assertiveness than their hypothetical character justifies. This will at least avoid tedious reassurances of the author's scientific reserve and enhance readability.

The reader is therefore asked to agree to two conventions. First, that assertive statements be read as meaning: *Such and such a clinical fact might be tentatively interpreted as suggesting such and such a hypothetical explanation.* The second convention is that the work of others who have expressed similar or identical ideas and who have contributed relevant scientific data be taken as being acknowledged. The author in his turn will uphold no claims for the originality of his facts or his views.

A.T.W.S.

Know then thyself, presume not God to scan;
The proper study of Mankind is Man.
Plac'd on this isthmus of a middle state,
A Being darkly wise, and rudely great:
With too much knowledge for the Sceptic side,
With too much weakness for the Stoic's pride,
He hangs between; in doubt to act, or rest;
In doubt to deem himself a God, or Beast;
In doubt his Mind or Body to prefer;
Born but to die, and reas'ning but to err;
Alike in ignorance, his reason such,
Whether he thinks too little, or too much:
Chaos of Thought and Passion, all confus'd;
Still by himself abus'd, or disabus'd;
Created half to rise, and half to fall;
Great lord of all things, yet prey to all;
Sole judge of Truth, in endless Error hurl'd:
The glory, jest, and riddle of the world!

Alexander Pope
Essay on Man
Epistle II, Lines 1–18

Each of us is in himself like such a building. In the lower storeys we live with our animal needs, animal greeds, and animal passions. Woe if we neglect the first, ignore the second, and pretend to be free from the last! No matter how high we rise we must never lose sight, never cease being aware, of the animal basis of our nature. If we do, we lose the sense of things. We get vapid, vague, hypocritical, arrogant, insolent. The tall structure that we have become turns into a tower of Babel, toppling over and confounding its builder.

Bernard Berenson
Sketch for a Self-Portrait

MAN'S PRESUMPTUOUS BRAIN

An Evolutionary Interpretation
of Psychosomatic Disease

Introduction

THE BRAIN has achieved its highest evolutionary development in the human cortex, the rind or covering of the cerebral hemispheres. The cortex is the seat of perception, memory and association. The complex interplay of these faculties is what is called the human psyche. To-day the psyche is held responsible for producing a large number of bodily or somatic disorders. These disorders are grouped together under the term psychosomatic. It is only during the last twenty years or so that the psychosomatic interpretation of disease has acquired the dignity of a scientific approach. Yet even in this short period it has become clear that the modern human psyche is the cause of a vast amount of bodily suffering.

Psychosomatic ailments account for the bulk of urban man's ill-health and are the most frequent cause of his death. Man shares this kind of affliction with no other living creature. A few similar conditions can be induced artificially in some laboratory animals by gross human intervention, but a disorder strictly comparable to a psychosomatic disease never occurs in any wild animal.

Once the principle that the psyche can cause serious bodily disorders had been clearly stated, it soon became necessary to include an ever-widening variety of diseases in this category. To-day it is easier and certainly safer to say which diseases are *not* psychosomatic than to enumerate those which are; their number is growing too rapidly.

Definitely excluded from the psychosomatic group is any disease which has an exact counterpart in wild animals. Also excluded are those ailments which result directly from the intervention of well-known and well-defined foreign agencies, such as injuries, poisons or an infestation with animal parasites. Tapeworms, malaria, sleeping sickness and scabies are no more psychosomatic than lice. In the case of bacteria and viruses the situation is not quite so neat and clear. Psychic factors may play

a considerable role in permitting micro-organisms to establish
themselves in the the human body and cause disease.

An example of this is asiatic cholera. Working in the midst of
an epidemic outbreak of cholera one cannot help noticing the
strange fact that the healthy adolescent, the busy mother and
the wage-earning father are more often stricken than the very
young children and the old and decrepit. Cholera is caused by
swallowing a microbe called a vibrio and it is known that the
cholera vibrio is highly sensitive to acids. The acid that is always
present in the normal human stomach is sufficiently strong to
kill the cholera vibrio almost instantly. How then does the
vibrio overcome this acid barrier which separates it from the
small intestines where, in the alkaline contents, it can thrive
and start its murderous activity?

The answer seems to be that it cannot. Only if the normal
flow of acid in the stomach is shut off is the vibrio able to reach
its destination. Now the one thing that stops the flow of acid
in the stomach is fear and panic. So it may come about that
those most terrified of death are just the ones the cholera kills,
while those too young to understand the danger and those to
whom life seems hardly worth living and who fatalistically tend
the sick and dying around them, may survive unscathed, because the secretion of their gastric juice is not emotionally
inhibited. Fear might thus play an important role in the selection of victims, and in this sense it would not be incorrect to say
that even in cholera psychosomatic mechanisms can be of importance. Similar factors may be involved in the sudden onset
of some cases of bacillary dysentery or in typhoid fever but not
in plague, where the bacillus is injected straight into the blood
by the bite of a rat-flea.

Excluded from the designation psychosomatic are all those
diseases directly due to enforced privations, be they nutritional
or environmental, such as famine, a lack of vitamins, climatic
extremes or lack of oxygen or sunshine. Obviously not psychosomatic are diseases due to abnormal anatomical formations of
the body existing from birth, such as malformations of the heart
or its main blood vessels, the blue baby for instance, a cleft
palate or the congenital dislocation of the hip-joint. Further
excluded are ailments that have been unexceptionally established as hereditary, such as some blood disorders, haemophilia

for instance, and the hereditary forms of paralysis. Certain disorders in which hereditary factors may be involved, such as
diabetes and obesity, may still be included under the term
psychosomatic, because in them it is often a psychic factor
which forces a latent disposition into overt disease.

The causes of cancer are not as yet fully understood. It cannot yet be claimed that psychic mechanisms play a part in its
causation. However, there is already some slight evidence to
suggest that they may.

The number of diseases to which a psychosomatic interpretation can be given is growing rapidly. Diseases which are not
caused by external agencies, diseases which are neither congenital nor hereditary and those which do not occur in wild
animals are all likely to have a psychosomatic background. We
are witnessing an alarming increase in the frequency with which
psychosomatic diseases, now recognized as such, are occurring
in modern urban man, and there is good reason to be apprehen-
sive about the sharp rise in the incidence of colitis, duodenal
ulcers, high blood pressure, coronary disease, diabetes, etc.

It does, therefore, seem worthwhile to enquire into the reasons
why man, standing as he does at the apex of evolutionary
accomplishment, should fall a victim to self-destructive processes of a kind utterly unknown in the rest of the living world,
past or present.

For a better understanding of the psychosomatic process it
seems necessary to discover the point in man's evolution at
which the imposing structure of his brain turned against the
body that upheld it. An investigation into the evolutionary roots
of this kind of human affliction is needed, and an attempt might
be made to interpret psychosomatic disease as having arisen
physiologically out of the peculiar evolution of the human brain.
In man the cortical evolution raced ahead, leaving far behind
those old but vitally important parts of his central nervous
system known as the brain stem. This unilateral development
of the human cortex and the cultural potentialities which this
entailed produced a dangerous disharmony within man's central
nervous system. The present study is an attempt to analyze this
disharmony and to evaluate its role in psychosomatic disease.

The evolutionary approach may yield a deeper insight into
how and when our pre-human ancestors broke away from a

biologically balanced evolution and branched out into an almost freakish development of their cortex. It will show how, about half a million years ago, at the dawn of culture, our human ancestors began to use this unique brain to overcome their physical limitations. They then rapidly refined abstract thought and built themselves an artificial environment to make up for their biological shortcomings. It was this trend towards an ever greater control over the world around him that led man into the appalling complexity of to-day's metropolitan life and into the psychosomatic diseases that are now threatening him with self-destruction.

PART 1

THE EVOLUTION OF MAN

I

The Evolution of the Human Body

The Science of Animal Evolution

ONLY a few decades ago most educated people believed that man owed his present form to a single divine act of creation. Only a hundred years have passed since Charles Darwin wrote *The Origin of Species*. In this and other great works he ordered all the evolutionary knowledge of his time and added to it an amazing array of facts which his fruitful theories led him to discover. Before Darwin, fossilized bones were looked upon as barely credible and in fact rather disgusting curiosities. Very few biologists foresaw the importance of these relics for our understanding of modern man. These finds seemed to have no bearing upon man's structure, his functioning, his place in nature and his diseases. Even after Darwin, many scientists still scoffed at the suggestion that men and monkeys have a common ancestry and regarded this theory as blasphemous nonsense. All that has changed. It is the biologist who now expresses scientific contempt of the supernatural origin of the human body.

A number of sciences have worked together to bring about this change. Paleontology grew out of a much more careful study of fossils, and it stimulated an intense world-wide search for new specimens. It learned how to reconstruct small scattered fragments into the complete skeletons of animals that lived hundreds of millions of years ago. Many conclusions could be drawn about the posture, the gait, the food and the habitat of the creatures that were thus resurrected. As the number of known extinct animals grew, they could be arranged into classes, orders and species, just as the zoologist systematically classifies living animals. But unlike the zoologist, the paleontologist can survey both the past and the future evolution of animals. As he follows the fate of many species through the ages, he discovers evolutionary laws. These laws help him to fill gaps

7

in his collection of fossils and tempt him to predict man's future and that of the living world around him.

In his vast field of research the paleontologist has been helped by the science of Comparative Anatomy. This branch of biology deals with single bodily structures. It follows an organ, a bone or a muscle in its evolutionary variations from species to species. It tells us, for instance, how a primitive fore-limb changed into the clumsy leg of a tortoise, into a seal's flipper, the wing of a bird or a bat, the clawed paw of a tiger or the hand of a man. Comparative Anatomy also describes the subtle differences that often make it necessary to divide animals which appear to be much alike into quite different species, orders or even classes. A whale looks like a fish but is a mammal, as is also the duck-billed platypus, in spite of the fact that it lays eggs. On the other hand, animals may have an entirely different appearance and yet be closely related. In the jungles of Celebes there lives a rare and tiny animal called Tarsius which has suckers on its fingertips to give it a firm hold on the branches, enormous nocturnal eyes and long hind legs on which it hops in the trees. Only Comparative Anatomy could discover that Tarsius is a close relation of the huge gorilla.

A third supporting science is Embryology, the study of the growth of the egg-cell from fertilization to the moment of hatching or birth. The great German biologist Ernst Haeckel first gave an evolutionary bias to Embryology. He suggested that every animal repeats the evolutionary history of its species in its embryonic development. Haeckel pointed out that the processes of fertilization and of early growth are nearly the same in all animals. He believed that even the human embryo grows through successive stages in which it first resembles a fish, then an amphibian and finally a reptile before characteristic mammalian features appear. He thought that, in foetal development, even the mammalian characteristics closely follow the evolutionary sequence in which primitive mammals grew into more advanced ones. Haeckel's famous theory is no longer tenable in its original form, but for many years it had a stimulating influence upon the study of man's animal ancestry.

Embryology, like Comparative Anatomy, plays an important part in zoological classification. It can tell whether a typical feature of an animal, for instance the neck of a giraffe, is part of a very ancient pattern or a more recent specialization. A giraffe has the same number of vertebrae in its neck as other mammals and it is only during the last weeks of its embryonic life that these verterbae become enormously elongated. It can, therefore, be concluded that the giraffe's long neck is a comparatively recent specialization. The embryo of a chimpanzee is much closer to the human body-pattern than this ape will ever be after birth. It is only in the very last embryonic phase that man and chimpanzee begin to go their own ways.

The study of the evolution of the crust of the earth is another ancillary science. Geologists can state at what time the strata of the earth's covering were formed by volcanic activity or the sedimentation of sand and gravel. They explain how the delicate skeletons of microscopic marine animals and plants rained from the water surface on to the ocean beds for millions of years, laying down enormously thick layers of chalk. In this chalk the remains of higher marine animals became embedded and perfectly preserved in the order in which they evolved among their contemporaries. It is often the fossilized fauna which a stratum contains that guides the geologist in dating its formation.

Geology discovered the history of the ice-ages, the glacial periods, and the great floods that had a profound influence on the evolution of plants and animals. It shows how the raising of steep mountain ranges and their subsequent levelling off by erosion brings lower and older layers, often containing the earliest fossils, to the surface and buries more recent layers.

Geologists have rendered great service to the study of animal evolution by being able to state which parts of the earth were at any period under fresh or salt water, which parts were dry land and whether this land was covered with ice, enjoyed a temperate climate, was an arid desert or bore steaming tropical forests. Geologists have drawn maps of the earth as it must have been in different geological epochs reaching back many millions of years. We thereby know which land masses were joined together, how they separated and when these changes in terrestrial configuration took place.

Islands that have long been separated from the mainland are particularly informative. They have preserved much of their primitive fauna, while on the larger continents new forms replaced the older ones far more rapidly. A typical example is the survival in Australia and South America of mammals that rear their young in a pouch, the marsupials, of which the largest is the kangaroo. In Australia the marsupials were the only existing mammals until modern man introduced more successful forms in which the young reach a high degree of maturity in the mother's womb. These are the placentals, to which belong most of the mammals familiar in the rest of the world.

Another example of the peculiarities of insular fauna are the giant tortoises of the Galapagos Islands. These animals can reach the fantastic age of four-hundred years and thus have the longest life of any living creature. In the Galapagos Islands 37 per cent of all the shore fish, 40 per cent of the plants and 96 per cent of the reptiles occur nowhere else on earth. Old islands also produce characteristic evolutionary trends of their own, for instance flightlessness of birds in the absence of carnivorous mammals. Examples are the Dodo of Mauritius, a species which man destroyed in quite recent times, and the surviving kiwi of New Zealand. The geographical distribution of living and prehistoric animals would be quite incomprehensible without the geological background.

Dating a Fossil

As soon as ancient bones are unearthed, the question of their age arises. Sometimes the paleontologist can identify the remains at once, and his knowledge of similar finds made elsewhere enables him to say roughly when the species lived. Frequently other, better-known fossils buried in the same stratum give him a helpful clue. But when there is no paleontological evidence to guide him, he turns to geology for information about the age of the bed in which his find was deposited. Occasionally the procedure is reversed, as when the geologist needs paleontological assistance in establishing the age of fossil-bearing strata. The combination of the two sciences makes it possible to say with considerable accuracy whether a given specimen was deposited before, after or at about the same time as other known fossils. But the method furnishes only a rough answer to the question of absolute age. It cannot prove directly that the fossil is exactly so-and-so many years old.

This drawback has to some extent been overcome by applying nuclear physics to paleontology. Many elements, such as carbon, potassium, fluor, etc., contain a sprinkling of radio-active atoms. These radioactive atoms are known as isotopes. They gradually lose their radioactivity, and the rate at which it is lost is known. By measuring the radioactivity of these isotopes it becomes possible to estimate their age. Under favourable conditions the age of bones can be calculated up to about 40,000 years. Beyond that the age of the mineral or peat bed in which the fossils are found can often be dated by measuring its radio-activity. The method is still in its beginnings, and much further progress may be expected. These atomic methods can, under certain conditions, reveal the absolute, not merely the relative, age of a specimen, and are then remarkably accurate. Since the introduction of these new methods, geologists and paleonto-logists have enjoyed the satisfaction of discovering how close to the truth their previous deductions had brought them. They are also relieved to know that the danger of paleontological fakes and hoaxes, such as the one perpetrated in the case of Piltdown Man, is over.

Modern views on animal evolution and the descent of man have a broad foundation in scientific fact, though there are as yet many gaps to be filled. Some large paleontological frag-ments still have to be held together with a little speculative glue. However, an imposing framework of the history of life has now been erected, in spite of these shortcomings. Future discoveries may be expected to fit into this framework without major alterations becoming necessary.

The Ruling Reptiles

Calculations based on the radioactivity of minerals have shown that the earth may be about four-and-a-half thousand million years old. Life began at an early date in the earth's his-tory. It is not known exactly when or how it started, but this extraordinary event occurred in the ocean more than two thou-sand million and probably less than three thousand million years ago.

This study will not be served by going as far back as the first dim evidence of life that we possess. A good starting-point is a time about two hundred million years ago. By then life had emerged from the sea. Some amphibians, having learned how to spend their whole life on land, had already developed into

reptiles. The reptiles were the first back-boned animals that
were able to breed on dry earth. They had developed real lungs
out of the simpler sacs with which amphibians breathe, their
skin had become dry and scaly and their eggs had grown a
tough protective shell. At that time the reptiles were already a
great biological success. They had increased in size and were
branching out into a large number of different species.

The Ruling Reptiles produced the biggest animal that has
ever walked the earth, Brachiosaurus, which could have looked
over the roof of a three-storeyed house and may have weighed
fifty tons. There were huge flying dragons that conquered the
air for the first time in the history of back-boned animals. There
were other forms that ran on two legs and had a long neck,
somewhat resembling an enormous ostrich. Yet others looked
like a rhinoceros, while some developed into ferocious, ram-
paging flesh-eaters that preyed on sluggishly browsing herbivora,
all of them often of gigantic size. Some of these early reptiles
returned to an aquatic life, for instance the marine turtles.
However, turtles must still come ashore to lay their eggs. This
single fact shows that they were originally land-living reptiles
and not amphibians, because amphibians lay their eggs in water
though much of their life is spent on the land. Thus the variety
among these reptiles was as great as that of present-day mammals and their dominance over all the other creatures of the
earth was undisputed. Among them lived the ancestors of our
tortoises, snakes, lizards, crocodiles and alligators. These few
forms have survived, but the whole crown of the reptilian family-
tree, the so-called Ruling Reptiles, vanished.

Pre-Mammalian Evolution

The beginning of the evolution of four-legged land-living
animals lies in the Carboniferous Age. Luxurious forests of
gigantic ferns and towering trees, often reaching a height of one
hundred feet, were piling up the vegetable matter that was later
to become coal. Just as the Ruling Reptiles were about to burst
into their gargantuan evolution, one small and still primitive
reptilian species broke away from the main stem. This aberrant
species took to the trees of the carboniferous forests and became
the first reptile to adopt an entirely tree-living mode of life.
For a long time these animals continued to be reptiles, but life

in the trees gradually brought about some remarkable bodily changes which were the rudimentary beginnings of typically mammalian features.

These small reptiles, destined to develop into mammals, found themselves faced with innumerable new problems. They had to learn how to maintain a precarious balance in the branches, and for this they needed quick muscular reactions in their limbs. Being defenceless, their survival depended on their ability to scutter away and hide when giant reptiles reared their heads into the trees or marauding winged dragons swooped down upon them from the skies. To detect these sudden dangers they needed good eyes and an acute sense of hearing, all attributes for which there was less need in the ponderous world of the earthbound creatures.

The working of a reptile's brain is sluggish, and sight and hearing are poor. Only the sense of smell is highly developed. This arrangement of the senses and the working of the reptilian brain were not at all suitable for an agile and timid creature living in the trees. The speed with which the brain could translate messages from the senses into action was far too slow, and a high development of the sense of smell was almost useless to an animal living on insects, fruits and buds.

Then as now, the reptilian brain was a highly organized central nervous system, in spite of its sluggishness. It was perfectly suited to control movement on the ground, feeding, mating, breeding and the internal functioning of the reptile's body. It performed these many duties by the interaction of a large number of nerve centres finely tuned to each other and arranged in the brain with amazing compactness. Each of these nerve centres had a very definite function to fulfil in the control of the body. For example, there was a centre which controlled breathing, another that adjusted the blood circulation to momentary requirements and one which regulated sleep and waking. Such centres can by natural selection from suitable mutations increase or decrease their specific activity to meet evolutionary needs, but none of them can take over the function of any other centre, nor can it change into a centre governing a completely new bodily function.

The problems of quick muscular reaction, of feeding and breeding in the trees and the many other difficulties that confronted the reptile could never have been solved by the mere enlargement of its existing brain-structure. Either the tree-living reptile was doomed to die out for want of a suitable brain, or an entirely new trend in brain-structure was needed to ensure the survival of the species. Man and all mammals owe their existence only to the fact that evolution adopted the latter alternative. This was one of the extremely rare instances in which evolution entered into a new phase to save an ill-adjusted species from extinction instead of sacrificing it.

In a reptile, the perception of smell is localized in two large bulbous outgrowths of the brain which we call the olfactory lobes. The olfactory lobes lie outside the rest of the brain, to which they are connected by a slender stalk. They are so far removed from all the other centres of the brain that a new nervous function could originate in them—and in them alone—without structural alterations in the rest of the brain becoming necessary.

The reptilian brain is so organized that it must respond to all incoming messages from the senses. On the ground these messages lead to purposeful actions, for instance burrowing for food or safety; but in the trees many of these actions became point-less. A reptile's behaviour is governed entirely by automatic reflexes. Its actions are not subject to reason. It does not have to make a choice between different ways of reacting. All its actions are due to sensory messages putting an ingrained reflex into operation, and over this process the reptile has no control.

A reptile, taking to the trees, carried with it all the ancient reflexes which it had acquired in millions of years on the ground. These reflexes which the change of habitat rendered useless must have been a terrible harassment to an already overworked reptilian brain. In the slow course of evolution these reflexes would have gradually changed into more suitable ones. But so desperate was the situation of the tree-living reptile that it would have become extinct long before normal evolutionary trends could have brought about a better adjustment to the new environment. Some sort of evolutionary shortcut was needed if the species was to survive.

The shortcut was biologically evolved out of just the right mutations occurring at this dramatic moment. It consisted of a mechanism which blocked useless messages from the nose and thus prevented them from reaching those centres of the brain which would have been obliged to react to them. In the olfactory lobes a few cells took over the function of a screening device, a sort of censorship or filter by which incoming olfactory messages were either suppressed or allowed to pass, according to their vital importance. This sorting or classifying of smells relieved the reptilian brain of the exhausting need to react to every message from the nose and thus, in the trees, proved to be an efficient labour-saving device.

The change in the olfactory lobe must have come about in the following way. Among the millions of individuals that lived through these ages, there occurred a mutation—a freakish change in the olfactory cells—which rendered such individuals able to withhold useless olfactory information. The freakish trait was inherited, and as the descendants of the mutated forms had a better chance of survival, those that had not inherited this new mechanism gradually died out, until only the forms that had the ability to censor smells survived.

An olfactory censorship that was able to prevent useless messages from reaching a nervous apparatus that would otherwise have been obliged to turn them into action gave the tree-living reptile's brain a new freedom from the tyranny of the sense of smell. Its brain used this freedom to proceed rapidly with many other problems of adjustment. It was not forced to wait for a slow evolutionary weakening of the sense of smell.

Among the most pressing problems of adaptation was the improvement of sight and hearing. But as these senses widened their scope and came to furnish more finely detailed information, a point was reached at which they too began to harass the brain with messages that had no bearing on vital needs. And so once again the brain needed protection from the senses. The innovation in the olfactory lobes had proved to be outstandingly successful in achieving this end, but evidently the eyes and the ears were unable to evolve a screening mechanism of their own. They were in an upsurge of evolutionary progress and probably had no idle nerve cells which could be diverted to a new function. Moreover, the centres of seeing and hearing were structurally much closer to the central part of the brain than the olfactory lobes. Instead of evolving a censorship of their own, they made use of the one which was already in operation for the sense of smell. This involved what may be called a complicated process of nervous re-wiring and led to an enormous enlargement of those parts of the olfactory lobe that were performing the screening function.

Gradually the automatic reflexes which made the muscles contract or relax in movement came to be similarly supervised, calling for a further enlargement of censoring brain-tissue. In higher mammals, finally, even the instincts themselves became subject to a process of censorship.

Out of such humble beginnings in the olfactory lobes of these first tree-living reptiles grew the cerebral hemispheres, the large domes which carry the cortex. These cerebral hemispheres have, in man, reached so great a size that they now almost smother the original brain. In higher animals the original reptilian brain is called the brain stem in order to distinguish it from the much more recent cerebral hemispheres. In the human brain, the brain stem has come to look like a mere appendage hidden under and between the two hemispheres.

Had not this remarkable change in a tree-living reptile's sense of smell taken place it is doubtful whether mammals and their ultimate achievement, man, could have evolved.

The Evolution of Constant Body-Temperature

Two classes of animals, the birds and the mammals, maintain an almost uniform body-temperature throughout their lives. The only exceptions are the mammals which hibernate. During hibernation there is a return to a thermal condition very similar to that in which cold-blooded animals lead their lives. However, hibernation is not a survival of reptilian cold-bloodedness. It is a new development which probably took place during the Glacial Periods. In its winter-sleep the animal needs no food and lives very economically on its reserves of fat. It is thus able to survive a long and cold winter.

A cold-blooded animal may show wide variations in the amount of food taken, intensity of movement and the duration of the incubation of its eggs. These fluctuations are due to changes in the temperature of the environment. The chemical and physical processes of life increase when the temperature rises and decrease when it drops. This has many disadvantages for tree-living animals. In the tree-tops the changes in temperature are more abrupt than on the ground, and there are much wider variations between night and day. In the reptilian egg incubating high up in the trees of the Carboniferous Age the embryo could not grow steadily and uniformly. During the warm day its growth was active, but during the cold night growth was almost arrested, greatly prolonging the period of incubation. This was clearly undesirable, as the many exigencies of life in the trees demanded the fastest possible maturing of the young. In a cold-blooded animal even the prolonged retention of the egg inside the mother's cold body would have offered no solution to this problem. Tree-living animals were thus in great need of some mechanism which would enable them to make their body-temperature less dependent on the environment. The advantages of installing a physiological thermostat in their bodies would be enormous.

Two problems were involved. One was the dissipation of excess heat when the sun burned down upon them, and the other was the generation of sufficient heat in their bodies on cold wintry nights. The problem was a tricky one because it called for a type of heat-insulation between the body and the environment which could be altered to suit two opposite requirements, the dissipation and the retention of heat.

In a cold-blooded animal food is only consumed to provide for growth, replacement of bodily tissues and to furnish the fuel required by the muscles in movement. When these demands are satisfied, the animal ceases to feed. In a warm-blooded animal a large quantity of additional fuel is needed to stoke the chemical fires which keep the temperature up and to lay down a stock of fuel in the form of fat. The intake of food must therefore be greatly increased, often to as much as twenty-five times the requirement of a cold-blooded animal of the same size. Even in a cold-blooded animal the body-temperature may rise a little above the temperature of the environment during the process of digestion after a large meal. It is probably this rudimentary relationship between food and body-warmth which the tree-living ancestors of the birds and the mammals elaborated into warm-bloodedness.

In the body of a small animal a further provision had to be made to retain as long as possible the heat generated by excessive feeding and by the rapid burning of fuel stored in the form of fat. There is a physical law which states that under equal environmental conditions the rate at which a warm body loses its heat depends on the ratio between the bulk and the surface of the body. When in a given environment two bodies of similar shape but of different size are heated to the same temperature, the smaller body loses its heat faster than the larger one. This is so because the smaller body has a much larger surface, compared to its bulk, than the bigger body, just as a cup of tea loses heat much faster than a bath-tub filled with water of the same temperature.

In animals this means that the smaller the animal, the better it has to be protected against loss of bodily warmth. It is for this reason that when a species, at home in a temperate climate, wanders north into a cold climate, its size increases and its body becomes more compact, thus reducing the ratio of its surface to its bulk. Inversely, when such an animal moves south into the Tropics where it must dissipate heat, it grows smaller and rangier and may even enlarge the surface of its skin by growing folds, such as for instance the long dewlap of tropical cattle.

If the ancestors of mammals had been as large as elephants, there would have been no need for them to evolve hair. But as they were very small, hardly as big as a mouse, they needed insulation. Insulation could have been provided by a thick layer of fat under the skin. This was the method adopted by the warm-blooded whales living in arctic seas. In the trees this form of insulation would have been useless, because it does not make provision for the opposite requirements of dissipating excess heat.

Hair, and in the case of birds, feathers, solved this dual problem. Attached to each single hair is a small muscle. When this muscle is relaxed, the hair lies flat against the body, but when the muscle contracts the hair stands on end. When the hair lies flat, the pelt is thin and contains little insulating air between the hairs. This allows bodily heat to dissipate more easily. When the fur is raised, the insulating layer is thicker and contains more air. Air being a poor conductor of heat, the raising of the pelt holds back the bodily heat.

All mammals except man seem to be able gradually to increase or decrease the length and the density of their coat according to the climatic requirements of their habitat. Modern

man is an exception to this rule, because his relative hairless-
ness has nothing to do with an adaptation to climatic conditions. It is the result of an entirely different process. Modern
man retains into adult life certain features which in apes are
merely an embryonic phase. For instance, about one month
before it is born the embryo of a chimpanzee has a hair-
distribution closely resembling that of a human child. It has a
thick crop on its skull, while the rest of the body is covered with
the short fine hair which in man is called baby-hair. Modern
man is born at this stage, but the chimpanzee loses this distribution of hair before it is born and develops the pelt which is
characteristic of its species while it is still inside the womb. This
strange evolutionary trick of retaining embryonic features into
adult life is important for the understanding of the evolution of
modern man and will be referred to again.

The Evolution of Placentals

Reptiles lay eggs and leave them to hatch by themselves. In
the trees this method of propagation was hazardous. The birds,
which also evolved from reptilian ancestors, solved the problem
by building nests and sitting on their eggs. Their warm-blooded
bodies kept the eggs at a uniform temperature, almost as if they
were still inside the mother's body. The female reptilian ancestors of the mammals adopted an entirely different method of
propagating and safeguarding their progeny. Instead of expel-
ling an egg shortly after fertilization, the female retained the
egg in her body until the embryo was ready to hatch in the
process we call birth. To this mammalian procedure there are
only two living exceptions, the spiny ant-eater and the duck-
billed platypus, the most primitive surviving mammals, who
still lay their eggs before hatching and then suckle their young.
Both these primitive species must have branched away from the
main stem of mammalian evolution at a very early stage. They
were probably the first mammals to descend from the trees, and
this appears to have arrested further progress in their method of
propagation.

Evolution progressed beyond the egg-laying stage in those
species which remained in the trees. The egg was retained in
the mother's body until the embryo broke out of its egg-
membranes and was born. In the earlier stages of this novel

system of giving birth, the new-born animal was still so immature that it was impossible for it to face the difficult life in the
trees without its mother. Instead of nesting over their newly-
hatched young and feeding them in the manner of the birds,
mammals adopted the method of growing areas of skin in which
the glands secreted a nutritious substance, milk. These glands
first developed inside a deep fold of the mother's abdominal
skin. The fold was like a sack. As soon as the tiny offspring was
born, it hauled itself up by the hair on its mother's belly until
it reached the pouch and slipped in. There it attached itself
to the milk-secreting area and continued to grow until it was
sufficiently developed to venture forth on its own.

The rearing of the young in a pouch provided with milk-
glands is the form of procreation known as marsupial. Though
marsupials still survive, their method of propagation ran into
an evolutionary blind alley and never got beyond the pouch-
bearing stage.

Much further progress was achieved by the placentals which
include man and all the higher forms of mammalian evolution.
At an early stage of pre-mammalian evolution there was thus a
division of the originally reptilian species into three branches
that went their separate ways. One small branch led to the egg-
laying mammals. A second more prosperous branch yielded the
marsupials. The third branch produced the so-called placentals,
which proved to be by far the most successful of all mammals.

Inside an egg, the embryo can grow only as long as it has yolk
to feed on. When the yolk is consumed and the embryo has
taken up all the room in the shell, it must hatch or starve. The
period of development inside the egg is thus limited by the
amount of yolk provided. However, merely increasing the
amount of yolk would not have solved the problem of prolonging pre-natal life; it would have been impossible to go beyond
what the birds have achieved in this direction. There are two
reasons for this. The first is that in an egg a growing embryo
produces waste-matter which it cannot get rid of. If the accumulation of its own excretions goes beyond a certain point, the
embryo inside the egg dies of self-poisoning. The second reason
why life inside the egg cannot be indefinitely prolonged is that
a growing embryo demands a rapidly increasing supply of oxygen. There comes a point at which this demand can only be

met by breathing with lungs. At this point the embryo must either hatch or suffocate.

In the embryo it is always the nerve-tissue which takes longest to develop. The mammals were particularly in need of the screening device in their brain. The screening device was the latest addition to the brain and was therefore also the last to develop in the growing young. In order to grow the large mammalian brain, the prolongation of pre-natal life had become a pressing need.

Once again man's ancestors teetered on the brink of extinction. And for the second time suitable mutations provided a most ingenious way out which completely solved the problem in a radically new way. Instead of sealing off the fertilized egg and its yolk in a shell, evolution did away with the yolk altogether, while the shell became a soft living membrane which grew as the embryo increased in size. In the womb the egg came to be surrounded with little pools of the mother's blood. Into these pools the embryo penetrated with finely-branched outgrowths, like little roots. Through these roots it was able to obtain all the nourishment it required directly from the mother's blood. Into the mother's blood it could also discharge all its waste-matter which the mother then eliminated for it. Moreover, an embryo that had direct access to its mother's blood was able to get all the oxygen it needed from that source.

In primitive mammals the little placental roots sprout from the whole surface of the egg. As this new mechanism is perfected in the course of placental evolution, the roots draw closer together in one spot. Tarsius, the rare little mammal that lives in the trees of Celebes, is the first living mammal that has gathered its placental outgrowths into a disc-like organ which is now a real placenta. In man, finally, the placenta is a large and highly complex structure of branching roots bathing in pools of blood. It weighs several pounds and is commonly known as the after-birth.

The placenta provides the means of prolonging almost indefinitely the duration of pre-natal life in the womb. Though man has extended this period to nine months, he is outdone by other mammals, such as the elephant, in which pregnancy lasts about eighteen months. The young of an elephant must be sufficiently mature at birth to be able to keep up with the fast-moving herd. The new-born elephant's only help is its mother's tail, to which it clings with its trunk. Man's ancestors led a more settled life in the trees. For them such a high degree of physical maturity was unnecessary. Their young could be carried about, while they clung to their mother. Without the placenta, mammalian evolution would have come to a halt at the marsupial stage, and man could never have evolved out of the marsupial pattern of procreation.

The Hunters and the Hunted

After the tree-living mammals had acquired hair, warm blood and a large brain and had split into marsupials and placentals, they developed some species which came down out of the tree-tops. By this time the giant ruling reptiles were thinning out and there was more room and more safety on the ground. The thick floor of the carboniferous forests provided the first ground-living mammals with ample nourishment, suited to their omnivorous tastes. They gradually increased in size and then moved out into the open plains. There they discovered that their better senses, their greater agility and their far superior intellectual equipment enabled them to outwit the remaining saurians. So it was not long before some of the mammals began to prey on the smaller reptiles and became flesh-eaters. Others gave up feeding on insects and veered towards a strictly herbivorous mode of life.

But gradually the reptilian prey of those mammals that had become exclusively carnivorous grew scarce. This forced the hunters into a habit which has always been the last desperate resort of hungry flesh-eaters. They developed cannibalism, in the sense that they started to prey upon their closest relatives, the smaller and weaker vegetarian mammals, whom they still resembled in all but a matter of teeth. Meanwhile, the browsing mammalian herbivora had become plentiful, but they were quite unprepared to defend themselves or to escape from the sudden danger that thus arose in their midst.

The hunting mammalian carnivora had an easy time. They grew bigger and stronger with well-filled bellies and soon branched out into a large number of different forms. But apparently life was too easy for them. They had no enemies, and so their further physical evolution was a luxurious exuberance rather than a dire necessity. It produced the largest land-living mammalian flesh-eater that has ever lived, a Mongolian species with a skull a yard long.

Flesh-eaters have two ways of hunting. One is out-running their prey, and the other is stealthily stalking it. Out-running requires superior speed, while stalking calls for superior intelligence. In these respects the early carnivora were no better equipped than their prey. But their herbivorous victims were so plentiful and so unsuspecting that the hunters had no need to develop either speed or intelligence. Moreover, life on the ground does not foster brain development as much as does life in the trees.

The situation of the hunted was very different. They were faced with a vitally urgent need for further adaptation. In them natural selection made full use of every mutation that provided longer and thinner legs, primarily designed for speed. The ancestors of the modern horse are an outstandingly successful example of this trend. Others specialized in hoofs, tusks, horns and antlers with which to defend themselves. Yet others took advantage of the herd-instinct, which enabled some individuals to watch and warn, while others fed and bred.

While the hunters were slow to make useful adaptations, the hunted progressed rapidly with their defensive and evasive evolutionary trends. Natural selection allowed the forms which made useful adaptations to flourish and weeded out those that did not. Finally a point was reached at which the flesh-eaters found it increasingly difficult to catch and kill their prey. One by one the early carnivora died out until extinction overtook them all—with only one remarkable exception.

It was about fifty million years ago when one species of these early carnivora seems to have done what its reptilian ancestors did millions of years before. It climbed back into the trees, and that saved it from extinction. It was a small and fierce little creature that looked like a cross between a miniature fox-terrier and a weasel. In the trees there still lived the numerous mammals that had stayed behind when their more enterprising relations descended to the ground. By this time the ancestors of the lower primates, the lemurs, the tarsoids and the monkeys were flourishing and the birds were already at the height of their prodigious evolution. The small tree-living mammals and the birds with their chicks and eggs provided a ready feast for a hungry flesh-eater that climbed into the trees and made itself at home there.

For the second time in mammalian evolution, life in the trees proved to be highly conducive to brain development. The 'dog-weasel', *Cynodictis*, soon started an evolutionary orgy of brain growing in which it almost caught up with the intellectually more advanced mammals that had never left the trees. Its brain developed far beyond anything achieved by the ground-living mammals who were at this moment enjoying a period of freedom from carnivorous persecution.

During its life in the trees, *Cynodictis* quietly nursed along quick muscular reactions, sensory precision and an outstanding intelligence. At last it was ready to venture back on to the ground and live there successfully. Its long sojourn in the trees may have played a role in man's evolution. Man's timid mammalian ancestors in the trees now had a dangerous, quick and intelligent flesh-eater in their midst, and this may have been a powerful selective factor in the further evolutionary perfection of their brain and their senses as a means of defence. The presence of *Cynodictis* in the trees may thus well have contributed to the evolutionary pattern which was later to triumph in the highest mammals, the apes and the direct ancestors of man.

When the descendants of *Cynodictis* were tempted to leave the trees, they found the land populated with fleet-footed, largely gregarious, hoofed and horned animals. There were already the forefathers of the hippopotamus and the rest of the pig family. The camels, giraffes, deer and the cattle family, which includes the antelopes, the sheep and the goats, were chewing the cud. Primitive horses were plentiful; early elephants had put the finishing touches to their trunks; the forebears of the whales, the seals and the sea-cows had already moved from the land into the ocean and the bats had learned to fly. At that time there were many dozens of other strange mammals that have long since become extinct. The mammalian fauna was thus highly variegated and numerous.

In this new world on the ground a superior tree-trained brain was for the second time able to outwit the intellectually more stationary ground forms. As before, the carnivorous newcomers battened, grew and then split up into highly diversified species which went their own ways in a new evolutionary crescendo. All land-living placental carnivora are descendants of *Cynodictis*. They are the large family of the cats, the dogs and their many relations, the bears, the weasels, the hyenas, the racoons and all their kin.

The Evolution of the Lower Primates

We possess fossil records of a large number of animals which cover almost every phase of their evolutionary progress. In the case of man's closest ancestors there are still a number of gaps waiting to be filled. One reason for this is that man's animal forefathers lived in the trees of tropical jungles in regions which have hardly been paleontologically explored. Moreover, the floor of hot and humid forests, teeming with vermin, only rarely provided conditions permitting the rapid inclusion of an animal carcass in a sedimenting mineral deposit, a quick-sand or a sticky bog in which it could become a fossil. One of the few ways in which fossilization of a tree-living animal could occur under such conditions was for it to drop dead out of the branches on to the bank of a sandy or gravel-bedded stream, just before heavy rains turned the water into a raging torrent, churning up sufficient gravel to leave the carcass permanently embedded. That is why some of the most important fossil finds have been made in deep gravel-pits on the banks of ancient rivers.

Another difficulty is that the closer we get to man, the shorter the evolutionary periods become and the more the evolutionary pattern seems to resemble the growth of a poplar. The branches closely hug the trunk and run parallel to it for long stretches of time, until they finally bend off in a horizontal evolution of their own. It thus becomes extremely difficult to establish the exact point at which the animal primates broke away from the stem which eventually led to man.

The highest mammalian order, the Primates, had its beginning in the tree-tops of the early Eocene, about seventy million years ago. One mammalian species that had never left the trees began to specialize in a further evolution of its brain. It retained its small size and with its pointed snout closely resembled the tree-shrews that still live in Far Eastern jungles. The inch-long skulls of these early shrew-like mammals have been found in Mongolian deposits that are forty million years old. Yet even those fragile remains show anatomical traits that exist only in primates. This small shrew-like animal that lived so long ago is the grandsire of all the lemurs, tarsoids, monkeys, apes and man.

The most primitive surviving primates are the tree-living lemurs of Africa, Madagascar and Asia. Except for their much larger size, the lemurs are so similar to their shrew-like fore-fathers that they are believed to have branched away at a very early date. Why the lemurs, now all but on the verge of extinction, remained almost stationary for millions of years while the main primate stem continued its spectacular evolution, is still a mystery. Perhaps too early an increase in the animal's size interfered with the latent possibilities of further development.

From where the lemurs branched off, the evolution of primates next led to the tarsoids, once a prosperous family, but now surviving only in the single species called Tarsius. This next great step yielded a small animal with a relatively enormous and highly differentiated brain. Tarsius lives in pairs, brings forth only one young at a time and is the first mammal to have a disc-shaped placenta, instead of the more primitive organ which covers the whole surface of the egg. In the tarsoids brain-development reached almost that of the lower monkeys. The snout regressed into a flat face and the large eyes moved close together, giving these animals, for the first time in evolutionary history, a true perspective vision. Tarsius has good ears and a very reduced sense of smell, features which are found at a further stage of evolution in the monkeys. Contrary to the extinct tarsoids of which there is ample fossil evidence, Tarsius has gone in for a number of specializations of its own which are found in no other primate. The long hind legs which give it a hopping gait and the suckers on the tips of its tiny fingers and toes with which the small furry animal grasps the branches are traits which it developed long after it had left the main-stem of primate evolution.

The lower primates are of great importance for our understanding of human evolution, but they are no longer a biological success. Their evolution has stagnated for millions of years, forcing them to give way to other forms which continued to develop. They have withdrawn into the seclusion of dense tropical forests and will soon become extinct.

The Evolution of the Higher Primates

After the tarsoids, the evolutionary sequence that led directly to man split off another branch which is still prospering. It led to the monkeys. Either this branch bifurcated very soon after its separation from what later became the human stem or, as a large body of fossil evidence suggests, it consisted of two distinct branches which grew in the same direction for a long time. One branch produced the American or New World monkeys, and the other the Old World monkeys. The New World monkeys have flat noses with widely separated nostrils directed laterally. They are without exception tree-living and have remained more primitive than the Old World monkeys. The placenta is disc-like and they have no cheek-pouches, but they have developed a prehensile tail which they use as a fifth limb. Their brain is superior to that of the tarsoids, but it is less highly differentiated than that of the Old World monkeys. The Old World monkeys have raised noses; the nostrils have moved close together and point forward. In both the New and Old World monkeys the eye has, for the first time, a *fovea centralis*, a central retinal pit, which enables them to see with a great precision of form, colour and depth when the gaze is fixed upon one sector of the whole wide field of vision.

Old World monkeys have a strong tendency towards terrestrial habits, though this transition has been fully accomplished only by the highly intelligent baboons. Only the Old World monkeys have perfected the sitting posture, and they all have callosities on their buttocks. The sitting posture freed the forelimbs from the burden of supporting the body, and this had a profound effect on the brain because it produced the hand which could be used for many purposes other than locomotion. Handling food, playing, reaching and flea-hunting required rapid and complex muscular co-ordination and opened a large variety of new activities which the brain had to direct and supervise. Among primates, sitting was also the first step to man's erect posture.

There are no monkeys of the Old World type found on the American continent, nor have any fossil remains of their immediate ancestors ever been found there. From the monkeys onwards, the evolution of man is a strictly Old World affair and is confined to the trees of tropical forests and the savanna which bordered on them.

Later again, roughly thirty-five million years ago, other branches broke away from the stem out of which man developed. These branches produced the apes. The surviving apes are the gibbon, the orang-utan, the chimpanzee and the gorilla. The lively gibbon, master-acrobat of the Malayan jungles, and the orang-utan, sad and ponderous, red-haired giant of the Indonesian jungles, soon went their own evolutionary ways. The chimpanzee, the gorilla and the direct ancestors of man stayed closer together for millions of years. This becomes particularly clear when surviving apes are compared with those that have become extinct. For example, thirty million years ago the extinct ape *Proconsul* lived in East Africa. About twenty million years ago a huge oak-ape, *Dryopithecus*, roamed the Siwalik Hills at the Indian foot of the Himalayas and became extinct only seven million years ago (unless it survived as the legendary Yeti of the Sherpas). The fossil remains of Proconsul and Dryopithecus are so similar to the chimpanzee, the gorilla and man's ape-like or pithecine ancestors that it is difficult to say which they resemble most.

The Evolution of Man

It is probable that when the primate stem broke up into the branches that led to the many known species of apes, there must have been one branch that finally produced man. It is not yet possible to say whether any one of the extinct apes belongs to that particular branch, though the careful study of fossilized bones makes this seem unlikely. It is not until much more recent times—about half a million years ago—that the first man-like beings appear to have lived.

In South Africa a few skeletal fragments about half a million years old were unearthed. The creature to whom they belonged was called *Australopithecus*, the South-Ape. Although its ape-like features were many, it had a brain capacity that was much greater than that of any known ape, living or fossil. It was chiefly for this reason that Australopithecus was believed to be the long-sought ancestor of the human species. To-day the most widely-held view is that the South-Ape was an unsuccessful side-branch of the stem that finally led to man—perhaps a sort of evolutionary pilot experiment that went wrong somewhere along the line.

But at about that time there lived the Eastern Pithecines. Elaborately chipped flint tools that could only have been fashioned by human hands were already in use by the Asiatic ape-men. Remains of these forms were found in Java and China (Peking Man). We know that Peking Man was a hunter and used fire. Compared with the highest apes, the brains of these ape-men were enormous and their gait was essentially human.

A sort of paleontological twilight still covers the evolution of man for the next 300,000 years or so. But then we find a race that spread over vast territories of Europe and the Middle East, and about these men our knowledge is much greater. The first remains of this early, now definitely human, species were found in 1857 in a cave in the Neanderthal, a valley through which runs a small tributary of the Rhine. *Homo neanderthalensis* was a 'cave-man' just as he is commonly pictured. Stocky, bull-necked and long-armed, his prominent brow-ridges, low sloping forehead and the lack of a chin gave him a brutish expression. While he seems to have been a fairly good hunter and liked to eat at his hearth, there is no glossing over the fact that he was also a cannibal who cracked human skulls and ate the brains. In the case of the earliest carnivora, cannibalism was perhaps a last resort which may have contributed to their extinction. In Neanderthal Man, cannibalism might mean either that he was not a biological success—the evidence points rather the other way—or that he was a more timid creature than his appearance suggests.

About 40,000 years ago Neanderthal Man was ousted by a new type of man, almost certainly an ancestor of the white race. This new type appears rather suddenly in Eastern and Central Europe. The race was tall and had a skull that was larger than that of modern man. The female was much smaller than the male, and her brain was not quite as efficient. These men had lost the prominent brow-ridges and the back-sloping jowl, and for the first time there appears a pointed chin. The new race had artistic trends and painted pictures on the walls of their caves. They also made fine tools out of patiently chipped flint and bone and may have been the first to use articulate speech instead of the grunts, grimaces and gestures that seem to have served Neanderthal Man. Where they came from is not known for certain, but it seems very unlikely that they descended from Neanderthal Man. This race is known as Cro-Magnon Man after a French cave in which some of their remains were discovered. Cro-Magnon Man flourished until about 15,000 years ago, but there is anthropological evidence to suggest that his blood still flows in modern European man.

Spread over the world, there are now a large number of different human races. But they all belong to a single species and can all interbreed successfully. Research into the origin of human races is still a vast, rather polemic, field and lies off the track of our present theme. In Cro-Magnon Man the evolution of the modern human body reaches a point beyond which no radically new anatomical features have developed. From this point onwards human evolution is the history of culture.

The Evolution of the Human Psyche

The Vertebrate Brain

THE EARTH is inhabited mostly by spineless animals which account for 95 per cent of all known species. The mere 5 per cent that have a backbone are on the whole larger and seem more important to man because their internal structure is similar to his own. The vertebrate body is suspended on the backbone, to which are attached the limbs, the chest organs and the belly. At its front end the spine is blown out into the large hollow of the skull which holds the brain. In spineless animals the nervous control is usually distributed over the whole body, while vertebrates show a strong tendency to concentrate all nervous control in the head.

Until the beginning of mammalian evolution, the vertebrate brain had a very slow development (see Fig. 1). A large number of nerve centres grew at the foremost tip of the spinal cord and consisted of clusters of nerve cells, closely linked to each other by an intricate network of nerve fibres. As the fishes evolved into amphibians and these later into reptiles, there was no need for the basic structure of the vertebrate brain to undergo radical changes. In fact, the brains of these lower vertebrates are extraordinarily alike.

The pre-mammalian brain supervised, controlled and co-ordinated every activity of the animal by automatic reflexes to sensory messages. But this brain, besides reacting to messages from the environment as reported by the senses, was also able to respond to stimuli coming from within the body in the form of hormones—chemical substances secreted by the endocrine glands such as the pituitary, the thyroid, the adrenals and the sex glands. The reptilian brain reacted automatically to hormonal stimuli by making the animal perform appropriate actions such as feeding, mating or sleeping. In these lower vertebrates every response to outer or inner stimuli was fully automatic and yet biologically appropriate for the species.

This high degree of perfection in lower-vertebrate reflexes was not achieved by reasoning or choice. It was the result of a long, cruel and relentless process of natural selection. Those individuals that inherited useful spontaneous changes in the nature of their automatic responses survived and passed on such traits to their progeny, while those that inherited changes which lowered their chance of survival were exterminated. The evolutionary fate of these lower animals depended—and still depends —entirely upon spontaneous genetic changes, known as mutations, taking place among them, and it was by a process of elimination that their brains became ever more perfectly adapted to specific needs.

The organization of the reptilian central nervous system was not abolished in the mammalian brain. The change that took place was the insertion of a censorship between the incoming stimuli and those parts of the brain which reacted to such stimuli. The censoring mechanism which became necessary for life in the trees originated in the reptilian olfactory lobes and began to suppress useless incoming messages to which the brain would otherwise have been bound to react in the old way. This first step was followed by a vast extension of censorship, which came to be applied to all the other senses, to movement and finally to hormonal and instinct stimuli. Thus when an important sensory or hormonal message called for an appropriate action, the action itself was screened through the censorship, making a choice from among several possible forms of action possible.

For instance, a small tree-living mammal might see a large bird circling high above the trees. Its primitive response to this sensory message would be to scutter away and hide. But the censorship would prevent this, because there was as yet no evidence that the bird was dangerous, and its presence would therefore be ignored. But if the bird came closer and proved to be an enemy, the mammal's brain took note and prepared the body for escape. The muscles tensed, the blood pressure rose, the animal stopped feeding and possibly evacuated waste-matter, but it did not necessarily start to run away, because the cortical sifting of the evidence informed it that the danger was not imminent. If, however, the bird of prey made a sudden

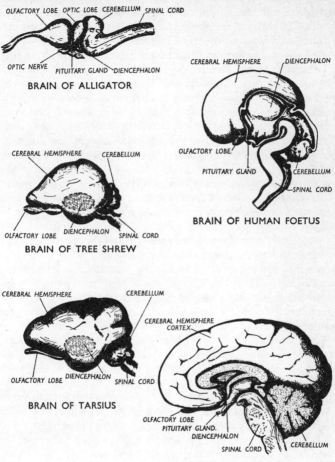

BRAIN OF ALLIGATOR

BRAIN OF TREE SHREW

BRAIN OF HUMAN FOETUS

BRAIN OF TARSIUS

ADULT HUMAN BRAIN

Note. The olfactory, the optic and the acoustic lobes (the latter are not shown in the diagram) unite to form the cerebral hemispheres, while the olfactory apparatus decreases in size as evolution proceeds. All those parts of the central nervous system not specifically designated as hemispheres are collectively known as the brain stem.

Fig. 1. THE EVOLUTION OF THE CEREBRAL HEMISPHERES

swoop in the directions of the animal, the censorship instantly permitted all the actions of defence or escape to run their course. In this way reasoning came to play an important role in the evolutionary process of survival.

In order to perform the function of a censor, the brain needed a huge storehouse of memories, so pigeon-holed that they were readily available. The brain also needed an elaborate system of highways and byways to accommodate a heavy associative traffic. Fragments of memory had to be combined into complex experiences to meet new situations. These experiences too had to be stored and kept available, in case similar situations called for the reaction-pattern that had proved to be satisfactory on a previous occasion. An efficient censorship also required a highly developed ability to learn from experience. Thus the elaboration of the function of censorship led to all the complicated processes of conscious perception, memory, association, learning and reasoning.

All higher cerebral processes are located in the large hemispheres which are peculiar to mammals and birds, though in birds they are far more rudimentary. The birds remained at a lower stage in brain development, because they never got beyond the egg-laying phase in the evolution of procreation and concentrated on flight rather than brain, as a way of solving the problems of life in the trees.

In mammals the cerebral hemispheres grew with astounding rapidity, but the primitive brain that runs the internal functioning and the reactions of the body remained almost unaltered. Subject to the newly imposed censorship, the old part of the brain still functions much as it did in all pre-mammalian vertebrates. This vitally important though now insignificant-looking part of the mammalian brain is called the brain-stem.

If a man had both his cerebral hemispheres carefully removed without damage to any part of the brain-stem, he would not necessarily die from such an enormous surgical mutilation. If he survived the shock of the operation, his body would still be able to perform the basic physiological functions of life. He would be unable to swallow food, as this requires a voluntary muscular action; but if food were placed in his stomach, it would be normally digested, assimilated and excreted. His kidneys would continue to secrete urine, which would be spontaneously voided when the bladder was full. His semen would be fit to beget a normal child, and a woman without cerebral hemispheres could go through a normal pregnancy and give birth to a healthy child. Breathing and circulation would continue to function satisfactorily, and the endocrine glands would adapt themselves tolerably well to the new situation. Such a man would not be able to move his skeletal muscles voluntarily, but these would still react to mechanical, thermal and electrical stimuli. He would be unable to perceive consciously any messages from his senses. He would be unable, for instance, to see in the ordinary sense; yet his pupils would still react to light and his eyelids would close at a sudden flash. He would react to heat by sweating and to cold with shivering and gooseflesh.

As the brain-stem runs all the basic manifestations of life, it would be impossible to remove the brain-stem and leave the hemispheres intact, as this would result in instantaneous death. Without the brain-stem the hemispheres are completely useless.

Anatomically the brain-stem is a conglomeration of nerve-centres, each of which consists of a large number of nerve-cells packed closely together. The diencephalon, from where all regulatory adjustments of the body take their origin, is the most vitally important part of the brain-stem and lies roughly in the middle of the brain. In the diencephalon animal instincts such as fear, rage, hunger and sex are translated into physiological activity, and it is chiefly with the diencephalon that this study will henceforth be concerned.

The brain-stem is the most conservative of all vertebrate structures. Such an old and efficient organ clearly could not submit to the revolutionary changes that life in the trees demanded. The brain-stem had reached much too high a degree of specialization ever to go back into the evolutionary melting-pot. The pre-mammalian reptiles could not hope to make for themselves an entirely new brain. They could only compromise by adding a new structure to their existing brain and thus influence its functioning to an extent that made their survival possible.

This new structure evolved in the most out-lying nerve centres of the reptilian brain, the olfactory lobes, where there were a number of idle nerve-cells to spare. As the olfactory lobes began to expand, their nerve-cells moved to the surface. The surface-layer of nerve cells in the cerebral hemispheres which grew out of the olfactory lobes is known as the grey-matter or cortex. The body of the hemispheres consists of white matter and is essentially a mass of nerve fibres which connect various parts of the cortex with each other, and also connect the senses with the cortex and the cortex with the brain-stem.

At first only the sense of smell was subjected to censorship. But gradually the other senses began to avail themselves of this useful device. The hemispheres that had been quite small grew rapidly to accommodate increasingly detailed sensory perception and to make room for the storage of countless sensory memories. When then the control of voluntary movement was later transferred from the brain-stem—where it had been localized in the cerebellum—to the cortex, a still further increase in the size of the cortex became necessary. Finally, when in early man the instincts started to be screened at the level of consciousness, the dimensions of the cortex became enormous.

In order to pack this huge expanse of cortical tissue into the smallest possible space, the surface of the hemispheres began to wrinkle at an early stage. The human cortex covers the hemispheres in deep and narrow folds. If the cortex were stretched smoothly over the hemispheres, a human brain would have to be the size of a beer-barrel.

One of the most remarkable things about the growth of the cortex was the incredible acceleration of this process. While the earlier phases took tens of millions of years to evolve, the later phases were covered in a few hundred thousand years. It seems to be a general law of evolution that once a trend towards a single successful specialization has become firmly established, the speed with which this specialization develops gets faster and faster and may even develop of its own accord beyond the limits of usefulness. Meanwhile, the rest of the body continues to evolve at a slow and steady pace, so that after a while a stage is reached in which all the other evolutionary trends are left far behind the outstanding specialization.

In modern man this development has already gone so far that there are signs of an evolutionary regression in the body in favour of a still more freakish growth of the brain. Modern man's body no longer reaches its full evolutionary maturity, as it did in Neanderthal Man. Though the modern brain develops further than that of Neanderthal Man, modern man's body remains behind in an earlier embryonic stage. He carries certain embryonic features on into adult life. An example of this has already been mentioned in connection with the distribution of human hair, but there are many other instances. One that interests us here is the relationship between the brain and the rest of the body.

In the light-skinned human races the development of the body is sharply braked in the last stages of pre-natal life, while the growth of the cortex is accelerated. There is some evidence to suggest that the negro's body is better adjusted to his brain. He is physically more mature at birth, and under ideal environmental conditions he averages a larger body. From an evolutionary point of view this makes his brain-body ratio more balanced.

Comparing the absolute size of animal brains does not furnish a useful index of brain development. For instance, the tiny brain of Tarsius is far more advanced than the bigger one of a whale or an elephant. It is only when the sizes of apes' brains are compared with human brains that there is a rough parallelism between volume and evolutionary advance. Thus the brain capacity of the gibbon is only 90 c.c., while that of a gorilla is 600 c.c.; the Ape-men—or Pithecines—had a brain capacity of 900 c.c., while modern man averages 1,500 c.c.

A more satisfactory index of evolutionary progress is the relationship between brain volume and the size of the animal's palate. Thus an adult male gorilla has 5.8 c.c. of brain for every square centimetre of palate surface. The skulls of ape-men or pithecines have as many as 30–38 c.c. brain volume for every square centimetre of palate surface. In modern man the corresponding figure is 60 c.c. Measured in absolute size, modern man's brain is about two and a half times as large as the brain of the gorilla; but when measured by the palate index the human brain is ten times as advanced.

In an adult male chimpanzee there are 8.5 c.c. of brain volume for every square centimetre of palate, while in a suckling chimpanzee the figure rises to 20 c.c. But in the eighth month of pregnancy the chimpanzee embryo has an index of 60 c.c., the same as that of an adult man. An adult man, therefore, has a brain-palate relationship which is an embryonic phase in the chimpanzee. In other words, the chimpanzee develops its body much further in relation to its brain than does modern man; or in yet other words, compared with his brain, man's body remains at what is an embryonic phase in his closest animal relations.

Yet even the brain-palate ratio does not reveal the whole truth. It applies to brain volume, whereas the brain's efficiency depends entirely on the size of the surface area of the cortex. Of two mammalian brains of equal size, the one which has more, finer and deeper folds will be the better. It is difficult to measure the dimensions of a folded surface which cannot be stretched, but it is significant that in the human embryo the first brain folds to appear are those which are found in adult monkeys. There follow those folds by which the brain of an adult ape differs from that of a monkey, while the last to be formed are the folds found only in the human brain. If one could compare the cortical area of an adult man with that of an adult gorilla, it would be found that the difference is much more than tenfold as shown by the brain-palate index.

Of all the surviving great apes, the gorilla's brain is most like that of man. But the gorilla, like Neanderthal Man, goes on to a further bodily development of strong limbs, long arms, a heavy jowl and what to us seems a brutish appearance, while the Cro-Magnon race learned to keep its body at a more delicate embryonic stage. It was this trick which enabled modern man to go further than his predecessors in the evolution of his brain at the expense of his body.

The Role of Leisure in Brain-Development

Two hundred million years of life in the trees produced better eyes, better ears, better movements and the purposeful control of all bodily reactions through the development of an intricate censorship localized in the cortex. But there is another factor which played a significant part in the evolution of the mammalian brain. That factor is animated leisure.

In the tree-tops the chase after winged food was short and fast. Grubs, caterpillars and other crawling insects, fruits and buds were plentiful and within easy reach all the year round in the tropical forests which man's mammalian ancestors inhabited. There was always water from rain or dew to slake their thirst. Hollow trees were freely available for shelter and the safe rearing of the young. Creatures leading such a life enjoyed many waking hours of replete leisure and freedom from mortal threats.

In comparison, most ground-living mammals never have a waking moment to spare and even their sleep is threatened. They are fully occupied with the constant struggle for the bare necessities of living, feeding, hunting or being hunted. The herbivora always have to be on the alert while they crop or ruminate huge quantities of green food. Every morning and every night of their lives they have to make an often long and perilous trek to the nearest water. This leaves them little leisure to indulge in the idle capers for which only the young they suckle have time.

In the trees there were none of these problems. Once a certain degree of cortical development had been reached, all vital needs could be fulfilled in a few short bursts of activity. During the rest of the time there was nothing of vital importance to be done. Yet a highly active brain compelled man's animal ancestors to perform some sort of activity in which this brain could be maximally employed.

Here again the higher tree-living mammals made use of the trick of continuing into adult life a trait that had hitherto been a privilege of the very young. They continued to play during their whole lives. They raced up and down the branches, chased each other for the sheer fun of it; they swung in the tree-tops and learned to leap from one precarious hold to another regardless of the void below. They learned to adopt the sitting posture, which made their forelimbs free for grasping, scratching, hunting for fleas and salt crystals left on the skin through the evaporation of sweat, or toying with morsels of food. Such activities that had little to do with the maintenance of life provided the best possible training for sensory acuity, all forms of advanced nervous control and muscular co-ordination. The ability to play skilfully may already at this early stage have been a powerful factor in sexual selection. The better players probably had better chances with the opposite sex, and so this trait was inherited with increasing frequency and rapidly perfected.

In modern man playfulness has gone to extremes. He plays from earliest infancy until he dies. It is only the nature of his toys which changes with the passage of the years. Modern man does not look upon those who perform vital duties as representing a flowering of human genius. The cook in her kitchen, the farmer behind his plough, the soldier on the battlefield, the policeman on his beat or the bricklayer with his hod have become mere servants. It is the painter, the poet, the musician and the actor who furnish most of the geniuses because it is they who enrich modern man's leisure. It is they who conform to the evolutionary trend which aspires to ever more time to play. Metropolitan man has largely solved the problems of bare existence. He now works mainly for life's cultural adornments which his brain so insistently demands.

The Diencephalon and the Cortex

In higher mammals the senses of hearing and seeing have developed far beyond the primitive reptilian state, while the evolution of the other senses has been neglected. The astounding perfection of sight and hearing has given mammals an extraordinary ability to interpret the nature of their environment and the events that are taking place in it. To make this possible the raw incoming messages from these senses had to be connected with the storehouse of memories and the associative conduits. The hundreds of thousands of light-receptive cells in the retina of the eye can each send only a single message of light or colour to the cortex. There, these punctiform messages have to be woven into a composite picture of light, colour, form and movement. It is this picture which is subjected to censorship. Only if it contains something which calls for bodily action is the message passed on to the brain-stem, which then acts upon it in the appropriate way by setting hormonal or autonomous nervous mechanisms in motion.

For example, a leopard is prowling in grassland at the edge of a forest. Its eyes send a continuous stream of messages to its cortex, where they are composed into complex images. The wind blows in a gust over the grass and sets it in motion, or a twig falls out of a tree. The leopard's cortex registers all these events, but it does not report them to the diencephalon for action. They are screened off. Yet if a deer steps out into the open, the need for immediate action is reported to the diencephalon, which at once goes to work. Automatically the leopard crouches. Its body is prepared for the rush and the leap by a tensing of the muscles, a sudden rise in blood sugar, and an increase in the pulse rate, salivation and a flood of gastric juice in the stomach. All these reflex reactions are managed by the diencephalon without any further participation of the cortex. Only after its body is thus prepared does the leopard pounce upon its prey.

Very similar reactions take place in the body of a deer if it is able to detect the danger in time. It has stepped out of the forest only after a long and careful survey of the environment. Having neither seen nor heard anything to be alarmed about, it moves forward cautiously and starts nibbling the grass. It is acting on a cortical level, while its diencephalon is merely going about its routine management of bodily functions. Suddenly it sees a glint of yellow moving stealthily along the edge of the forest. Alarm is at once reported to the diencephalon. Without any voluntary effort the deer freezes into immobility. Its ears are pricked, its head is turned straight into the direction of the danger and it sniffs the wind. Its muscles tense, its heart beats faster, its blood sugar rises and its pelt is raised. The deer's only hope of escape lies in its ability to run away with the utmost possible speed, and for this its diencephalon instantly prepares it.

In the leopard all the diencephalic reflexes are geared to attack, kill and devour. Its intestinal tract is prepared for food, and it suddenly feels hungry. In the deer all the automatic reflexes are geared to flight. The hunger that led it out into the open is gone in a flash. It empties its bowel in a sudden attack of diarrhoea so that it can run faster. Only after these complicated bodily reactions have been put into operation by the diencephalon is the deer ready to break into the headlong flight which may save its life. The muscular effort involved in flight uses up the excess of blood sugar and the additional supply of blood provided by the increased blood pressure and the faster heart-beat. If it reaches safety, its cortex will inform the diencephalon that the danger is over. The appetite immediately returns, the bowels resume their normal function, excess sugar is no longer poured into the blood-stream, the heart slows down and the diencephalon settles back to its management of routine bodily functions. Thus in both animals there is a perfect coordination of cortical and diencephalic mechanisms, finely adjusted to the best interests of their survival.

In lower vertebrates such as the reptiles the movement of the body is controlled by that part of the brain-stem which is called the cerebellum. Reptilian movements are comparatively simple and uniform. A tortoise can protrude or retract its legs under the carapace. It can move forwards, backwards, to the right or to the left, but its gait is always uniform, and for such movements the interplay of its muscles is perfectly co-ordinated.

But the cerebellum, the small hind-brain, would never have been able to initiate the rapid, complex movements with which a squirrel darts about or which enable a gibbon to swing gracefully among the branches. The new problems of balance and agility which life in the trees brought with it demanded a far superior nervous apparatus to govern movement. Movement too had to be connected with memory, association and the ability to learn. Each movement needed censoring before it was put into operation, and it was for this reason that newer and higher centres of movement developed in the cerebral cortex.

The new cortical centres of movement are clustered round the middle cortical fold of the hemispheres, running from the crown down both sides of the head in the temporal region. In these central folds movements are put into operation after they have been carefully screened to suit the needs of the moment. But the cortex only directs that a certain movement shall be performed —for instance, the reaching up of an arm to grasp a branch— it does not pass on detailed information how this movement is to be accomplished by the muscles.

The whole complex sequence of contracting and relaxing the groups of muscles which oppose each other in movement is still managed by the cerebellum and therefore remains entirely below the level of consciousness. The performance of complicated movements, such as searching each other for salt-crystals, flea-hunting, peeling a banana or swinging in the tree-tops, requires cerebellar training under cortical guidance. At first each single muscular movement must be initiated by a voluntary cortical effort, but gradually the cerebellum learns to perform a whole sequence of muscular feats without cortical supervision. Once a practiced movement is voluntarily initiated by the cortex the entire action runs off automatically. Here again there is a perfect co-operation between the cortex and the brain-stem.

In man's pre-human ancestors the close and harmonious co-ordination of cortex and brain-stem was a highly satisfactory means of assuring survival and evolutionary prosperity, as it still is in all wild-living mammals. But when, about half a million years ago, man began very slowly to embark upon the road to cultural advance, an entirely new situation arose. The use of implements and the control of fire introduced artifacts of which the cortex could avail itself for purposes of living. These artifacts had no relationship whatever to the organization of the body and could, therefore, not be integrated into the functioning of the brain-stem.

The brain-stem's great body-regulating centre, the diencephalon, continued to function just as if the artifacts were non-existent. But as the diencephalon is also the organ in which instincts are generated, the earliest humans found themselves faced with a very old problem in a new garb. Their instinctive behaviour ceased to be appropriate in the new situations which the cortex created by using artifacts. Just as in the pre-mammalian reptiles the new environment in the trees rendered many ancient reflexes pointless, the new artificial environment which man began to build for himself at the dawn of culture made many of his animal reflexes useless.

In the tree-tops of the Carboniferous Age the insertion of a censorship between the raw incoming sensory messages and the diencephalon had proved to be a splendid solution to the problem, and in 150 million years this system was developed and made almost perfect for mammalian life. Then, only half a million years ago, many of the old dangers which body and brain had co-operated to meet lost their peril and the normal reactions to old threats became obsolete. One might have expected the existing censorship to have learned how to suppress sensory messages that no longer called for a bodily state of emergency, but this, unfortunately, did not happen. Ancient dangers that artifacts rendered harmless continued to pass the normal cortical censorship and to put the diencephalon in a state of alarm.

There may have been two main reasons for this failure to extend the old censorship of the senses to the new conditions of culture. One reason is that culture developed at a pace which was too fast for the old interpretation of danger to be broken down when, in rapid succession, one threat after another was eliminated. The second reason is that the censoring mechanism was by now too highly specialized and perfected to submit to a revolutionary re-organization. A similar evolutionary law prevented the old brain-stem from changing into a new brain in pre-mammalian evolution, so that a new steering device had to be super-imposed on the existing brain. Similarly, at the dawn of culture the old reflexes could not suddenly be eliminated.

The human brain solved the difficulty by creating a new type of censorship. Hitherto sensory and hormonal stimuli had been censored only with regard to the bodily reactions which they produced. Once such reactions were permitted to run their course they were fully conscious. But under the influence of culture a censorship began to be applied to the reactions themselves, as well as to the sensory and hormonal stimuli that had evoked them, after they had already been cleared by the normal animal censorship. The new development was that culture imposed a second censorship at the level of conscious awareness. This meant that instincts and bodily reactions thereto could be operating without any conscious knowledge of the fact, whenever there were cultural reasons for repressing them. This new type of censorship was thus an extension of an old principle that had proved its worth in a long process of pre-cultural evolution.

The new censorship at the level of consciousness probably began with the instinct of fear. As culture progressed, rage, then hunger and sleep, and last of all sex came to depend on cortical approval. Without this cortical approval the instincts could not become conscious; and unless they were consciously perceived, instinct-gratification could not run its course.

An example will illustrate this. An early Stone Age Man is squatting beside his precious camp-fire at night. Suddenly he sees a pair of gleaming eyes just beyond the circle of light, then another pair and then more. He realizes that wolves are prowling around him in the darkness. This sensory perception has been composed out of raw optic messages in his cortex. As it constitutes a threat, it is immediately passed by the lower censorship and conveyed to the diencephalon for action.

The diencephalon goes into its normal emergency routine. It raises the pulse-rate, the blood pressure and the blood sugar; it stops hunger and may produce a liquid evacuation of the bowel; it may raise gooseflesh and will tense the muscles. This is the normal preparation of the body for flight and the appropriate bodily response to fear. Yet the Stone Age Man is not consciously aware of any panic, nor has he any intention of making a dash for the safety of his cave.

Leisurely, he picks a flaming brand out of the fire and hurls it at the closest pair of eyes. The eerie lights vanish, and he returns to the patient chipping of a flint. The new thing that has happened in his brain is that, while the old terror of the wolves is still there, the new censorship at the level of consciousness has screened off the instinct of fear because his artifacts—in this case the fire—have rendered the natural instinctive reaction unnecessary.

Instinct and Emotion

Modern educated man has a fairly clear idea what he means when he speaks of emotions, but these powerful impulses are difficult to interpret physiologically. Physiologists, psychologists and philosophers have tried to explain and classify human emotions. So far there has been little agreement among the many theories that have been put forward. One of the difficulties seems to be a matter of terminology and definition. The term *emotion* is often used to cover two entirely different psychic phenomena. For the purposes of this study it is necessary to make a clear distinction between these two forms of feeling, of which the one will be called an instinct and the other an emotion.

An instinct is a very old impulse which is generated in the diencephalon by a combination of hormonal and sensory stimuli. In this process the cortex is involved only to the extent that it censors the raw incoming messages from the senses. An emotion, on the other hand, is the conscious or subconscious elaboration of a diencephalic instinct by the cortical processes of memory, association and reasoning. Emotions are thus generated in the cortex out of crude instincts.

Animals have only very rudimentary emotions. In them the instincts can pass without further cortical embellishment into consciousness. In early primitive man many raw instincts were still consciously acceptable, but in urban man this is no longer so. When a raw instinct such as fear, rage or sex breaks through all cortical barriers, it is usually interpreted as insanity or crime, because raw instincts threaten the cortical authority with which man runs his artificial world. A horse which resists training and continues its natural tendency to shy at the slightest provocation is useless and dangerous as a domestic animal. In the same way, a man who cannot cortically control his animal instincts is a threat to a society built upon such control.

Animals have cortical control over their instincts, but they differ from modern man in that their control is directed exclusively to biological and not to artificial requirements. Moreover, man not only controls his instincts, but also represses them, together with the emotions they engender, at the level of consciousness. The cortical control of conscious instincts and emotions is useful, but their repression by a censorship which has become too severe is dangerous, because this leads to psychosomatic disease, arising out of a conflict between diencephalic and cortical behaviour.

The difference between an instinct and an emotion can be illustrated by a simple example. A peasant comes to the city for the first time and pays a visit to the zoo. He arrives at the lion-cage and stares at an old tawny male. Suddenly the lion bares its fangs and rushes with a blood-curdling roar at the bars. The peasant's instinct-ridden diencephalon reacts at once. The reaction is that of stark terror, and instantly his body is prepared for flight. His muscles tense, his blood pressure, pulserate and blood sugar rise, he gets gooseflesh, etc. Before his cortex can put a check on these unnecessary instinctive reactions, the peasant may have staggered back a step or two.

Yet in a moment the cortex regains control and informs him that the beast is imprisoned behind sturdy iron bars. The peasant feels ashamed of his instinctive behaviour and smiles sheepishly. But later he will recount the incident at the village inn and describe it as a wonderful thrill which he enjoyed immensely. There will be no mention of the momentary panic. In this example the stark terror and the reaction it produced were a matter of instinct—primitive, crude and uncontrollable. The enjoyable thrill is a cortical elaboration, and only this can correctly be called an emotion.

In the above example there was an audible and visible lion of which the peasant was fully aware. He knew that a lion is a dangerous animal which only an artifact, in the form of the cage, rendered harmless. If the peasant had been a city-dweller, accustomed to seeing caged lions since his childhood, he would not have staggered back. The primitive fright would still have been there, but it would not have broken through the better-trained cortical censorship of diencephalic instincts. The bodily reaction would have been immediately registered as a pleasant thrill. The censorship would have been tighter.

In modern man the cause of the panic to which his diencephalon reacts often remains below the level of consciousness. In animals this does not happen, because their diencephalon reacts only to sensory and hormonal stimuli. But in modern man an emotion that was elaborated out of a primitive instinct can in its turn put the diencephalic mechanism into operation, regardless of whether the emotion is above or below the threshold of consciousness.

For instance, a puny factory worker may have a primitive physical fear of his loud and hefty foreman. Whenever the foreman approaches, the sound of his voice and the sight of his huge body make the worker's diencephalon prepare for flight. Of this the worker is not consciously aware. The instinct of fear is suppressed, because the cortex knows that the foreman will not harm him physically; yet in spite of this knowledge the instinctive fear is still there.

On this suppressed fear the cortex now goes to work and turns it into an emotion, such as disgust with the job, worry about finding another one, or jealousy of the foreman's pay and position. Only when thus disguised can the primitive fear become conscious.

But there may be other emotional elaborations which the censorship at the threshold of consciousness considers unfit to be allowed to pass, though they may still be free to express themselves in the worker's dreams. Such emotions might be a wish that the foreman would get cancer, wither away and die or that he get caught in a machine and be crushed to pulp. Such violent emotions the worker is quite unable to face consciously, and so his cortex screens them off. Yet all these emotions evoke the diencephalic reflexes that are geared to the primitive instincts of rage or flight.

If these instincts break through all cortical barriers, the worker

will either run amok or start screaming and jump out of the
window. He will then find himself in jail or in a mental hospital.
If instincts do not break through, the perfectly normal diencephalic responses begin to pile up, and sooner or later the
worker will suffer from such psychosomatic diseases as high
blood pressure, diabetes, chronic diarrhoea, or a coronary
thrombosis. The addition of ill-health further increases his
alarm; and since his diencephalon can only react to alarm in
accordance with its ancient mechanisms, the symptoms get
worse.

Another example is the successful businessman who knows
that after years of hard work he has made enough money to
cover the costs of his tastes for the rest of his life. His diencephalon temptingly suggests instinct-gratification, such as lying abed in the morning, promiscuous sex, leisure, play and
solitude. If he can consciously take note of these primitive desires
and consciously resign himself to the fact that they cannot be
fulfilled because he accepts his obligations to his wife and children, he will avoid psychosomatic ill-health.

But all too often urban man's sense of duty to his family and
to the business he has created is so great and so deeply ingrained
that his cortex censors the promptings of instinct before they
can become conscious. In this case they are cast back from the
threshold of consciousness on to the diencephalon, which primitively interprets the situation as one of dangerous confinement
and sets the appropriate reactions in motion according to its
lights. It prepares the businessman for physical flight and escape.

But as these preparations are never used for what they are
intended, and as there is no let-up in the need to escape, the
bodily reactions continue to pile up, and the businessman may
become unbearably irritable or irascible. He may fly into a
rage if his dinner is ten minutes late, not because this is in itself
a calamity, but because to him it is a subconscious reminder of
the prison from which there is no escape. Eventually he may
fall a victim to one or several of the same psychosomatic disorders from which the worker suffered.

The Human Instincts

It is often said that animals act by instinct, whereas man is
motivated by reason. Generally speaking that is correct; but put

in this way it might be taken to mean that man has lost his primitive instincts, and this is certainly not the case.

In modern man all the instincts are still there as they were millions of years ago, but they have become imprisoned in the diencephalon in the sense that they no longer have a free outlet into consciousness. Before they can become conscious they must undergo a process of cortical refining, grooming and bridling which turns them into emotions. Finally, they have to pass another censorship at the conscious threshold where all those emotions that are conventionally or ethically unacceptable are screened off. In the modern cortex this censorship is becoming ever more meticulous and finicky, while the repressed instincts appear to be growing more and more turbulent, as their outlet into action and their exposure to conscious reasoning is blocked.

It is a basic rule of all life that the survival of the species is the supreme consideration to which all else is sacrificed. The propagation of the species is served by the instinct of sex. The sexual craving and its gratification have no significance for the survival of the individual. The survival of some individuals is necessary for the purposes of propagation, but other individuals are mercilessly sacrificed when their death enables the species to flourish.

The parasitic tapeworm produces hundreds of millions of fertile eggs in its lifetime. If only two or three of these eggs accomplish the hazardous passage from host to host and so reach maturity, the purposes of the species are fully served, though at a fantastic cost of individual lives. Fishes produce enormous shoals of baby fish. The progeny must be sufficiently numerous to allow predatory fish to satisfy their hunger and still spare a few baby fish which may then survive into maturity. In the whole animal kingdom the prosperity of the species ranks above the prosperity of the individual, and the instincts are adjusted primarily to the survival of the species.

A threat to the species is present when sex is involved, as in rivalry for the possession of a mate or in the defence of a helpless brood. The reaction to a sex-threat is always rage and never fear, regardless of how ill equipped to do battle the animal may be. This must necessarily be so in the over-riding interest of the species.

In sexual rivalry battle is joined by two members of the same species having the same armament and the same tactics. Therefore the stronger opponent always wins and temporarily or permanently eliminates the weaker from the act of procreation. If fear entered into the reaction to a sexual threat, the weaker would run away from the stronger and pass on his feebler traits to an inferior progeny. The blind rage which a sexual threat provokes prevents this.

Similarly, a threat to the brood calls forth rage and selfless heroism, because fear and flight would mean sacrificing the progeny for the sake of the individual parent. The survival of a parent at the cost of the brood would be of great disadvantage to the species, as the potential fertility of the brood is greater than that of one parent. Thus in the sexual sphere, and only in the sexual sphere, there exists a type of rage from which fear is totally absent.

When the individual is threatened with hunger, pain or death in the absence of sexual implications, the instinctive behaviour is different. In this case fear always precedes rage. Only when a threat to individual survival goes beyond a certain point does fear change into rage. The point at which this happens varies vastly from species to species and is largely a question of defensive or aggressive armament. The better armed the animal is, the sooner it will turn to attack. The greater the chance of victory in close combat, the sooner the animal will fight to remove the threat.

But there is a large group of animals so poorly equipped with biological weapons that they must at all costs avoid combat and concentrate on escape. They do this either by running away or by making themselves invisible. They may hide or melt into their environment by colour-adaptation or mimicry, which makes them look like something different from what they are; or they may, like the cuttlefish, eject an inky cloud in which they disappear. Only in the extreme emergency of finding themselves at bay will timid animals turn and fight with whatever weapons they have.

On the gradient that runs from animals in which fear soon provokes rage to those in which this switch takes place only when they stand at bay, man's position is at the extreme end of timidity and physical defencelessness. Man has only had a brief time to adapt himself to life on the ground, unlike the horse, which is one of the most successful escapists.

Measured by animal standards, man's gait is still clumsy and awkward and his highest speed is moderate. Man has none of the elegant agility with which the gibbon does a super-trapeze act in the branches. Man has a strong scent, which other creatures can smell from afar, while he himself has an almost worthless nose. He is a rather poor swimmer and is unable to hide under water for any useful length of time; he cannot take off into the air and, being devoid of any protective colouring, he is always conspicuous.

These and many other disadvantages, however, are fully compensated by the extraordinary development of his cortex and the perfection of his eyes and ears. Man's optical and acoustic perception and the associative ability of his cortex have enabled him to interpret his surroundings so well that he can establish the exact nature of a threat from afar. This gives him valuable time to take such protective measures as may be necessary.

Before the beginning of culture man's only response to a threat was very early flight—the earlier the better. In order to survive he had to be extremely pusillanimous. Any recklessness, carelessness or a temptation to indulge in sex, feeding or sleep when he should be on the run would have been extremely dangerous.

In those animals in which danger quickly evokes rage because they are well equipped to fight, the sex-urge is more powerful than fear; and this is in the interest of the species, for if the danger becomes great there are two individuals to fight in partnership. In the less well-armed animals that have to seek safety in flight, the fearless continuation of copulation in the face of a threat might mean the death of two individuals. Thus in timid animals—and man is one of them—it is of advantage to the species if fear interrupts copulation.

Dogs growl and the large cats roar menacingly when threatened during feeding. If the danger increases they eat faster; fear does not destroy their appetite. But the animals that run away are unable to feel hunger and fear simultaneously. In them fear dominates and wipes out their appetite. This automatic reflex saves them from having to choose between the pangs of fear and the pangs of hunger. At the approach of danger they are instantly relieved of hunger and are thus free to run without hesitation. Similarly, fear and sleep are incompatible in such animals, and in all but extreme exhaustion it is always fear that dominates.

The bodily mechanisms by which fear banishes sex, hunger and sleep are managed by the diencephalon. They are fully automatic and require no cortical intervention. Modern civilized man has surrounded himself with a complicated and most efficient system of artificial defences. Under ordinary circumstances he no longer needs to run for his life, and his primitive bodily reflexes that were all geared to flight have become meaningless. His cortex, having censored the diencephalic reactions at the level of consciousness, is unable to interpret the bodily preparations for flight correctly. Feeling perfectly safe inside its artificial fortifications, modern man's cortex cannot understand that his primitive diencephalon still reacts in the old way to threats which the cortex no longer accepts as such.

When these once normal and vitally important reactions to fear do reach his conscious awareness, he interprets them as something abnormal and regards them as afflictions. He speaks of impotence or frigidity when the sex-instinct is suppressed by fear, of indigestion when apprehensiveness kills his appetite, and of insomnia when fright keeps him awake at night.

Modern man also fails correctly to interpret the physical preparations for flight, because his cortex sees no reason to run away from threats which his senses are still reporting to the diencephalon as an emergency. A few thousand years have not nearly been long enough for the old censorship of the senses to adjust itself to the artificial environment. The once appropriate clenching of his back muscles which have to hold him erect while running he calls lumbago. The increased heart-beat becomes palpitation, the rise in blood pressure he notices as a headache, the sudden elimination of waste-matter he calls diarrhoea or a urinary disorder, and so forth. It is man's civilization which prevents him from realizing that such bodily reactions may be merely the normal results of diencephalic alarm and the mobilization of those marvellous flight-mechanisms to which he owes his existence as a species.

These now largely useless reactions, and their misinterpreta-

tion as signs of disease, produce a new—this time conscious—
state of alarm: the dread of disease. If the cortex were consciously able to understand why such reactions occur, it would
inform the diencephalon that cortical intelligence has proved
the original alarm to be false, whereupon the diencephalon
would immediately demobilize. This is exactly what the mammalian cortex is for and the way it operates in animals.

But the modern human cortex has put iron bars between the
body and the lion. It has erected artificial, non-biological
defences, and of these the diencephalon knows nothing. The
diencephalon still reacts to the lion as if there were no bars. To
the cortex such behaviour seems senseless and unintelligible.
These normal diencephalic reactions cause the cortex concern
and alarm, this alarm or anxiety is flashed back to the diencephalon as a new emergency, and the diencephalon must
always react to a message of emergency received from the
higher authority of the cortex. It does this in the only way it
can, which is an ever more intensive preparation for headlong
flight. More wires are set humming throughout the body, thereby increasing just those symptoms which are upsetting the cortex. These normal diencephalic reactions which the cortex considers a sign of disease increase and create more terror. It is in
this way that the vicious cycles which cause psychosomatic
disease become established.

At the root of all this cortico-diencephalic misunderstanding
lies the introduction of non-biological artificial weapons and
defences into the perfect equilibrium of the pre-Stone-Age
human body-brain organization. In the millions of years spent
in the trees, the diencephalon had learned to serve superbly the
most timid of mammals and to protect it from making wrong
and dangerous decisions. In this it could rely implicitly on perfect co-operation from the cortex. But when biologically timid
man started to arm himself with inorganic armour to which
the diencephalon had no functional relationship, he suddenly
grew bold. His body and his brain-stem, having spent eons
specializing in timidity, could not adjust themselves to the new
courage. Their once normal responses became ever more in-
appropriate as culture and civilization swept onward.

Surprisingly, paleontology shows that the more timid a
creature is, the greater is the longevity of the species. Gone are

the fierce giants of the early world. Our present-day carnivora are comparatively young and are already threatened with extinction, while the very timid and incredibly old duck-billed platypus still lives in its secluded burrows in the banks of Australian rivers. The horse is another example of the long, steady and successful evolution of a very timid animal, and man clinches the point.

When timid and hence biologically successful man made for himself an artificial world in which he could live free of the dangers that beset his ancestors, he suddenly became ferocious. Ferocity was quite contrary to his evolutionary nature, which was pusillanimous and non-violent. He learned to make up for his lack of natural weapons by impatiently creating an invincible armoury of artificial defences. He began to live as if he possessed all the hoofs, horns, fangs and claws with which evolution had armed the animal world and to act as if he were the most aggressive creature on earth.

Modern man's diencephalon is as yet unable to cope with the perverse situation of a life entirely different from that for which its evolution had prepared it. The more modern man's cortex drives him out of his natural environment into an artificial one, the more he will become prone to psychosomatic disease, unless he realizes the extent to which he is an animal straining in a cortical harness.

The Human Emotions

While the basic instincts of sex, hunger, sleep and fear are diencephalic, the wide range of human emotions such as pity, sadness, shame, regret, hope, curiosity, guilt, awe, etc., are cortical elaborations of these basic instincts. Many emotions are clearly of sexual origin, such as romantic love, devoted friendship, groundless jealousy, conceit and vanity. Delight in culinary refinement is an elaboration of hunger. Some emotions are derived from the cortical urge to animate leisure with play, such as the enjoyment of the arts, sport, hobbies, etc.; but by far the most numerous are cortical elaborations of fear.

Man's lofty virtues of courage and bravery, when sex is not involved, are a product of civilization. In early Stone-Age Man any show of valour would have been a dangerous and despicable vice. Even to-day, when non-sexual honour evokes heroism, it is psychologically pertinent to enquire whether the real motive is not the fear of disgrace. We are always ready to shower material rewards upon those who pander to our leisure, while those who risk their lives for us must be content with a medal, significantly called a 'gong'. Their sacrifice is never really and deeply appreciated, because it runs contrary to all the biological trends of our essentially pusillanimous nature. A medal is a label by which we distinguish the man who is unnatural enough to put the needs of civilization before the needs of survival. A medal is an award, not a reward.

From a cortical point of view man is at his best when he is on the defensive. Timidity enormously enhances his inventiveness, while the security he is always striving for renders him unproductive. The tragedy of the rut into which man's brain has slipped is that his cortex cannot content itself with unproductivity. It is never satisfied with whatever security it achieves and must needs embark upon fresh intellectual adventures in the hope of achieving still greater security. In this process he is continually widening the gap between his diencephalic evolution and his cortical activities.

The emotion of sadness is an example of one way in which the cortex elaborates the instinct of fear. Basically, sadness is always self-pity, and self-pity is a long-drawn fear. The fear may be a dread of privation or loneliness, sickness or the death of a loved person, or it may be engendered by the cortical identification of the sad person with the suffering of others. These processes are below the level of consciousness, because the admission of fear in this context is unacceptable and has to be disguised. That is also why the suggestion that sadness is a form of self-pity is often fiercely resented.

Why the emotion of sadness should stimulate the tear glands to excessive secretion is unknown. Weeping must certainly once have been a useful function, but its purpose has been lost in the past of human evolution. As weeping exists in animals—if at all —only in a very rudimentary form, it would appear to be a rather recent acquisition. The elimination of water in the form of urine, diarrhoea and cold sweat is a normal reaction to fear when the body prepares for flight. Perhaps the shedding of tears once belonged to that category of reactions.

Under normal conditions tears prevent the surface of the

eyeball from drying out and wash away dust that settles on it. Tears also afford some protection against the glare of the sun or its reflection from snow, the heat of a forest fire or the smoke of a hearth in a cave. A strong flow of tears also flushes the nose into which the tears are drained from the eyes, and it is only when the flow is stronger than that with which the drainage system can cope that tears spill over the eyelids. It is probable, though hard to prove, that an animal in headlong flight also has a stronger secretion of tears. In flight the eyes are torn wide open with terror and the evaporation from the surface of the eyeball is greatly increased, calling for a more copious flow from the tear-glands. Perhaps man weeps because he no longer runs. Sitting still there is no increased evaporation, and so the excess lacrimation spills over.

Though sadness is a cortical elaboration of fear, the act of weeping is put into operation by the diencephalon. Weeping is one of the very few bodily reactions to fear, anxiety and tension which urban man considers legitimate and to which his diencephalon can still give free rein without incurring too much cortical displeasure. Perhaps the diencephalon made the most of this rare privilege and fondly developed weeping as the one remaining outlet for its pent-up frustration. In modern man weeping was the only all-round satisfactory emotional vent until verbalization on the psychiatrist's couch was introduced and began to replace it.

When considering the origin of weeping it should also be remembered that the excessive secretion of tears is associated with the crying of an infant. In this case the association with fear is very obvious.

Other Bodily Reactions to Fear

In his long evolutionary history man has perfected all those mechanisms with which his diencephalon helps him in his dash for safety. The usefulness of these reactions becomes clear as soon as the extreme timidity of early Stone-Age Man is fully appreciated, but there are a few very old diencephalic reactions to fear which are not so easily interpreted.

An example of such an evolutionary relic is the puckering of the skin known as gooseflesh. Physiologically, gooseflesh results from the contraction of the tiny muscle attached to each hair.

This contraction makes the hair stand on end. It has been explained that the mechanism is necessary for the regulation of body temperature in small mammals. But why should not only cold, but also fear, produce this bodily reaction? Probably the erection of the pelt proved to be a useful protection against the talons of the birds of prey and the fangs of snakes and mammalian marauders that hunted in the trees, because it made them misjudge the real size of their prey.

The raising of the hair is an instantaneous response to danger which man has retained, though he has lost most of the hair that made it effective. Moreover, hair has always been a sensory organ of touch which considerably extends the tactile reach of the skin. The whiskers of a cat are a further development of this principle. In the porcupine and the hedgehog hair became a weapon of defence, and in both these cases its mobility was of utmost importance. In the rhinoceros the united tuft of hair which forms the horn has become an immobile weapon of attack. There is thus a close connection between hair and danger.

An enquiry into the evolutionary origin of such a seemingly useless and embarrassing reaction as blushing is beset with even greater difficulties. Blushing is caused by the sudden dilatation of the small blood vessels of the skin of the face. It is the diencephalon's strange reaction to the cortical emotion of shame. Shame is a mild form of fear, calling for hiding rather than flight; indeed, another expression of shame is hiding the face or turning away. Perhaps blushing is a form of camouflage, a rudimentary colour adaptation rendering the face less conspicuous, or was it once a signal used to communicate sexual excitement?

Some other reactions to fear have a clearer evolutionary background. For instance, trembling with fright or cold is an effective method of stoking up for flight or of increasing the body temperature. The muscular effort involved raises the temperature, increases respiration, heartbeat, blood sugar and blood pressure, all useful preparations for running. Trembling does not occur when flight is resorted to at once; but when flight does not take place, as in urban man, the diencephalon intensifies its preparations. Rather pathetically, it does the best it can by mustering its last resources to force the body into the only reaction it knows—headlong flight.

Similarly, being paralysed with fear is an exaggerated dien-cephalic reaction to panic. Though the story of a bird being hypnotized into suicidal immobility by a snake is apocryphal, it is nevertheless a happy human fiction, because man can in-deed be paralysed by fear. The explanation seems to be that the normal tensing of the muscles in preparation for flight may go beyond the point of usefulness.

A few facets of the complicated evolution of the human psyche have been discussed. They may suffice to show that in man fear is of over-riding importance. This primitive instinct and its many cortical elaborations such as shame, dread, anxiety, worry and apprehension, produce bodily reactions which were once highly appropriate and, indeed, a vital necessity.

The function of the mammalian cortex has been interpreted as being basically one of censorship. This censorship was for millions of years confined to the senses. Gradually it began to be applied to movement and later still to the instincts. In the last stage of this trend a censorship was established at the threshold of consciousness, when half a million years ago man started on the road that led to civilization. Throughout this development there is a clear tendency for the censorship to be-come stricter, and this is particularly marked in the censorship at the threshold of consciousness.

In modern man the decision on what is allowed to pass into consciousness and what is not, no longer follows the dictates of biological necessity. Determining what the cortex allows into consciousness are conventions, habits and the postulates of civilization. Of these postulates the brain-stem and its centre, the diencephalon, have remained completely unaware; they are therefore no longer in harmony with the conscious mind.

It is improbable that there has been any organic change in the human brain during the last 30 thousand years. The difference between modern and Paleolithic Man is one of cere-bral training and not of biological or anatomical advance. In later Paleolithic Man there was already all the room for memories, all the associative capacity, the reasoning power, the ability to learn and the perceptive acuity of modern man. The main difference is that primitive man projected all these func-tions into his natural environment, while modern man concentrates on the artificial world with which he has surrounded himself.

The floundering terror of a pygmy suddenly transferred to Piccadilly Circus would be no greater than that of a London professor marooned in the Congo jungles. Londoners would think the Pygmy a poor fool, but to the Pygmies the professor would present a sorry spectacle of fear and helplessness. The average city-dweller and the average primitive jungle-dweller have the same congenital intelligence, but the way they use it is entirely different. As long as he is not exposed to modern civilization the Pygmy's way is conducive to mental health and balance, because he uses his cortex exactly the way his biological evolution intended him to use it. He thinks so as to survive in hostile natural surroundings, and only to this end does he censor his instincts and emotions. The professor, on the other hand, knows no hostile natural environment. He has been raised in an artificial environment, to which his brain has no organic relationship. He uses his brain to conform to the rules of civilized conduct—not for vital exigencies. These rules are purely cortical constructions, and for them he has had no evolutionary preparation. His body and his diencephalon react just as the Pygmy's do, and this his cortex resents. The end-result of this conflict is psychosomatic disease.

It is only conceit and presumption which tempt modern civilized man to assume that he has a better brain than any member of the most primitive human race on earth. Organically the brains are identical; the apparent difference is merely one of application and training.

3

The Spread of Culture

The Paleolithic Age

THE BEGINNINGS of culture reach back about half a million years. The first men were meat-eating hunters that lived in tropical grasslands. It was during the age of the second great glacial period in which the ice spread south of the Arctic Cap that the severe cold first taught man to appreciate the comfort of fire. He knew fire from the craters of volcanoes and he learned to carry it with him. Fires were also started by lightning, the rubbing together of dead branches in the wind or the self-ignition of fermenting vegetable matter. From such fires man may have collected glowing embers and discovered that by adding dry wood he could perpetuate the fire on his hearth.

Early man may have tasted the flesh of animals caught and roasted by forest fires and found it to his liking long before he deliberately roasted his food. Fire was used for hundreds of thousands of years before man learned how to kindle it by friction. Even to-day there exist primitive tribes, on the Andamans and among the Papuans for instance, who are unable to make fire. They only know how to preserve the fire which they obtain from other tribes, and they often have to make long journeys to get it. For them the extinction of their fire is a major tribal disaster.

Early man found that fire protected him from the cold and from dangerous beasts. Branches charred to a point, wooden clubs and the stones he learned to hurl gave him the possibility of defending himself against animals which he could never have tackled with his bare hands. His weapons also increased the variety of the game he could hunt, adding to his diet many animals that had hitherto been out of his reach.

For thousands of years man threw the whole animal he had killed into his fire. In the heat the skin burned and burst, and he cracked the skulls and the bones with a heavy stone to get at the brain and the marrow. As the ice of each successive glacial period advanced, man suffered from the freezing cold as soon as he moved away from his fire in search of food; and this may have forced him to migrate south each winter, until some pre-historic genius had the brilliant idea of using animal skins for protection from the cold. Once the idea was conceived, there arose the problem of skinning the animal before it was roasted. With only teeth and fingernails to work with, that presented a considerable difficulty.

Early man had found the hard, ball-like flints particularly handy as a missile. He noticed that when such flints struck another hard surface, they shattered into sharp-edged flakes. He collected such flakes if they were of a handy size, particu-larly if they had a sharp point, and used them for ripping open the skin of the animals he killed and for scraping off the fat. Collections of such stones have been found on the earliest Paleolithic sites. The first stone implements were not manu-factured but assiduously collected whenever they were found, the collections being handed down from generation to genera-tion long before they were deliberately fashioned.

The application of fire, animal skins and these crude stone implements was such a startling innovation that their use spread rapidly to all parts of the world where man needed them. Many thousands of years had to pass before man began to shape flints by patient chipping and flaking to suit the purpose for which he required them, and for a long time clubs, branches and bones were his chief weapons. In spite of these weapons, early man was still a timid hunter. He could not attack and kill the larger and more dangerous beasts that threatened him. The bones of many ferocious animals have been found on the sites of early human dwellings, but it is questionable whether man killed these animals. It seems more reasonable to suppose that he found them dead or dying and dragged them to his cave. Man's evolutionary history is quite contrary to the notion that he was the great and fearless hunter he is so often pictured to have been, and the fact that he frequently resorted to cannibal-ism suggests that he was often hungry.

In the lower Paleolithic Age, which started about 500,000 years ago, naturally shaped stones used as tools were replaced by manufactured stone tools; and it is at about this time that different Stone-Age cultures can be distinguished by definite traditions in the shape and workmanship of their tools.

Four times the ice fringe moved south, and three times it retreated in interglacial periods. Its movement produced alternating wet and dry periods in Africa and alternating arctic and tropical conditions in Europe. It was during the third interglacial period, when the hippopotamus was thriving in the tropical waters of the River Thames, that earliest Neanderthal Man appeared and began to spread over the whole of Europe, North Africa and the Middle East. When then the ice returned for the last time about 70,000 years ago, he was well established with fire, furs, good stone tools and was able to survive the cold winters by moving into caves. And then quite suddenly prosperous Neanderthal Man was replaced by the new and entirely different race known as Cro-Magnon Man about 40,000 years ago.

The erratic movements of the ice-cap and the alternating wet and dry periods which they produced in Africa had a profound influence upon the cortex of Paleolithic Man. The men who lived near the glacial fringe, with their few precious cultural achievements, were kept continually on the move to find living conditions in which they could survive. This wandering north and south brought Paleolithic Man in contact with an ever-changing fauna and flora to which he was forced to adapt himself. The periods in which he had to make such adjustments were much too short for any biological adaptations of his body to have taken place. In an environment in which periods of paradisaical plenty and warmth alternated with almost arctic weather, where endless torrential rains, storms and floods alternated with years of scorching aridity, hunger and privation called for a high degree of cortical ingenuity and inventiveness if man was to survive.

In thousands of millions of years of animal evolution Paleolithic Man is the first instance of survival depending on artifacts and not on biological adaptations. Yet if man's diencephalon had not reached the highest degree of perfection in its automatic bodily responses, the human cortex would have been unable to assure his survival. What saved man was the perfect co-ordination of cortical reasoning and diencephalic reaction.

But even at this early stage the first seeds of disunity between the cortex and the diencephalon were sown. The discrepancies were still of a very minor order, owing to the paucity of artifacts, and hardly made themselves known to Paleolithic consciousness. Only much later, when these artifacts were developed to the extent of completely dominating man's environment, did they lead to psychosomatic disorders.

The Mesolithic and Neolithic Ages

In the post-glacial period in which we are still living there was a continual withdrawal of the arctic ice. The retreating ice left behind fertile, well-irrigated plains enjoying a stable temperate to sub-tropical climate. In the valleys of old rivers—the Nile in Egypt, Tigris and Euphrates in Mesopotamia, and the Indus in India—the astounding change from Paleolithic to Mesolithic and finally to Neolithic Man took place about seven to eight thousand years ago.

The age called Mesolithic produced great improvements in the old stone implements. Compound tools, such as stone axes with a wooden handle and stone-tipped arrows and spears, had been invented. Remarkable though this was, the Mesolithic improvement of stone implements was far less important than the Neolithic achievements of the men that inhabited the Indo-Mediterranean river valleys. This cultural revolution brought mankind agriculture, pottery, domestic animals and warfare.

It is hard to say why Indo-Mediterranean Man had the remarkable upsurge of inventiveness which brought him so many great cultural achievements in rapid succession. Perhaps it was because he enjoyed for the first time a stable, warm climate and because plant and animal life around him was so plentiful that he no longer needed to wander from place to place in search of food. As a result he had far more leisure than any of his ancestors had ever had. In this leisure he used his wits, which had been sharpened during the glacial periods, to satisfy his innate curiosity and to experiment, at first playfully, with his environment.

Towards the end of the Paleolithic and in the Mesolithic stage man was already collecting the grains of wild grasses, pounding them into flour and making an edible paste with water. This paste he then spread over hot stones and so baked his first bread.

Such food must have been a rare delicacy requiring many hours of hard work to collect the wild grains. In the Nile Valley man first learned to seed and cultivate those wild grasses which became our barley, wheat and millet. In the Indus Valley the men who created the great pre-historic Indian cultures learned to cultivate indigenous wild rice. Once the principles of seeding, transplanting, harvesting and storing had been mastered, this knowledge spread rapidly throughout a large part of the inhabited world. The new craft of agriculture was applied to all wild plants that were in one way or another useful to man. Seed could be transported over long distances and so grew the vast variety of plants which man now cultivates.

For the first time man could provide himself with ample vegetable food without having to face the many dangers of ranging through the forests in search of roots, berries, nuts and grasses. As agricultural knowledge increased, the earlier wandering from place to place, the burning down of a patch of forest, the raising of a single crop, collecting the seed and then moving on to repeat the process elsewhere, began to be abandoned. This wasteful form of early agriculture is still used by some primitive races such as the Veddas of Ceylon, but elsewhere it gradually gave way to permanent settlement when it was realized that the same land could be used over and over again if it was ploughed. The discovery that turning over the surface of the soil gave the earth back its fertility was another brilliant cortical feat, and it is chiefly the result of this discovery that man came to live in villages, towns and cities, i.e. became civilized.

The domestication of wild animals and their controlled breeding was another great Neolithic achievement. The first animals to be tamed were dogs, who had long ago attached themselves to human habitations to scrounge for scraps of food. The taming of the dog was probably accomplished independently in many parts of the world.

The next animals to be domesticated were cattle, sheep, goats and pigs. Various races of these animals existed over the whole world, but domestication was achieved in Central Asia. The breeds that were tamed are found only in Asia, and it is from these breeds that domesticated animals were imported into the Mediterranean area, where the indigenous varieties continued to exist in the wild state only. At the fringe of the ice-cap the reindeer was tamed. The camel that once lived in the Old and the New World was one of the earliest animals to be used by man in Eastern Europe and Asia. Its close relative the llama was tamed independently on the American continent. Among the animals used for transport the ass was an early domestication; the horse was tamed somewhat later, as was the Indian elephant.

Domestication provided man with a constant supply of animal food and made him independent of hunting and canni-balism. The tending of his flocks and herds changed man's life completely, because it imposed upon him work that had to be performed at regular hours. His day had to be divided into fixed periods which were devoted to work, sleep and feeding. It it probable that man learned the causal connection between the sex-act and pregnancy from his animals. Only a few years ago tribes living in a Mesolithic stage of culture in Australia still knew nothing of this connection. Agriculture and domesti-cation taught man to measure and to count. He learned to reckon in time, first in days and seasons, and soon made the great discovery that these periods were correlated to the move-ment of astral bodies and the changes of the moon.

A third great Neolithic achievement was the invention of pottery. This discovery spread so rapidly throughout the Neo-lithic world that it is now impossible to say where the feat was first accomplished. It is also difficult to say how this knowledge originated. It may have arisen from the plaiting of long leaves and stalks into basketwork which was caked with mud and left to dry in the sun and used for storing grain. It may have been discovered that certain kinds of mud would hold together with-out the basketwork. Firing may have been discovered acci-dentally. On the other hand, pottery may have been the result of man's need to store water and to boil it for cooking his food. Man probably discovered the extraordinary properties of boil-ing water long before he knew how to make a pot. He may, for instance, have experimented with boiling water by using a human skull or an ostrich's egg-shell as a recipient. Whatever the origin of pottery, the later invention of the potter's wheel ranks among the greatest early technical advances.

For reasons that have been explained, it is very unlikely that pre-Neolithic Man was a belligerent creature, though he will always have fought a sexual rival, and neighbouring clans may have mutually adducted young women. The land was thinly populated and there was room for all. There can have been no motive for primitive clans to slaughter each other, and this would have been contrary to the natural laws governing the survival of the species. Killing each other for non-sexual reasons is an exclusive and very recent human trait, though man has managed to train some of his domestic animals such as cocks and dogs to overcome their natural instincts and to behave as he does in this respect. Wild animals may chase away members of their own species that stray into their hunting grounds or pastures, but they never kill them. Only some of the highly socialized insects such as ants practise robbery upon their own kind, in this case because there is something worth stealing.

Man's timidity and peacefulness towards his fellow men changed when in Neolithic times the clan began to own valuable possessions, such as fertile fields, herds of domestic animals, pots, houses and the skilled men who knew how to provide such riches. These cultural possessions were so important for a better chance of survival that men for the first time were trained to sacrifice their lives in order to obtain or retain the new luxuries for the clan.

The need to survive in a now much more competitive world forced man to overcome his innate timidity and to suffer pain and death voluntarily. The fruits of Neolithic civilization were so valuable that it became worthwhile to sacrifice individual lives in order to rob or to defend the new possessions in the greater interest of the species. Those who stayed behind the battle line —the chiefs, the elders, the magicians, the farmers and the women—held their warriors in the highest esteem, for warriors were the new means of providing more security, leisure, food and wealth.

But whenever the threat of invasion was remote or when further conquests could add little that was worth having, the standing of the warrior slumped. At the height of Indian, Chinese, Egyptian, Greek and Roman culture when, as in our days, war brought loss and destruction to both sides, the standing of the physically timid was in the ascendant. Priests, politicians, scientists, artists and women were more appreciated than the soldiers and their warlords.

It may well have been the Neolithic spurt of inventiveness and the new dread of losing its material fruits that irrevocably set the cortex of Mediterranean Man on its specialized trend towards ever greater warlike ferocity and technical proficiency. Warfare and non-sexual robbery were thus a fourth Neolithic novelty. Man became brave, not because there was any change in his biological make-up, but because the cultural artifacts which his cortex had created forced him into internecine strife. To this new development the human diencephalon could make no evolutionary adjustment because the Neolithic revolution was far too sudden. The diencephalon continued to behave as it had always done and so fell out of step with cortical progress. It still reacted to danger with all the old bodily reflexes that were geared to flight, but harsh military training taught the cortex to ignore these reflexes. As long as battles were fought in hand-to-hand combat, many fear reactions proved useful to sustain the physical exertion of fighting; but when later warfare ceased to be a matter of muscles, these reactions became pointless. From the Neolithic beginning of warfare the human cortex has tried to infuse a sexual motive into valour, and this has always been a stimulus. Many ancient sagas, the Homeric epics and the fair ladies of the medieval knights reflect this tendency in literature.

Though Paleolithic Man hunted with clubs, stone weapons and fire, he was as yet no match for the stronger and more dangerous beasts such as lions or tigers. Even to-day when a hungry leopard chooses to roam in an Indian village, the peaceful inhabitants who possess no fire-arms can only tremble in helpless panic, hoping and praying that the beast will not break through the wall of a hut but content itself with a stray dog, a goat or a calf. It was not until the use of metals was discovered that man began to dominate the entire animal world. The Age of Metals started only about 5,000 years ago when some unknown genius discovered that a piece of native copper, with which he may have been playing, was malleable with a stone and could be hammered into any desired shape. Perhaps he found the metal smelted out of the brightly coloured stones which he is known to have collected to make his hearth.

At first man used copper for ornaments, then for tools and finally for weapons. Armed with cutting swords and metal-tipped spears and arrows, he could at last risk close combat with any animal foe. Moreover, copper implements could be manufactured much faster than the finely chipped flints he had hitherto used. For a long time copper and its natural alloys were used as they occurred in ores. The degree of hardness was entirely a matter of chance, and so stone implements continued to be indispensable for purposes for which copper was too soft.

Nearly another thousand years had to pass before the much harder bronze was deliberately manufactured by adding 6–10 per cent of tin to copper. This more useful alloy was probably invented in the regions of present-day Saxony and Bohemia, where the two metals occur in the same ancient mines. From there bronze spread over the whole Eastern Mediterranean, together with the already highly prized gold. It was chiefly the relative scarcity of tin which prompted early trading and adventurous seafaring to Ireland, Wales and Cornwall, where there were rich deposits of tin and gold.

Iron was known to man long before it came into general use. A few iron beads and an iron tool which are authentically 5,000 years old have been found in Egypt. But as far as we know they are a curiosity, for iron did not come into use until about 1,000 years before the birth of Christ. The smelting of iron ores vastly increased man's knowledge of the use of fire. The ability to make a very sharp, long, cutting edge out of a hard metal gave man a weapon much more formidable than anything nature had ever devised. The use of iron brought about another revolutionary change in human civilization.

While the Paleolithic Age lasted half a million years, all these great Neolithic innovations—agriculture, the domestication of animals, pottery, warfare and the use of metals—occurred in the brief span of a few thousand years. There was thus a sudden and almost incredible acceleration in the process of civilization which enormously widened the gap between natural, diencephalic living and cultural, cortical life.

Historical Times

Four thousand years ago villages had already grown into towns and cities. Social structures had become highly complicated, with an ever finer specialization of labour. Seafaring, writing, building, religions and the arts flourished. Commerce and continual wars brought about a rapid diffusion of technical achievement. The great cultures of ancient India, of China and of Latin America were at their height. In the huge land masses bounded by sea, by forbidding mountain ranges and in the north by an inhospitably cold climate, there was hardly any stimulating peripheral contact. These cultures became static because of self-sufficiency and so lost touch with the rest of the world. Further progress soon became almost entirely confined to the countries surrounding the Mid- and Eastern Mediterranean, a racial and cultural melting-pot out of which modern civilization was finally distilled. In this part of the world there were a number of early peaks: the Egyptians, the Assyrians, the Etruscans, the Hebrews, the Greeks, the Romans and later Arabian Islam with its vast expansion to the east. Around the Mediterranean, Christianity spread rapidly northwards and produced a period of relative cultural rest lasting nearly one thousand years—the Middle Ages.

If the Middle Ages had lasted one hundred thousand years, they might have given Western man's diencephalon time to catch up with his cortical activity. In the 'Dark' Ages there was only slow technical progress and life was led according to a fixed pattern, as it was until quite recently in India, China and Africa. In this technically and intellectually conservative environment man could begin to adjust himself physically and emotionally to what his cortex had previously achieved. He would not have been forced to make a readjustment of his cortico-diencephalic relationship, under the impact of a fast stream of technical innovations. Had it lasted long enough, this period of cultural slackening might eventually have brought about evolutionary changes in diencephalic function. The useless reactions with which the diencephalon prepared the body for flight when there was nothing to run away from might have become subjected to a censorship similar to that established long ago for raw sensory messages. If man had had a chance to complete this process there would have been far less psychosomatic disease.

But man never got this chance, because the medieval cortical calm was shattered by the invention of printing in the middle of the fifteenth century. This was about one hundred years after the invention of fire-arms. Printing and gun-powder were known in China long before they were re-invented in the West, but in China these discoveries did not lead to revolutionary changes in the civilization of that staid country and were used almost playfully. Chinese civilization had evolved very slowly and uniformly long before Western civilization entered into the Middle Ages. The Chinese were therefore more closely tied to an established pattern of life which was not so easily upset by technical inventions.

In Europe the intellectual upheavals of Humanism, the Reformation and the Renaissance followed. Man took off to a new and energetic start from the heritage of Greece, Rome and early Christianity. The discovery that the earth was indeed round and that upon its surface there were unimaginably rich and vast new worlds was in that effervescent period just as inspiring as the conquest of space is in our own day. Moveover, Copernicus and Kepler had discovered the mechanics of the solar system, and around 1600 Galileo Galilei was using a crude telescope to probe into the universe and bring it closer. Eighty years later Newton propounded the laws of gravity, and in another hundred years Watt's steam engine was in use, inaugurating the Machine Age. The great electrical discoveries of Galvani, Faraday, Röntgen, Edison, Marconi, Curie and many others followed rapidly.

In 1903 Orville Wright took to the air for the first time in a power-driven machine. At the outbreak of the First World War the far-reaching consequences of Einstein's Theory of Relativity were beginning to be realized. The liberation of untapped energy confined in the structure of the atom had its ghastly announcement in Hiroshima. In 1957 the first man-made satellite was successfully hurled into space rapidly followed by others, and man is now in touch with the moon.

Once again a new peak of civilization is arising with a fantastic crescendo and this time with the participation of practically the whole world. Such widespread participation is not an entirely new phenomenon. It happened with the making of stone implements, agriculture, the domestication of animals, pottery, the use of metals, the necessity of armed robbery and the change of courage from folly into virtue. In ancient or modern times some cultural achievements such as religion and art remained much more closely confined to their place of origin. They were not so unhesitatingly accepted by all, because they served man's spiritual and bodily comforts rather than the survival of his species.

The sudden upsurge of technical civilization during the last 500 years is making it unnecessary for man to be afraid of anything but himself. The threats from savage beasts, climatic catastrophes, hunger and pestilence are almost gone. Man's weapons against his neighbours have reached a destructive power that will soon make war too absurd to be seriously contemplated. War will disappear as did the valiant knights, the robber barons, the pirates, the warlike kings and the fierce tribal chieftains. Proud regiments and mighty battleships are already obsolete. The short historical phase in which new-found weapons and possessions seduced man into committing acts of physical bravery is all but over, and indeed, in the Gandhian concept of non-violence, the ethics of a not too distant world without war and bloodshed have already been laid down. Among men there will once again be peace on earth as there always had been until the birth-pangs of Neolithic civilization provoked hatred and envy.

Once again it will be the timid man with flaccid muscles and turgid brain, now operating panels of switches and gauges, who holds man's power in his delicate fingers, as did the expert flaker of little flints in the Stone Age. This man earns his salary and pays his taxes; they provide him with a personal security and a standard of luxurious living far higher than that enjoyed by the richest kings and princes of the past. And yet there remains one mystery of nature which terrifies him, and that is his own body. About his body and the working of his brain he knows far less than he does about his electronic devices. Indeed, he is using these devices as a means of finding out more about himself. He can construct an electronic brain in many ways superior to his own cortex, about which he still knows so little. He has not understood that, domineering though his cortex is, its reign over the functioning of his body is by no means absolute and that the rumblings of revolt against the would-be cortical oppressor are becoming louder. Perhaps he will one day learn to construct an electronic diencephalon. Only then will he be able to understand fully many things that now seem unfathomable.

According to Western man's concepts a machine, well oiled and tended, runs smoothly. Any grating in the gears, any sparking at the terminals, harasses him, for it may mean taking the machine to pieces and putting in a new part. He knows he cannot do this with his body. His closest approach is to let a surgeon do a mechanical repair-job. This gives him a far greater satisfaction than a chat with a psychiatrist, an injection or a bottle of pills, which seem to him like oiling a broken-down engine. The removal of an appendix, even if it was quite healthy, is something done well, finally and satisfactorily to his mechanical way of thinking. He is not so impressed by having an anxiety removed as he is by having his appendix cut out. When the painless psychological operation is dramatically successful, it seems to him like a miracle. He feels that he has been outwitted and that a sort of conjuring trick has been performed; there is something about it which seems to him unreal. But when he is shown his dead appendix, he feels that a good job has been expertly accomplished and he is satisfied to reward his surgeon handsomely for a few minutes of routine work.

This mechanical attitude towards the body exists only in the descendants of European man, who are, with but few exceptions, those responsible for recent advances in civilization. This is not the attitude of those races who have remained in stiller technical by-waters. They use technical equipment as it rolls out of the factories and use it well, but their emotional attitude to the machine is entirely different. The machine is not their creation and it does not thrill them; it is not a part of themselves. Their cortex does not think primarily in mechanical terms, and thus when they are ill, priestly incantations and the magic rites of medicine-men give them a much deeper satisfaction than the knife of the mechanical repair-man—the surgeon. This is certainly not because they are ignorant, backward people; indeed, they may be highly educated and even brilliant engineers; but their cortex has not been drilled into a wholly mechanical way of thinking as far as their body and its ills are concerned. A similar attitude still exists in our own young children and womenfolk, but even in them a change is now coming about. The modern psychiatrist has rather belatedly taken over the functions of priests and medicine-men in curing essentially emotional ills, but he inspires none of the deep-felt awe that his ancient professional colleagues aroused. The patient pays his psychiatrist to do a specific job, in much the same frame of mind as he pays the plumber. The psychiatrist is obliged to bore his way in reverse through a close cortical censorship. He has no direct access to diencephalic processes as have priests and magicians and, in the case of Western man, the surgeon.

Man's technical evolution may be interpreted as a result of a cortical urge to extend his physical being into his environment. This is the direct continuation of a trend that started from the earliest tree-living days of his ancestors. Then, as now, the extension of the physical being is basically a means of defence through better integration with the surroundings. It has been shown how man's ancestors achieved this on a biological level through an advanced development of the senses of seeing and hearing and by the elaborate interpretation, through memory and associative thinking, of what these senses reported. The sensory evolution took hundreds of millions of years, during which it was continually accelerated so that the most spectacular results were achieved in the last ten million years. Until about half a million years ago these adaptations fully satisfied cortical demands, but at about that time the pressing urge for further integration with the environment outran biological possibilities. The comparative slowness of these evolutionary processes ceased to satisfy the cortex. It was then that the human cortex turned to the use of artifacts to achieve a better control of the body's natural environment.

The cortex did this in many ways. First it replaced body hair by fire and later skins, clothing and shelter. It extended the range and the strength of the arms with spears, clubs and stones, which in due course led to the blow-pipe, the dart, the boomerang, the bow and arrow and finally fire-arms. Muscular strength was increased by the invention of the lever, the wheel, the pulley, and then by engines driven by water, wind and later steam, electricity, oil and nuclear fission, and by such appliances as cranes, pile-drivers, steamrollers and bulldozers.

Timid man must always have envied the horse for its speed. Having no hope of ever being able to compete with it on a biological level, he brilliantly did the next best thing, which was to catch the horse, tame it and climb on its back. When mere horse-muscles became too slow and inconveniently in need of rest and food, man, ever impatient and on the run, invented mechanical transport, ungratefully bringing the noble steed he had loved so well to the brink of extinction. He tamed the ass, the camel and even the elephant to carry him and his burdens when speed was of no account and then invented the cart and power-driven vehicles. He extended the volume and the range of his voice with drums and trumpets and all sorts of musical instruments and then invented modern methods of telecommunication.

Being a strictly ground-bound creature, he mastered the water with ships, submarines and diving equipment. He took to the air first in the balloon, then in aircraft and is now reaching into space. He has learned how to burrow deep into the earth's crust and to live on and under the ice of arctic wastes. Perhaps greatest of all is the extension of his sight. His huge telescopes enable him to see astral galaxies millions of light-years away, showing him things which actually took place at a time when he himself was still a mousy, tree-living mammal. He has learned to change light into electricity and vice-versa, enabling him to see things no light waves could ever reveal directly to his eyes. He can thereby see through solid objects with X-rays; in the electron microscope he can enlarge the invisibly small 100,000 times and in television and radar see things that are entirely out of his sight.

Man's thermometers measure temperature variations that his skin cannot perceive, and in his analytical balances he can weigh a speck of dust which his sense of touch cannot feel. Finally, he has recently learned to extend his memory, his associative capacity and reasoning power with the electronic brain which can in minutes, without error, solve problems which would take the living cortex years to do. Interestingly, he has neglected the senses of taste and smell; they have so far escaped mechanization and thus still offer possibilities of biological refinement and enjoyment without much cortical inteference.

As soon as man's missiles, his aircraft, his visual and auditive communications achieved global dimensions, he set about the conquest of space in dead earnest, because he is an inveterate escapist and has an abject horror of any kind of confinement. It is still the old primitive urge to run away. When there is nothing left to run away from, he hurriedly sets his sights on a new haven of security, trying to get closer to the infinity he will never reach.

This peculiar urge is particularly developed in the white races of European stock. The East Indian mystic, too, seeks infinity, but he does not do this on a mechanical level. The drive towards the mechanical enlargement of the individual body was a very early feature of occidental civilization. In the Egyptian and later in the Greek, Roman and the Moslem world it existed in the institution of slavery. Using men as a sort of domestic animal or machine was unknown in the rest of the world, except in a few African tribes. It disappeared almost completely during the Middle Ages only to be revived when the need for more 'man-power' arose after the conquest of the New World. Slavery was finally abandoned when machine-power proved to be more efficient and more economical to run than the muscle-power of man or beast. In modern occidental civilization the machine fulfils the role of the slave. Just as the ancient Mediterranean civilizations would never have reached the heights they did without slavery, so modern civilization would collapse without the machine.

Except in the Middle Ages when wars were really fought for ideas, Western wars have been mainly fought for the acquisition of more mechanical power and more room. Once slaves were the richest spoils of war; more recently these spoils have become coal, iron and oil. But since very shortly nuclear fission will provide mankind with unlimited and easily transportable power, and since the conquest of space will provide unlimited room, the old motives for belligerent bloodshed will vanish. Man's present position may be compared with that of a desert-dweller for whom water is the most precious thing he knows. All the desert-dweller's energies, his inventiveness and most of his fears are directed to the finding and the conservation of water. Nuclear fission and the entry into space will do for us what suddenly being moved to the edge of a large lake would do for the desert-dweller. The precious liquid on which survival depended will suddenly have become abundant. There will be more of it than we can ever use. The stuff we fought and died for will have lost its value and can then be shared by all and even squandered.

Man's technical accomplishment, his government by law, his social orders and his commerce are all the outcome of fear. They are fortifications against dangers that were known in his earlier evolutionary stages but soon forgotten when protection against them became complete. Until technical or scientific advance fully relieves him of a threat, man seeks protection against that threat in magic or religion. He uses the comforts of religion to span the gap between the realization of a threat and its conquest by scientific means. Once the threat has been fully removed by technical advance, it ceases to call for divine intervention. Civilized man no longer prays that he and his family may be spared the horrors of plague or famine. He invokes divine aid only against the perils with which he is technically unable to cope. With the progress of civilization the emphasis of religion shifts more and more to the hereafter, because death remains the one dread against which man has no hope of permanently protecting himself. Without the belief first in magic and later in a propitious deity safeguarding him against dangers from which he cannot escape, timid man's life would be intolerable once he realized the extent of the dangers to which he is exposed. Modern religions hold forth a promise of infinite beatitude for which the human cortex is forever striving as a protection from the finality of death. In the typically cortical manner of progressing through increased censorship, religious man hopes to achieve everlasting bliss by bridling his instincts by the increased cortical control which he calls ethics and morality. Ethics, like laws, are a mutually protective convention. Without their observance communal living would be impossible; they are thus essential to modern civilization. Morality changes with every advance in civilization and must be adjusted to it. The observance of an ethical code is a necessity of life, regardless of whether after death good conduct will be rewarded in Heaven or misconduct cruelly punished in Hell.

In the static Middle Ages, religion pervaded almost every human activity, as Hinduism still does in India. Religious dogma was not discussed, and doubting or heresy were considered tantamount to insanity. Under such conditions religion provides a very satisfactory way of coping with diencephalic instinct-pressure. In modern urban civilization the situation is not the same. Dissenters abound and are fully accepted socially, even in religious circles. A man's religion and the degree of his piety are largely a matter of choice and often a source of deep conflicts. Yet even to-day a man who, in religion, has preserved an outlet for his secret impulses, dreads and anxieties in cortical communication with his God, will generally be psychosomatically healthier than one who has allowed his reason to clog these channels. The mystic has much easier access to those profound diencephalic mechanisms which are out of the cortical reach of atheists. The very recent re-awakening of religious needs among the most highly mechanized nations is a healthy sign. One can only hope that it will make sufficient headway to offset some of the fast-rising dangers to health caused by the rapid widening of the gap between man's natural diencephalic world and the artificial world his cortex is creating. Religion is still one of the few bridges that span the gap.

Man has inherited the urge to play from his earliest tree-living ancestors. This need to fill his ample biological leisure with something which keeps his brain and his muscles alert he has elaborated into the games, competitions and exercises which we call sport. In competitive sport the player reacts physically to the fear of defeat with biologically normal primitive mechanisms. He puts all the old diencephalic reactions to fear—increased muscular tension, pulse-rate, blood pressure, blood sugar and respiration—to their normal uses with full cortical consent. This temporarily establishes a perfect cortico-diencephalic equilibrium and is therefore highly beneficial from a psychosomatic point of view. If the athlete or sportsman performs well, he becomes the popular idol of his less fortunate fellow-men; and this is as it should be. It seems futile to indulge in sophisticated deprecation of this 'Cult of Brawn', because the admiration that is felt for the champion and the Olympic record-breaker has much older and deeper roots than our cynicism. The spectator, on the other hand, experiences vicariously waves of fear and relief from fear. But he can only express his thrills in hoots, applause and nervous fidgeting. The event does him far less good than it does the player.

There is, however, one kind of human play—the arts—into which fear hardly enters, unless it is in the form of an escape from painful reality. The artist, as he appears from the evolutionary point of view, is one who has exceptional means of cortically releasing diencephalic pressure. He is fortunate in having a looser censorship at the cortical level of consciousness than his contemporaries; hence also his frequent contempt for current conventions. The artist is able to perform a very fine cortical elaboration of his sensory perceptions, and in this respect he is humanly outstanding. Works of art are appreciated, apart from the technical excellence of their execution, because they offer a legitimate lead by which the audience can find a path through the maze of their own cortical obstructions to a greater degree of diencephalic freedom from cortical oppression. Instrumental music, being entirely abstract, does this in the most completely satisfactory manner, because it does not directly prompt or suggest fixed cortical associations. This absolute freedom in the evocation of memories and emotions by an abstract acoustic stimulus is largely responsible for the pleasures of harmony, melody and rhythm. The desire to give cortical processes of memory and association a wider freedom also underlies the modern trend towards abstract painting. Modern man can feel a profounder artistic satisfaction when his cortex is lifted out of its common associative ruts and is free to respond in its own individual way to composition, form and colour without being squeezed into an associative channel by representational rendering. A similar effect can be achieved by so fantastically distorting reality that grotesqueness blocks the run of common associations, as in much of Picasso's work, leaving the cortex free to interpret much deeper feelings than could be aroused by the faithful reproduction of what is already familiar.

Civilization is thus an artifact and not a biological phenomenon. The only physiological result it has had in man is the insurgence of psychosomatic disorders. It has produced no new organs and no new functions. Civilization is the method of perfecting artificial means of escape. It has now gone so far that it almost entirely prevents urban man from reacting to danger in a way which is evolutionarily and physiologically normal. Modern man is so overwhelmed with his cortical achievements that he has forgotten that his body is still functioning on a level that was normal before the dawn of culture. The diencephalic reactions of his body, which no longer make sense to his cortex, he misinterprets as disease, and thereby lays down the pattern that eventually leads him into psychosomatic suffering.

Man's cultural evolution is brought about by the ever better training of the cortical ability to learn. He is the only living creature that has brought its natural evolution to an end. Man has ceased to adjust his body to his environment; he now adjusts his environment to his body. It is therefore highly improbable that a new human or superhuman species will ever appear on earth, as new species can only be produced by natural selection. No living being can pass on to its progeny any attribute it has acquired during its life, because this can never form part of a creature's genetic structure, immutably laid down before birth.

PART II

THE EVOLUTIONARY BACKGROUND
OF SOME PSYCHOSOMATIC DISORDERS

4

Disorders of the Upper Digestive Tract

FROM THE LIPS to the anus man's digestive tract is a long
and winding tunnel; strictly speaking, the contents of this tunnel are outside his body, just as a train is not a part of the
mountain through which it runs.

Food which passes through the digestive tunnel consists of
highly complex chemical compounds and is unable to enter
the body in its original form. In order to pass from the inner
lining of the digestive tract into the blood and lymph which
circulate in the intestinal wall, food must be broken down into
very much smaller and simpler molecules.

The mechanical breakdown of food is achieved by chewing
and by the kneading action of the stomach, while the chemical
demolition of complex molecules is performed by the stomach's
hydrochloric acid and a large number of ferments or enzymes
which are poured over the intestinal contents from most parts
of the digestive tract. Finally, the disintegrating action of tril-
lions of bacteria which live and multiply in the large intestine
plays an important role in preparing food for absorption. All
these complicated functions of the alimentary canal are covered
by the term *digestion*.

Apart from water, salts and vitamins, there are only two
nutritional substances which can be absorbed without undergoing any further chemical breakdown: glucose and alcohol.
These two substances can be drawn directly through the cellular
membranes which line the digestive tract. In this way they
reach the blood which circulates in a microscopically fine network just below the inner layer of cells.

All other food—the proteins, the fats, the complex sugars
and the starches—have molecules which are too large to pass
through the cellular membranes and have to undergo many
chemical changes before they can be absorbed. The absorption

of the chemically simple end-products of digestion through the lining of the intestinal tract and the passage of nourishment into the blood and lymph is known as *assimilation*. Food thus becomes incorporated into the living tissue of the body only after the process of assimilation.

The simple end-products of normal digestion are always the same, regardless of the form in which protein, fat, sugar or starch is eaten. Provided poisons and gross nutritional deficiencies are avoided, the form in which food is eaten makes very little difference to the inner chemistry of the body. That is why the countless and often contradictory dietary taboos that abound throughout the world have little or no physiological foundation, however much their advocates may cherish them.

Races, nations, towns, villages and even individuals have different superstitions about which foods are good and healthy and which should be avoided, which are easy and which are difficult to digest, and which are apt to produce certain disorders of the body and which are not. Most of these notions are based on hearsay, uncritical self-observation and the cortical habit of jumping quickly to causal conclusions, however scientifically implausible.

It makes remarkably little difference to the digestive process whether protein is eaten as meat, fish, eggs, cheese or milk. The digestion and assimilation of starches is the same whether they are taken in the form of bread, potatoes, rice or spaghetti. Regardless of whether fats are taken in the form of lard, oil, butter or margarine, the digestive end-products which are assimilated are always the same.

Figure 2 shows the various parts of the human alimentary canal. Of these only the mouth has the ordinary striated muscles which are entirely under voluntary control. The rest of the intestinal tract is furnished with smooth or involuntary muscles. The wall of the digestive tube contains throughout its entire length two sets of these involuntary muscles. One set is circular and surrounds the tube, while the other set runs lengthwise.

The interaction of these two sets of muscles controls the ever-changing width of the tube and its shortening or elongation. When the circular muscles contract the tube becomes narrower, and when they relax it dilates. A contraction of the longitudinal muscles shortens the tube and their relaxation lengthens it. The rhythmic play of the two sets of muscles contracting and relaxing produces the intestinal movement, a kind of milking action known as *peristalsis*, which transports and churns the intestinal contents. These muscles also furnish the motor power which expels the faeces.

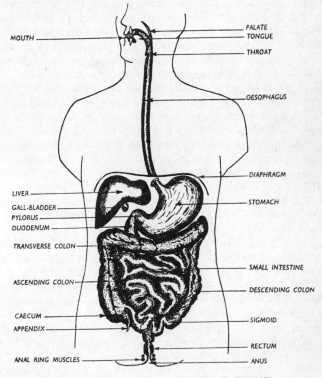

MOUTH

PALATE
TONGUE

THROAT

OESOPHAGUS

DIAPHRAGM

LIVER

GALL-BLADDER
PYLORUS
DUODENUM

STOMACH

TRANSVERSE COLON

ASCENDING COLON

SMALL INTESTINE

DESCENDING COLON

CAECUM
APPENDIX

SIGMOID

RECTUM

ANAL RING MUSCLES

ANUS

Fig. 2. THE HUMAN DIGESTIVE TRACT

At the mouth, and to some extent at the anus, there are three levels of nervous control. In this nervous hierarchy the local automatic regulations are the lowest. The immediate increase in salivation which occurs when an irritant such as mustard or pepper comes in contact with the oral lining is such a local automatic regulation in which the brain takes no part.

The body has a large number of such automatic regulations and reactions which can operate without participation of the brain. They are all run by the autonomous or vegetative nervous system which is distributed throughout the body.

Though the autonomous nervous system is ultimately under diencephalic control, it has a large number of nerve centres of its own, one of which is the solar plexus. These sub-centres are able to act on their own account without the reflex having to be relayed through the central nervous system. They manage the routine operation of most of the inner organs, and it is only in the case of an emergency that the diencephalon takes over by producing reactions which lie outside the competence of a nerve plexus. Thus on the second level of nervous control, diencephalic reactions, such as a decrease in salivation in response to fear, are superimposed upon the local reflexes.

Finally, at the summit of nervous control over mouth and anus, the cortex can dominate the local and the diencephalic reactions. We can therefore eat, swallow or allow a stool to pass at will.

Moving downwards from the mouth, cortical control ends just beyond the throat, and moving upwards from the anus it ends in the rectum. From the beginning of the oesophagus and upwards from the anus, all central nervous control is diencephalic and no longer cortical. There are thus only two levels of nervous control in these parts, local and diencephalic.

The diencephalon can over-rule local reflex mechanisms down the length of the oesophagus, in the stomach, at the pylorus, in the duodenal cap and in the first part of the duodenum (Fig. 2). From the lower half of the duodenum on, diencephalic authority rapidly wanes, so that the whole small intestine, the caecum, the ascending colon and the first half of the transverse colon are governed only by their own local nerve centres and are therefore almost free of direct diencephalic interference.

From an evolutionary point of view the middle of the human digestive tract is the oldest part. It has undergone no recent structural changes, and its function is so perfectly regulated by its own nervous control that the need for diencephalic interference no longer arises.

In the second half of the transverse colon diencephalic

domination begins to re-establish itself, and down the length of the descending colon its power rapidly increases. In the sigmoid it is again in full control and at the rectum it is once more joined by cortical supervision.

Thus diencephalic stimuli strongly influence the ends, not the middle, of the alimentary canal. This distribution of central nervous control in the intestines explains why psychosomatic diseases of the lower duodenum, the small intestine, the caecum and the first half of the colon are unknown. They are confined to those regions over which the diencephalon holds sway.

Under normal conditions it is the body's demand for sustenance—felt as hunger or thirst—which controls the upper reaches of the alimentary canal. This demand has now been cortically harnessed into fixed meals and dietary habits, neither being essential to the body's welfare. On the contrary, if man would eat only when he is hungry and only as much as he requires to allay his hunger, this might be cortically, socially and domestically inconvenient, but it would certainly be salutary.

The institution of regular meals probably dates no further back than early Neolithic times. The whole structure and functioning of our digestive tract suggests that man is by his evolution a casual and continual eater of snacks and was never intended to gorge himself at intervals as do the carnivora. Characteristically, the cortex of modern man almost viciously condemns this natural habit and tries, often in vain, to eradicate it ruthlessly in the infancy of his children. Modern man forgets that he only recently invented meals as a labour and kitchen convenience and he is, therefore, grimly determined to preserve his little Neolithic invention by pretending that it is a law of Nature and that eating between meals is bad for him. Primitive races who have not yet reached a Neolithic level of culture, such as the African Bushmen, do not eat regular meals as we do, nor does our closest animal relation, the gorilla.

Man's intestines have a digestive power that goes far beyond his requirements, provided his digestion is unhampered by interference from the brain. It is common knowledge that mental defectives who are unable to reason about what they eat hardly ever have digestive disturbances, even if they have eating habits that would horrify civilized man. If an Eskimo, accustomed to eating fish and blubber, is suddenly switched to an Indian diet of milk, rice and hot pickles, or vice versa, neither would be digestively any the worse off after a day or two, provided his cortical likes and dislikes, his superstitions and his fears could be eliminated. During famine man can and will eat anything even remotely edible—putrid meat, stinking, weevily grain, rotting fruit and human flesh—without suffering from indigestion. In two hundred million years of evolution man's intestinal function has become superbly adapted to omnivorous feeding. A carnivorous tiger fed on greens and potatoes would very soon die, as would the herbivorous horse if fed on steaks, but man can exist on almost anything—even locusts and wild honey.

Yet the structure and the chemistry of man's alimentary canal is closer to the carnivorous than to the herbivorous intestine. Man could healthily lead a purely carnivorous life, provided he ate the flesh of herbivorous animals raw and included their bones and their filled entrails in his diet. On the other hand, man cannot follow a strictly vegetarian regimen, as he is unable in the long run to survive without some animal protein in the form of meat, fish, eggs, milk or cheese.

In all creatures who seek safety in flight the instinct of fear over-rules the instinct of hunger. In the presence of danger the diencephalon abolishes hunger by stopping the secretion of digestive juices and by a contraction of the circular muscles in those parts of the intestinal tract over which it has control. The mouth drops open so that the teeth can no longer chew. The flow of saliva is shut off, making the mouth go dry. The oesophagus contracts, making swallowing impossible and producing the feeling known as 'choking with fright'. In the absence of gastric juice, the strong ring-muscle that controls the outlet of the stomach, the pylorus, snaps shut and the flow of bile and pancreatic secretion into the duodenum is checked by a tight contraction of a small ring-muscle.

With all these intestinal mechanisms clicking into operation at once, there is neither the desire nor the ability to swallow another bite in the presence of fear. As always in physiology, the safeguards for survival go far beyond what seems to be necessary and such vital diencephalic devices are therefore not only foolproof, but also work with an enormous margin of safety.

At the other end of the intestine—in the descending colon, the sigmoid, the rectum and the anus—mild fear produces a sudden contraction of the involuntary muscle-fibres which encircle the tube, and then evacuation becomes impossible. But when fear turns into terror or panic, there is in addition a sudden outpouring of water and mucus into the sigmoid.

The small glandular cells in the lining of the sigmoid always produce a certain amount of mucus in order to ease the passage of a formed stool, and this secretion is locally controlled. But under the influence of diencephalic emergency-intervention the mucus becomes watery and is secreted in huge quantities, liquefying the contents of the sigmoid. The result is the uncontrollable ejection of a liquid evacuation. It is thus that mild fear produces constipation, while terror produces diarrhoea.

The great biological importance of these mechanisms in timid animals is that fear stops them from eating, even if they are hungry, and that they involuntarily evacuate just before they break into flight. In modern man, who no longer runs for his life when he is frightened, these ancient reflexes are nothing more than a source of embarrassment when he is consciously aware of being frightened. But when such normal reactions occur in response to a subconscious fear, they are always wrongly interpreted by the cortex as an intestinal disorder, because no other explanation is forthcoming.

Psychosomatic Disorders of the Mouth

The mouth is not subject to many psychosomatic disorders, because it is largely under conscious cortical control. Diencephalic interference with oral functions is almost confined to disturbances of salivation. A dry mouth, a coated tongue and a 'bad taste' may be purely psychosomatic, and this is always so in patients who are over-anxious about their digestion.

There is no physiological evidence to suggest that these symptoms are in any way, other than psychologically, connected with the functioning of the bowel.

We know that there is no such thing as intestinal auto-intoxication, but even if such hypothetical toxins did exist there is no conceivable way in which they could be eliminated at the speed with which a coated tongue becomes clean once the anxiety is relieved. When a coated tongue clears up after an evacuation which the patient considers to have been satisfactory, it is the relief from anxiety and not the defecation as such which removes the coating. The elimination of faeces which are already outside the inner working of the body could not possibly bring about a change on the surface of the tongue.

When a patient gets frantic because he has not had a stool for three days his tongue gets coated. He then takes a strong purge and after the purge has worked his tongue clears. This convinces him that a clogged bowel caused the coating, and he always attributes the betterment to the purge instead of to relieved anxiety. He finds it hard to believe that his ugly tongue had nothing whatever to do with his bowel, but was entirely due to that diencephalic change in salivation which is an old normal reaction to fear.

The same reasoning applies to those cases in which a coated tongue is believed to be caused by a bad stomach. A white tongue and indigestion may well occur together as a diencephalic reaction to fear, but one is never the cause of the other. Such faulty interpretation of bodily phenomena merely increases the anxiety and leads to the grotesque and often absurd diets, useless medicines and fantastic restrictions with which patients suffering from psychosomatic digestive disorders are so apt to plague their bodies.

A Psychosomatic Disorder of the Oesophagus

In the oesophagus, which is entirely beyond cortical control, there is a common psychosomatic disorder which old French authors, with more insight than tact, called *boule hysterique*. The patient complains of a lump in his throat or chest which prevents him from swallowing, yet when, with a great effort of will, he forces himself to swallow food, there is no obstruction and the sensation is momentarily relieved.

The most unpleasant feeling of a lump is a cortical misinterpretation of the normal contraction of the oesophagus in response to fear, one of the many mechanisms that prevent the intake of food in the presence of danger. But this the reasoning cortex has long forgotten; all it now knows is that a muscular contraction of the oesophagus is required to transport a bolus of food from the mouth to the stomach.

An oesophageal contraction which occurs when no food has

been swallowed is utterly perplexing to the cortex, particularly when the fear that caused the cramp is not consciously admitted. But the cortex is never baffled for long; it must find an answer, even if the answer is hopelessly wrong. As no food has been swallowed, the cortex reasons that there must be a lump or a 'growth', as normally only a lump of food produces such contractions. This wrong notion is extremely alarming, and, of course, makes the contraction worse. In human pathology there do exist real lumps in the oesophagus, but in these cases the obstruction does not disappear when food is swallowed and an X-ray examination reveals the difference at once.

There are many examples of this type of cortical misinterpretation in psychosomatic disease. For instance, an abnormally contracted, empty urinary bladder is cortically interpreted to be full. The patient feels a strong urge to urinate, but he can produce only a few drops of urine at a time. A cramped, empty sigmoid is erroneously interpreted to be full of faecal matter, so that the patient tries desperately and in vain to evacuate stool which is non-existent.

A good example of erroneous cortical interpretation of this type is the old parlour-trick of rolling a dried pea between the crossed tips of the index and middle finger. When the eyes are shut there is a distinct feeling of rolling two peas. The cortex cannot conceive of a single pea being felt at the same time by the outer side of the index and the inner side of the middle finger; so it jumps to the unwarranted conclusion that there are two peas.

In the case of the pea, the eye can check the cortical error, and that is why it is a parlour-trick. But when the eye cannot check the cortical error concerning something that happens inside the body, the result is psychosomatic disease.

Fortunately, in the case of oesophageal cramps the eye can be allowed to check by making the patient swallow barium behind an X-ray screen and watching what happens in a mirror. Seeing the barium pass unimpeded down the food-pipe will not relieve the anxiety which caused the spasm, but it does relieve the anxiety about an obstructing lump. Accompanied by the necessary explanations, the demonstration brings the symptom and its correct interpretation to a fully conscious level at which it is understood by the patient. As soon as the reasoning mind understands the diencephalic action, the cortico-diencephalic vicious cycle of fear ceases to operate, because conscious alarm has been abolished.

If by this time the original subconscious fear that initiated the process has subsided, the patient will be cured, but if the subconscious fear continues it may find expression in some other form of psychosomatic disorder. In that case a simple explanation may be insufficient and further psychotherapy directed at making the repressed fear conscious becomes necessary.

Psychosomatic Disorders of the Stomach

The stomach is a large and powerful muscular sack which is able to make great changes in its shape, size and position. It is lined with microscopic glandular cells, of which some produce mucus, others digestive enzymes such as pepsin, while yet others have the astounding ability to secrete inorganic hydrochloric acid so strong that it will burn a hole in a piece of marble.

The stomach ends in a large ring-muscle, which opens and closes it. This ring-muscle is known as the pylorus (the gate-keeper). Beyond the pylorus lies the duodenal cap, followed by the short duodenum.

Like the rest of the intestinal tract, the stomach has many automatic reflexes and reactions of its own. The regulation of normal gastric secretion, its movements, the opening and closing of the pylorus can all work automatically. Superimposed on these routine functions lies the much more powerful diencephalic control which takes over in an emergency.

The stomach is mechanically and chemically an extraordinarily robust organ. If it were cut off from cortical interference and left to normal diencephalic supervision, there would be no such thing as chronic indigestion or a 'weak stomach'. Short of the ingestion of poisons, the human stomach can cope perfectly with all the exigencies of omnivorous feeding and the physiological reactions to fear. But as soon as the heavy-handed, blundering cortex tries to interfere with the management of these delicately poised mechanisms, they are grossly upset.

The cortex, having no direct nervous access to the stomach, can only interfere by making use of diencephalic mechanisms, and these mechanisms it does not understand. For example, a healthy person gets an acute attack of indigestion on account of an incident which produced rage or fear. The cortex does not see this connection. Mistakenly, it assumes that the indigestion, caused by the tight closure of the pylorus and the interruption of gastric secretion, must be due to something in the food. After some anxious cortical deliberation a scape-goat is picked upon, perhaps the dozen cherries that were eaten after lunch. To the cortex this seems an entirely satisfactory explanation, and so the anxiety subsides and the indigestion is rapidly relieved with or without bicarbonate of soda.

A few days later the person is again tempted by luscious cherries, but now his cortex warns him: 'Be careful; remember what happened last time.' Yet the sight of those cherries is too tantalizing, and so a compromise is struck. The cortex says: 'Let's be brave and try an experiment to find out whether this stomach really cannot digest cherries.'

Gingerly the first cherry is picked up and eaten. It tastes delicious. A second cherry follows, and then more. By this time the cortex is screaming: 'Enough, enough, you'll suffer for this!' Thereupon the diencephalon promptly registers emergency and goes into its usual action. Within half an hour the unhappy experimenter is writhing with stomach-ache.

Cortical conclusion: Never another cherry!

After a while another emotional upset occurs and again there is that indigestion. This time no cherries were eaten; so it must be something else. Again the cortex goes to work and finally clusters its suspicious on a glass of milk or perhaps the potato chips, and the whole rigmarole is repeated. By now the cortex is well on its way to the elaborate frame-up which so commonly accuses a perfectly normal stomach of being a dyspeptic wreck.

For what were once very good reasons, fear stops the secretion of gastric juice and tightly closes the pylorus. When this happens to an actor on a first night, he correctly interprets the cramp in the pit of his stomach and a disgust for food as being caused by the fear which he calls stage-fright. With his entry on to the stage the discomfort vanishes, and after the curtain falls for the last time he is ready for a hearty meal.

Similarly, a voyager on a rough sea correctly interprets the alarming symptoms of sea-sickness. He would not dream of consulting his family physician about the violent nausea he felt, as might a seafaring landlubber who had never been told of sea-sickness and who would therefore be terribly alarmed. But when

similar symptoms occur in response to a fear which is not cortically admitted into consciousness, the normal fear-reaction is
interpreted as a disorder, and this sets up a psychosomatic
vicious cycle.

An unadmitted fear produces the primitively appropriate
diencephalic reactions not recognized as such by the cortex. The
sensations which these reactions evoke cause conscious anxiety.
This anxiety in turn induces the diencephalon to adopt more
energetic measures which again increase cortical alarm. When
then finally a specialist is consulted and he cheerfully tells the
patient that there is nothing wrong with him—just nerves—the
situation becomes utterly chaotic to the patient's way of thinking.

When a diencephalic reaction to fear blocks the secretion of
gastric juice, food which is eaten in spite of the lack of gastric
secretions cannot be digested. It may stay in the stomach much
longer than normal and cause a feeling of fullness, heaviness or
indigestion. Food that has not been digestively prepared in the
stomach is unfit to be acted upon by the enzymes of the middle
and lower intestines. When such unprepared food reaches the
colon, it is apt to be rapidly eliminated as waste-matter. This
condition, in which deficient stomachic digestion leads to
watery evacuations, is called gastrogenic diarrhoea. It can be
controlled by administering artificial gastric juice in the form of
dilute hydrochloric acid.

The diencephalic blocking of gastric secretion and the associated closure of the pylorus produce most unpleasant symptoms,
even when no food is swallowed and the stomach is empty. These
symptoms are usually grouped together under the misleading
designation of aerophagia, air-eating (Fig. 3).

Swallowing air is perfectly normal and is done all the time,
because the stomach needs plenty of air to churn the food
properly, just as the contents of a bottle filled to the cork are
difficult to mix by shaking. Normally, an excess of air escapes
through the pylorus into the duodenum and the small intestine,
where it is absorbed. Exceptionally, it may be brought up in a
belch, but this is difficult because the entry of the oesophagus
into the stomach acts like a valve. Swallowed air passes easily
into the stomach, but it can only return into the oesophagus
when the valve is open, as when the stomach is weighed down
with a heavy meal or at the moment when air is passing into it.

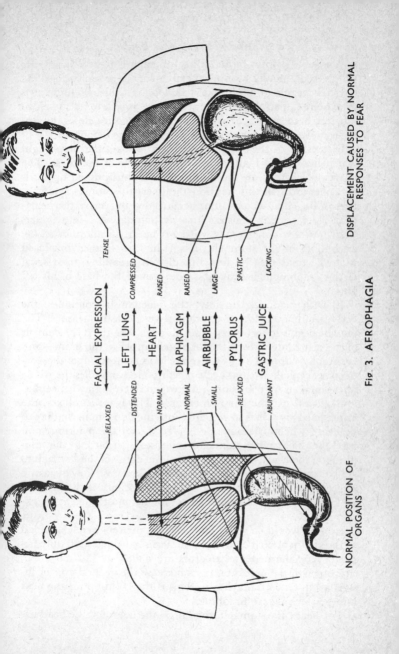

NORMAL POSITION OF ORGANS

DISPLACEMENT CAUSED BY NORMAL RESPONSES TO FEAR

	RELAXED		TENSE
FACIAL EXPRESSION			
LEFT LUNG	DISTENDED		COMPRESSED
HEART	NORMAL		RAISED
DIAPHRAGM	NORMAL		RAISED
AIRBUBBLE	SMALL		LARGE
PYLORUS	RELAXED		SPASTIC
GASTRIC JUICE	ABUNDANT		LACKING

Fig. 3. AFROPHAGIA

When the pylorus of an empty stomach is tightly closed, air which is continually swallowed can no longer get out, and so the stomach begins to dilate like a balloon. In this condition it is even more difficult than normal for the stomach to release air in a belch, because the air which is under pressure closes the lips of the valve which controls the entry into the oesophagus.

Distension of the stomach with air presses the diaphragm which lies over it high up into the left side of the chest. The heart, which rests on the diaphragm, is thus pushed upwards and outwards. In this position the heart-tip thumps against a part of the chest which is not accustomed to receive the heart-beat. The patient registers this as palpitation. He wonders what has now gone wrong with his heart, in addition to the discomfort in his stomach. His fears are further increased when he finds that he has difficulty in breathing, the raising of the diaphragm having also compressed the base of his left lung.

If, with mounting anxiety, this mechanism continues, the body is ultimately forced to adopt a very drastic measure. The patient begins to feel dizzy—possibly because the displacement of the heart interferes with the blood supply to the brain—and eventually faints. The loss of consciousness interrupts the cortico-diencephalic vicious cycle of fear which underlies the whole phenomenon. All fear is instantly wiped out and the diencephalon calls off its emergency measures. The pylorus relaxes, the imprisoned air rushes so violently into the duodenum that it can be heard when a stethoscope is placed over the pyloric region and the ballooning stomach collapses, permitting the diaphragm, the heart, the left lung and the dome of the stomach to get back into their normal positions, while a fresh flow of gastric juice is released. After a few seconds consciousness is regained and the patient is none the worse for his most unpleasant experience.

Now all would be well if at this point matters were explained to the victim of such an attack, but usually he and his family become very alarmed and doctors are called in. All too often, doctors with the best intentions increase the general apprehensiveness instead of allaying it. This is the build-up for the next attack which is sure to follow.

The heart, the stomach, the lungs, the liver and the head are then passed in clinical review. When all the laboratory tests, X-rays, the electrocardiogram and examinations by specialists turn out to be entirely negative, the patient is plunged into an abyss of hopeless despair. Either he feels accused of imagining things which he knows to be very real, or he begins to think that he is suffering from some rare and obscure disease which the doctors are unable to diagnose. He and his family have probably read that cancer may be difficult to diagnose in the early stages. He dare not mention the dread disease to his doctor for fear of the notion being pooh-poohed, and yet there is the gnawing uncertainty that perhaps something will be overlooked until it is too late.

Such an attack is sometimes mistaken for a coronary occlusion. The difference is that though it is very uncomfortable there is never real pain associated with 'aerophagia'. In coronary disease there is usually pain, and in any case a thorough blood examination and an electrocardiogram can always clarify the situation.

There are several ways of dealing with aerophagia. The most radical is to make the repressed initial fear conscious or, in the phraseology of this study, to give the diencephalic pressure a conscious outlet by opening the mesh of cortical censorship a little wider. But that may be a long and tedious procedure.

In the past a bogus diagnosis with a complicated medicinal and dietary regimen often produced good results, because the medical prescription was unquestioningly accepted. That is how in the old days the good family doctor, often unwittingly, did it. With modern urban patients this is neither possible nor ethical. It is all too easily unmasked by the sceptical patient who knows all about diagnostic tests and is very apt to check on his doctor's diagnosis.

In an attack of gastric distension the sequence of symptoms can be interrupted in a matter of minutes by administering a strong dose of suitably diluted hydrochloric acid, the most important ingredient of gastric secretion. When such artificial gastric juice is swallowed, the pylorus reacts as if the emergency had passed and it opens through reflex mechanisms of its own. The effect of this simple trick is the same as the wiping out of cortical influence in fainting, and relief is almost immediate.

The Peptic Ulcers

Any part of the stomach or of the upper duodenum may be the site of an ulcer, but by far the most common localization is in the vicinity of the pylorus. There is now almost general agreement that peptic ulcers are a psychosomatic disease, but there is as yet so much discussion about the mechanics of their causation that it is still permissible to cast yet another theory into the ring.

The psychiatric investigation of many ulcer patients suggests that this disorder is associated with a feeling of guilt rather than of anxiety. The emotion of guilt is basically the cortical elaboration of a conflict between the instincts of hate and love.

The basic pattern of guilt can be traced back to a primitive animal level. When a mammalian cub is rejected by its mother, the rejection consists of a withdrawal of teat or food. The favoured cub is generously suckled and gets the choicest tidbits, while the cub that is rejected is pushed aside.

From the standpoint of the welfare of the species, the instinct to suck is just as important as the instinct of sex in later life. Thus when sucking is thwarted, hate and rage are engendered and the hatred is directed towards the mother who refuses instinct-gratification. Opposed to this hatred is the biologically essential close binding to the mother without which the cub must die.

When in man a conflict of this type reaches a cortical, though not necessarily conscious, level it evokes the emotion of guilt. Repressed guilt is the result of hating where such hatred is biologically or cortically inadmissible because the hated person must be loved.

A maternally rejected cub is hungry, and in its stomach there is a profuse secretion of gastric juice in anticipation of a meal. When the meal is refused, powerless rage is generated and triggers the usual diencephalic mechanisms. In flight-conditioned animals rage produces the same reactions as fear. Thus there is a closure of the pylorus and an inhibition of the secretion of gastric juice. But in the primitive guilt situation there is the difference that the stomach is already full of strong digestive juices with a high acidity.

It has been explained that a high gastric acidity induces the stomach's own regulations to open the pylorus. It is for this reason that administering hydrochloric acid unclenches the pylorus when there is a lack of acid in response to fear. As there is no such lack of acid in the primitive guilt situation, the diencephalon is forced to put much more power into the pyloric closure in order to overcome the stomach's local mechanisms working in the opposite direction. There is thus a sort of tug-of-war between the local regulations and the diencephalon. To win this struggle and achieve its object of closing the pylorus as a normal reaction to fear the diencephalon must use a much stronger nervous impulse than in the case of fear. Primitive guilt thus produces a maximal contraction of the circular musculature in the region of the pylorus.

A spasm of the intestinal muscles interferes with the blood circulation which serves the inner lining of the alimentary canal because the veins and the arteries coming from the outside of the intestine have to pass through the mesh of the longitudinal and circular muscles before reaching the inner lining (Fig. 4).

When the spasm is moderate only the veins are strangled, because they have thin, soft walls, while the hard-walled arteries which feed the blood into the intestinal lining remain open. A strangulation of the veins, caught in a contracted muscular net, prevents the normal reflux of venous blood, though blood continues to be pumped into the lining of the pyloric region through the arteries. This causes a congestion, clinically known as gastritis and duodenitis, a condition which is often due to a prolonged state of anxiety.

But when the spasm is maximal, as in the case of guilt, it is possible even for a hard-walled artery to become strangled. The result is that the arterial blood-supply to a small area of the inner lining is cut off, causing the death of the superficial cells in that area, owing to a fatal lack of oxygen.

The destruction of the superficial layer of cells in a small area of the intestinal lining served by an arterial ending exposes the lower layers to erosion by the gastric acid against which these cells have no protection. Once this process has been initiated it is liable to continue and will then lead to a peptic ulcer.

If the guilt-induced cramp persists, the complete perforation of the whole intestinal wall may take place in a few hours, calling for immediate surgical intervention. Fortunately, this hap-

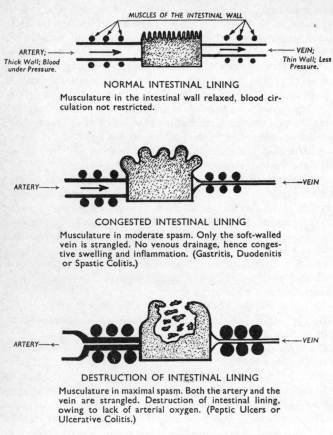

MUSCLES OF THE INTESTINAL WALL

ARTERY;———→
Thick Wall; Blood
under Pressure.

VEIN;
←——— Thin Wall; Less
Pressure.

NORMAL INTESTINAL LINING

Musculature in the intestinal wall relaxed, blood circulation not restricted.

ARTERY——→   ←——VEIN

CONGESTED INTESTINAL LINING

Musculature in moderate spasm. Only the soft-walled
vein is strangled. No venous drainage, hence congestive swelling and inflammation. (Gastritis, Duodenitis
or Spastic Colitis.)

ARTERY——←   ←——VEIN

DESTRUCTION OF INTESTINAL LINING

Musculature in maximal spasm. Both the artery and the
vein are strangled. Destruction of intestinal lining,
owing to lack of arterial oxygen. (Peptic Ulcers or
Ulcerative Colitis.)

Fig. 4. THE ACTION OF INTESTINAL SPASM ON
CIRCULATION

pens only rarely. Usually the cramp is not continuous. The guilt may be temporarily smothered by cortical distraction in work, or the ingestion of food may for some hours absorb the excess acidity.

As soon as the spasm relaxes, normal repair mechanisms can get to work. If the reparation of the damage is not interrupted by another wave of guilt causing a renewed spasm, a fresh ulcer can heal in a few days. This does not always happen because the conflict of opposing instincts which causes the emotion of guilt is rarely resolved.

The notorious chronicity of peptic ulcers is due to the fact that fresh waves of repressed guilt, always causing excessive acidity and spasm, keep recurring before the body's healing mechanisms have had time to complete the repair of the damage caused by the foregoing wave.

Wild animals and primitive man may be exposed to a guilt-provoking situation, but they do not suffer from peptic ulcers, nor does the modern man who feels consciously guilty of crime, misdemeanour or sin. In this connection, it is interesting that calves bred in modern dairies, where they are prevented from sucking, occasionally develop typical peptic ulcers, because domestication has repressed their instincts. The effect of this is the same as in modern man, who suppresses his instincts by cortical censorship at the level of consciousness, a mechanism which certainly does not exist in bovines.

In man an ulcer develops when the emotion of guilt is repressed. In wild animals there is no such censorship and in primitive man the censorship is very lenient, while in urban man it is extremely strict and rigid.

The instinct-conflicts which produce an ulcer are usually concerned with sex or family relationships. The modern cortex refuses to admit such conflicts and to expose them to the processes of reasoning. Guilt of this type, therefore, continues to build up behind the censoring screen and forces the diencephalon into the drastic action which causes the ulcer.

This interpretation of the peptic ulcers suggests an obvious psychotherapeutic approach. Censorship at the level of consciousness must be so far relaxed that the conflicting instincts, and the emotion of guilt which they engender, can be ushered into conscious awareness. Thereafter the psychological situation becomes identical with that of a person who has a guilty conscience on account of something he knows he has done, a situation which never produces an ulcer. If such a psychotherapeutic manoeuvre is successfully accomplished, ulcers may heal with surprising rapidity, often in a matter of days, and do not recur unless an entirely new guilt-provoking situation arises.

It is a well-known fact that ulcers may persist in spite of months of expert medical treatment and then quite suddenly and unexpectedly heal without any treatment while the patient is eating just those foods which he has been told strictly to avoid. When such cases are carefully investigated by a clinical psychiatrist, it is very often found that the reason for a feeling of guilt has been eliminated by circumstances.

The psychiatrist dealing with an ulcer patient should concentrate on uncovering guilt and nothing else. In experienced hands five to ten sittings are usually sufficient, because the conflict which is causing the ulcer is quite close to the surface of consciousness and because there is always a close relationship in time between the arising of the conflict and the onset of the first symptoms.

Deep-seated guilt reaching far back into infancy may be a factor in the personality-structure of the ulcer patient, but it is never responsible for the actual occurrence of an ulcer. Thus when psychotherapy is used with the object of curing a peptic ulcer, analytical procedures need only be directed towards uncovering a recent event. Raking back into infancy should be strictly limited to what may be necessary to achieve this end.

Two clinical case histories will illustrate the type of conflict which can lead to an ulcer.

A prosperous businessman, aged 34, married to a beautiful and charming wife who had borne him three fine children, was admitted to hospital complaining of increasingly severe indigestion for about six weeks. Examination revealed a fair-sized ulcer on the posterior wall of the duodenal cap.

The patient assured the clinical psychiatrist that he 'hadn't a worry in the world', that he adored his wife and loved his children and that there was no flaw in his sex-life.

Further enquiry into recent events revealed that two months ago his wife's younger sister had come to spend the summer with them. The whole family often went bathing together, and he admitted after some hesitation that he had often seen his pretty sister-in-law in rather careless négligé. However, he flatly denied that he felt any infatuation for the girl; she just happened to be 'a bit sexy', that was all.

It was possible to make the patient realize the connection between his sister-in-law, a feeling of guilt towards his wife and the formation of an ulcer in his duodenum. As soon as this connection was consciously accepted, all medication was stopped and the patient was put on general hospital diet. He never felt another twinge of intestinal discomfort, and an X-ray check two weeks later showed that the ulcer had healed with a normal scar.

The second case is that of a married woman, aged 48, who was admitted to hospital with a fairly large duodenal ulcer. With her she brought old X-rays dating back eight years which showed an ulcer on the opposite side of the duodenal cap.

She gave the following personal history: Eleven years ago she had obtained a divorce from her first husband. At that time her daughter was 12 years old. Two years later she remarried, and it was then that she began to suffer from the indigestion which was finally diagnosed as a duodenal ulcer eight years ago.

She underwent orthodox treatment in hospital and was pronounced cured three months later. Since then she had occasionally suffered from indigestion, but the symptoms were quite different. Radiological checks had always proved to be negative and her indigestion was ascribed to 'nerves'. Her present symptoms, which reminded her of what she had suffered eight years ago, had begun during a trip abroad and had been getting steadily worse for two months.

The patient was at first quite refractory to any psychotherapeutic approach. She had no worries and was 'wonderfully happy' in her second marriage. Her daughter was a 'fine girl', also happily married; indeed, her trip abroad had been undertaken to attend the wedding. She emphatically avowed that there could not possibly be anything in her life which might account for any emotional difficulty.

However, after a few days the clinical psychiatrist obtained the following story: She had been deeply in love with her first husband, who was 'a really fine man' and had always 'been good to her'. One day she surprised him in an adulterous

situation. From that moment on all her love had turned to
hatred and revulsion. She had immediately left the house and
obtained a divorce.

At the time of her daughter's marriage her first husband,
whom she had never seen since the divorce, had written to say
that he would like to be present at his daughter's wedding. To
this request she had replied imploring him to stay away as she
could not bear to see him again. However, at the ceremony the
first husband was in the church. This had given her 'a terrible
shock' and she had 'nearly fainted'. But she had pulled herself
together and had even exchanged a few banal words with him
after the service. That night she began to have indigestion.

On the day following this disclosure she admitted that, having
grown older and knowing more of the world, she could forgive
her first husband's unfaithfulness and that the memory of their
life together still meant something to her, but that she did not
like to think of it as she had found such complete happiness with
her second husband.

From that moment on it was relatively easy to make her see
a guilty motive towards her second husband arising from the
fact that she still loved her first husband. As it was clear from
her behaviour that she had grasped the point, it was not thought
necessary to insist on her admitting the insight in words. Up to
the day she left the hospital she maintained that none of this
was true, and no attempt was made to dispel her smoke-screen.

Once the conflict was brought into the open, all her symptoms
vanished within twenty-four hours and she resumed a normal
life without medicines or dietary restrictions. Control radio-
graphy two weeks later showed, much to the radiologists' sur-
prise, two healthy scars and only a slightly deformed duodenal
cap. Since two years there has been no further complaint.

It is of evolutionary interest that even in modern man the
diencephalic reaction to repressed guilt still follows the primitive pattern of the rejected hungry cub. It still produces an excessive secretion of highly acid gastric juice in an empty stomach
and a tight closure of the pylorus to prevent this acid leaking out.
The condition of the stomach is thus identical with that which
occurs when a very hungry person anticipates a hearty meal. The
ulcer patient describes this as 'hunger-pain' and soon learns that
it can be almost instantly relieved by taking food. Yet as soon

as the stomach has emptied, the situation builds up again. The patient usually attributes this recurrence to the food he has eaten, with which, of course, it has little or nothing to do.

In a recent careful survey a large number of ulcer patients were divided into two groups. One group was given a strict, old-fashioned ulcer diet, while the other was given normal hospital diet. No psychotherapy was used and the medicinal treatment was identical in both groups. In the end-result there was no difference between the two groups, but it was noticed that the patients on the strict diet were more rapidly relieved of pain than those that ate normally.

The reason for this difference is almost certainly psychological. Whenever there is a sense of guilt, be it conscious or repressed, atonement brings some relief. The ulcer patient usually settles on dietary restrictions, brazenly flaunted at home and in company, as a way of making amends. That is also why patients whose ulcer has healed without a resolution of their guilt-producing conflict may continue to diet for years as a sort of preventive measure against a relapse.

Dieting does, in fact, serve this purpose, but this is not because dietary indiscretions may bring on a new ulcer. The prophylactic value of dietary restriction lies entirely in the use of chronic invalidism as a means of appeasing a guilty subconscience. There is not the slightest clinical reason why a patient who has once had an ulcer should watch his diet after the ulcer has healed.

Peptic ulcers do not occur in pregnancy. The reason is that during pregnancy diencephalic behaviour changes completely. All the otherwise normal responses to rage, fear or guilt are abolished. During gestation diencephalic reactions are geared to hide rather than to run away or fight. Primitive pregnant women and many female mammals seek a lair where they are hidden and safe. They creep away from danger and expect the male to defend them. There is thus no need for the mechanisms which prepare the body for flight or fight, and such mechanisms do not occur during pregnancy.

As long as she is with child, a woman is therfore fully protected against all those psychosomatic diseases which arise out of the normal fear or rage reflexes that civilization has rendered useless or inadmissible to consciousness.

It is characteristic of Western man's mechanistic attitude towards his body that a simple ulcer is still in many quarters considered an indication for major surgery. In the treatment of peptic ulcers there are only three absolute indications for surgery: the perforation of the intestinal wall, because it may lead to death from peritonitis; a penetration of the ulcer into other organs, because such ulcers can no longer heal without surgical repair; and the formation of so much scar-tissue that the passage of food is mechanically obstructed, even after the spastic factor has been eliminated. The bleeding of an ulcer is only in the rarest case an indication for surgery.

Past clinical experience has shown that ulcers treated with a full array of dietary and medicinal methods alone will usually heal but very often relapse. Even when relatively conservative surgery is performed by short-circuiting the affected area, new ulcers are apt to appear. These disappointing results led to ever more radical surgery, culminating in the removal of the whole area that could possibly be affected—the lower two-thirds of the stomach and the upper duodenum. The reasoning behind this mutilating operation is to save the patient once and for all from further suffering on account of peptic ulcers.

One can but marvel at the magnificent development of these radical surgical techniques which are now performed by specialists with a minimum of risk to the life of the patient. So much technical brilliance and ingenuity has gone into the surgical treatment of ulcers that it is bitterly disappointing to the Western mentality when it is forced to admit that a good clinical psychiatrist can, in cases of simple ulcer, usually achieve identical results by 'mere talk' at far less cost, with no risk and in less time than it takes a patient to recover from the operation. It is now but a matter of time—time needed to overcome cortical reluctance to give up a cherished achievement—until surgery of the uncomplicated peptic ulcer will become as obsolete as the once famous Sippy milk-diet is to-day.

That thousands of stomachs are still being resected unnecessarily is because surgeons, by the very nature of their calling, are inclined to think mechanically rather than psychosomatically and because there are so few good clinical psychiatrists. A good clinical psychiatrist is not one who carries the teachings of his favourite psychiatric school into the medical and surgical wards. He is not one who blunders into the gossamer web spun in years of conscious living. He knows that the human cortex is as sensitive as an Aeolian harp and therefore needs no plucking. He crosses and recrosses the bridge that spans the gap between physician and psychiatrist and is welcome and at home on both sides of the abyss. The bridge he uses is built out of a sound knowledge of diencephalic physiology.

Psychosomatic Disorders of the Upper Duodenum

In common with the stomach, the upper duodenum is prone to congestive inflammation, known respectively as gastritis and duodenitis. Congestion occurs when a moderate contraction of the muscular wall of the intestine strangles the soft-walled veins and thus interferes with the reflux of venous blood from the inner lining of the stomach or duodenum. This condition is a diencephalic response to fear or anxiety. The upper duodenum also shares with the stomach a liability to peptic ulcers when guilt provokes the maximal spasm that can choke an artery long enough to kill the small area of tissue which it feeds.

But the upper duodenum has psychosomatic conditions of its own.

The liver produces a constant stream of bile which flows down a small pipe, the bile-duct, until it reaches the upper duodenum. On its way from the liver to the duodenum the bile-duct has two side branches (Fig. 5). One leads to the gall-bladder and the other to the pancreas.

The pancreas is a large intestinal gland which produces a number of powerful digestive enzymes. Its secretion flows only when stimulated by a digestive process going on in the stomach, much as the sight, the smell, the taste, the feel and even the thought of food stimulate salivation. The flow of pancreatic secretion is not constant, as is the flow of bile from the liver, and the body therefore needs no reservoir to store pancreatic secretion.

Bile differs from pancreatic secretion in that it is not merely a digestive juice necessary for the breakdown of fats, but also an important outlet of waste-matter from the liver. Bile must therefore be discharged even when it is not required for digestive purposes and is then stored for future use in the gall-bladder.

The flow of the mixture of bile and pancreatic secretion into

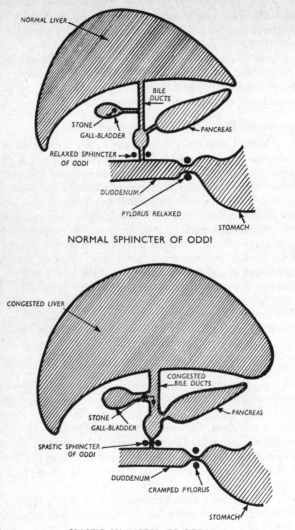

NORMAL LIVER

BILE DUCTS

STONE
GALL-BLADDER

PANCREAS

RELAXED SPHINCTER
OF ODDI

DUODENUM

PYLORUS RELAXED

STOMACH

NORMAL SPHINCTER OF ODDI

CONGESTED LIVER

CONGESTED
BILE DUCTS

STONE
GALL-BLADDER

PANCREAS

SPASTIC SPHINCTER
OF ODDI

DUODENUM

CRAMPED PYLORUS

STOMACH

SPASTIC SPHINCTER OF ODDI

The organs in these sketches are not given their correct anatomical position for the sake of clarity

Fig. 5. THE SPHINCTER OF ODDI

the duodenum is controlled by a ring-muscle—the sphincter of Oddi—which encircles the bile-duct just before it enters the duodenum. When this muscle is closed, the bile coming down from the liver cannot get out of the duct and is forced into the side branch that ends in the gall-bladder.

In the gall-bladder the thin, watery liver-bile is thickened into a dark, viscid fluid—bladder-bile—through the absorption of some of the water which the clear liver bile contains, and in this high concentration bile is digestively more potent.

When fat arrives in the upper duodenum, the sphincter of Oddi opens and the gall-bladder contracts sharply. Thereby three different substances flow into the duodenum: the thin liver-bile which is in the duct, the thick bladder-bile which is squeezed out of the gall-bladder and the pancreatic secretion which joins the bile just above the sphincter of Oddi.

Under normal conditions all these functions are regulated by the local centres of the autonomic nervous system and function perfectly without central nervous intervention. Yet in an emergency the diencephalon can overrule these local centres. It stops stomachic digestion in response to fear, and as soon as the flow of gastric juices is turned off the pancreas ceases to function. There is a tight contraction of the sphincter of Oddi, preventing any further entry of bile and pancreatic secretion into the duodenum. When the sphincter of Oddi is tightly closed for a long time, the pressure in the bile-ducts becomes so greatly increased that these thin tubes are forced to dilate.

If small stones have formed in the gall-bladder, such a stone can slip out of the bladder into the dilated duct and may thus bring on a gall-stone colic. Expert questioning after the pain of a gall-stone colic has been relieved more regularly reveals a preceding emotional disturbance than a dietary indiscretion. In this sense even a gall-stone colic may be psychosomatically induced.

But even when no stones are present in the gall-bladder, the diencephalic contraction of the sphincter of Oddi has a number of repercussions. The contraction can be so violent that the patient feels a severe pain in the gall-bladder region which is clinically almost indistinguishable from a gall-stone colic.

More common is a moderate spasm of the sphincter which merely inhibits the flow of bile and pancreatic secretion into the

duodenum. The absence of bile interferes grossly with the digestion of fats, while the pancreatic enzymes can to some extent
be replaced by other enzymes secreted from the intestinal wall;
yet when the flow of pancreatic secretion is cut off the digestion
of proteins and starches is less satisfactory than normal.

In this case digestion may be improved by the oral administration of pancreatic enzymes, but far better results are achieved
if the cramp of the sphincter of Oddi is relieved by administering dilute hydrochloric acid, which seems to have the effect of
signalling to the diencephalon that the emergency is over.
Except in the case of very rare destructive processes in the pancreas, there is probably no such thing as a genuine primary
pancreatic deficiency. A deficient pancreatic function seems invariably to be a secondary result of a deficiency of gastric
secretion or an abnormal clenching of the sphincter of Oddi. In
other words, it is usually psychosomatic.

When the diencephalic contraction of the sphincter of Oddi
lasts for a long time, it may lead to a congestion of bile in the
liver. The liver then becomes slightly, but palpably, enlarged.
A slightly enlarged liver associated with indigestion is often
interpreted as liver disease, suggesting that there is something
very wrong with the liver as such. A diagnosis of liver disorder
heaps new terrors on an already frightened patient whose liver,
as judged by all clinical tests, may be normal.

A normal flow of bile from the liver which fails to get past the
sphincter of Oddi can often be demonstrated radiologically.
The radio-opaque medium which the patient swallows in order
to make the gall-bladder radiologically visible fills the gall-
bladder and shows this organ to be perfectly normal in shape,
size and position.

When then a fatty stimulus—in the form of egg-yolk—is
given, the normal response is an opening of the sphincter of
Oddi and a sharp contraction of the gall-bladder. But when
the sphincter is diencephalically clenched, the gall-bladder's
contractions are in vain because the bladder-bile cannot get out
of the duct. The visible contraction is therefore only slight and
sluggish, not necessarily because the gall-bladder itself is sluggish or diseased, but simply because the flow is blocked by the
cramped sphincter of Oddi.

A spasm of the sphincter of Oddi can be released by strong

anti-spastic medication, but a more rational approach is to concentrate on allaying the underlying anxiety and to obtain almost immediate relaxation by using the same simple trick that has been recommended in dealing with the moderate pyloric cramp occurring in response to fear—i.e., the introduction of a suitable amount of diluted hydrochloric acid into the stomach.

The diencephalon cannot distinguish between gastric hydrochloric acid and the same acid out of a bottle. It can only interpret this manoeuvre as a resumption of the flow of gastric juice, and it is thereby persuaded to react as if, for the moment at least, the emergency had passed. It at once releases its emergency grip on the functions of the upper intestinal organs and confidently hands them back to their own local control, whereupon they immediately resume normal behaviour.

If treatment with dilute hydrochloric acid is continued regularly for some weeks, the absence of digestive disturbances breaks the vicious cycle of subconscious alarm, diencephalic reaction thereto, conscious awareness of the symptoms produced by the diencephalic reaction, increased alarm and increased diencephalic emergency measures.

In many cases this result can be achieved without psychotherapeutic intervention. In others relapses continue to occur until the underlying subconscious anxiety has been psychotherapeutically resolved.

5

Disorders of the Lower Digestive Tract

The Lower Intestines

·THE LAST two-thirds of the duodenum, the whole small intestine, the caecum, the ascending and the first half of the transverse colon are run by their own local regulations. These local regulations are so efficient and so little concerned with what goes on outside the body that they have fully emancipated themselves from diencephalic interference. It follows that the middle parts of the human alimentary canal are never the site of psychosomatic disorders.

The functional disturbances which sometimes occur in these organs are always secondary to an abnormal behaviour in those parts that are under diencephalic control in the upper and lower reaches of the intestinal tract. The middle of the intestinal tract does not respond directly to any diencephalic signals of emergency. Psychosomatic diseases again begin to appear in the second half of the transverse colon and become increasingly common in the descending colon, the sigmoid, rectum and anus.

Partially digested food coming from the small intestine enters the colon at the caecum. There it undergoes a number of important changes. In the small intestine food particles are suspended in very watery digestive juices. This suspension is sterile. The highly acid gastric juice has killed and digested all the bacteria with which the food was contaminated. Even the numerous germs that inhabit the mouth are killed in the stomach. As it enters the caecum the sterile food suspension is brought into contact with a luxuriant bacterial flora. From this point on the forward transport of nourishment is very slow. The passage of food through the long and narrow small intestine is rapid, taking but a few hours, while the journey from the caecum to the sigmoid normally requires forty-eight hours or more.

The length of an adult's colon is more than 4 ft. and its

normal diameter is 3 inches. The colon, therefore, holds an enormous mass of food, several pounds in fact. The colon must always be filled to capacity; otherwise it cannot function normally. A colon which is empty, after a high colonic irrigation for instance, takes four to five days of hard feeding without an evacuation taking place to get back to a normal degree of fullness.

It is not generally realized how little residue is left after the process of digestion and assimilation. Many people still believe that a large meal remains in the intestines as eaten until it is evacuated. This is not at all so. For instance, a potato consists of about one-third water and two-thirds starch. If the potato has been boiled, mashed or well masticated, most of the water and the starch are assimilated long before the remains of the potato reach the colon. The water has been eliminated as urine, sweat or moisture in the breath, while the starch has been burned up to furnish muscular energy or body-warmth. Almost the whole bulk of the potato has vanished about two to three hours after it was eaten; all that remains is a small quantity of indigestible cellulose fibres, amounting to about as much as a match-head. It takes a lot of match-heads to fill a pipe the size of the human colon. To a greater or lesser degree all food is rapidly reduced to a very small residue in the course of normal digestion. If the faeces consisted only of food residue, it would be quite satisfactory to evacuate about once every two weeks. That this is not so is due to the fact that normal human faeces contain only a small amount of food residues, 20 to 40 per cent perhaps. The rest of the bulk of the normal stool is made up of bacteria, dead cells shed from the ever self-regenerating surface of the intestinal lining, excretions, chiefly from the liver, gas bubbles, mucus and water.

The process of digestion is completed when the colonic contents finally reach the sigmoid. There has then been enough time for the bacterial disintegration of vegetable and animal fragments and for the digestive enzymes to complete their work. Assimilation has been going on throughout the entire length of the alimentary canal, but the final extraction of nourishment takes place in the sigmoid, and here most of the water of the semi-solid colonic contents is absorbed. The withdrawal of the last, fully digested food and surplus water changes the colonic contents into solid waste-matter, the normal faeces. It takes the sigmoid about twenty-four hours to accomplish this change. If the colonic contents stay in the sigmoid less than twenty-four hours, the faeces are not normal, because they then contain too much water and some nourishment of which the body is deprived by premature evacuation. If, on the other hand, faecal matter stays in the colon more than twenty-four hours, no harm is done. There are many people who habitually evacuate only once a week, though they eat as much as others. Such persons are perfectly healthy, and as long as they do not worry about their slow rhythm they suffer from none of the dire consequences popularly believed to be caused by so-called con- stipation. Their weekly stool is not much larger than a daily evacuation, from which it differs only in that it contains more food-residue and other waste-matter and less bacteria and water. As long as such persons resist the blandishments of laxatives they have nothing to fear.

A strong muscular motor expels the faeces from the sigmoid into the rectum and out through the anus, and a clear under- standing of this mechanism is essential for the interpretation of the psychosomatic disorders of evacuation. The sigmoid has powerful circular and longitudinal muscles which bring about the ejection of stool by a short sequence of well-co-ordinated contractions and relaxations (Fig. 6).

Before defecation, the juncture between the descending colon and the sigmoid is open. The other end of the sigmoid where it joins the rectum is so tightly closed that only gases can escape. Normal defecation is initiated by a relaxation of the muscular closure at the entrance to the rectum. At the same time the circular muscles at the colon-sigmoid juncture contract tightly and seal off the upper end of the sigmoid. Between evacuations the sigmoid is thus a tube which is open at the upper and closed at the lower end. When defecation starts the situation is reversed.

The second phase is a contraction of the longitudinal muscles of the sigmoid. This draws the open end of the sigmoid back over the head of the solid faecal mass. Owing to the closure of the colon-sigmoid juncture, the mass cannot escape back into the descending colon and so the faeces are forced into the previously empty rectum. This operation is accompanied by a

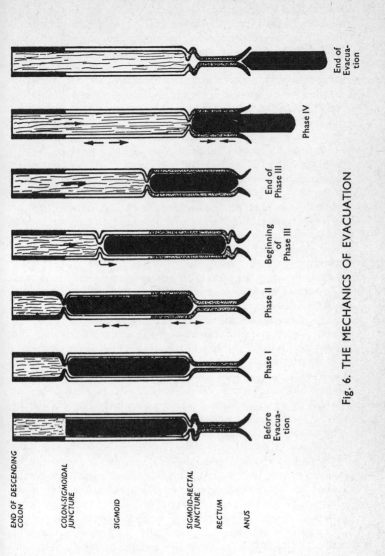

END OF DESCENDING COLON

COLON-SIGMOIDAL JUNCTURE

SIGMOID

SIGMOID-RECTAL JUNCTURE

RECTUM

ANUS

Before Evacuation

Phase I

Phase II

Beginning of Phase III

End of Phase III

Phase IV

End of Evacuation

Fig. 6. THE MECHANICS OF EVACUATION

longitudinal stretching of the rectum to allow for the shortening of the sigmoid. Thus the lower end of the faecal cylinder is already in the rectum before the upper end has moved away from the closed colon-sigmoid juncture.

In a third phase the circular muscular constriction at the colon-sigmoid juncture starts to move and runs down the whole length of the sigmoid. This peristaltic movement pushes the faeces out of the sigmoid into the elongated rectum. When this downward travelling constriction reaches the rectum, it stops there, once again sealing the sigmoid from the rectum. The beginning of a fourth and final phase usually overlaps the end of phase three. It consists of a relaxation of the contracted longitudinal muscles of the sigmoid, which thus resumes its normal length. Meanwhile, the anal ring-muscles have opened, while the stretched rectum contracts back to its normal size and thus expels the whole faecal mass. The position and the state of these organs are then once again the same as before evacuation. As the colon-sigmoid juncture remains open, fresh matter can flow down from the colon into the sigmoid, where, in the course of a day or more, the process of turning it into faeces is repeated. The normal mechanism of defecation requires about five seconds to run its full course.

Under normal conditions, a tentative beginning of the first phase of evacuation is felt as an urge to evacuate. The relaxation of the longitudinal muscles of the sigmoid when it stretches in the fourth phase produces the feeling of satisfaction which occurs after normal defecation. It is obvious that this mechanism cannot function when the colon and the sigmoid are empty, as there is then no solid faecal cylinder on which the musculature can act, nothing over which the sigmoid can retract and nothing which a peristaltic wave can expel.

Modern civilized man does not necessarily evacuate the moment he feels an urge to do so. Normal evacuation can be delayed or initiated at will. This may seem surprising, as the cortex has no direct influence on the mechanism beyond its ability to clench the peri-anal muscles. Yet indirectly the cortex can, by a long period of training, force the lower centres to go into action in response to a cortically controlled situation or action. To do this the cortex makes use of a nervous mechanism known as a conditioned reflex, which may be local or diencephalic. A normal reflex can be 'conditioned' when it is regularly associated with the same act, situation or sensory stimulus. The cortical stimulus has nothing to do with the reflex, but once conditioning has been established by careful training, the cortical stimulus alone can be sufficient to put the local reflex into operation. Persons who regularly go to stool after the first cigarette, a glass of hot or cold water, a cup of coffee, shaving or reading the newspaper, are examples of good conditioning. The conditioning of defecation is socially and conventionally useful, and its only drawback is that an empty cigarette case, a breakdown of utility services or a postal strike may cause dreaded 'constipation' because the stimulus to which the evacuation has been conditioned is lacking at the right moment.

Man is not born with the many conditioned reflexes which he uses in civilized life to obtain cortical control over bodily functions with which his cortex has no right to interfere. Conditioning must be taught. Western man begins to condition the defecation of his children in their earliest infancy. Baby is punctually put on the pot and woe betide it if its little sigmoid refuses to be bullied. As is the case with the institution of meal-times, the modern cortex clings tenaciously to non-biological order and convenience by foolishly pretending that recent cortical contrivances are actually laws of health and nature.

Even after long and severe training the old and biologically infallible diencephalon may disobey cortical demands which are based on an entirely wrong interpretation of an internal situation. For example, when the sigmoid is empty and cramped, the cortex is always ready to believe that it is overfilled, though it is merely distended with gas blocked by spasms. The cortex then orders an evacuation which the diencephalon is mechanically unable to perform. The cortex interprets this as insubordination and petulantly reacts by evoking grim forebodings. With the terror which forebodings of impending intestinal disaster generate, the cortex once again gets a hold over the diencephalon and forces it to react with the diarrhoea of fear. In case the desired evacuation does not take place, the cortex resorts to a purge, with which it thinks it can outwit the diencephalon. The fatuous insistence of the cortex on disciplining the diencephalon always causes a psychosomatic conflict.

Habitual Constipation

Wild animals do not suffer from constipation, but domesticated carnivora such as lap-dogs often do. For this there are
several reasons. One is that the fresh, filled entrails of herbivorous animals are an important ingredient of a normal carnivorous diet. The herbivorous intestine is full of vegetable
matter in the process of chemical and bacterial digestion. When
a dog eats this matter, the bacteria are rapidly killed and digested in its stomach. The bacterial disintegration of the vegetable
fragments is stopped. In the short and small carnivorous colon
there is no time for bacteria to resume this disintegrating action,
and so vegetable fragments are not further digested; however,
they usefully increase the bulk of the faeces, in which meat
leaves hardly any residue. Moreover, the digested bacteria are
of great nutritional value. That is also why putrid meat which is
teeming with bacteria is good for dogs. But such canine delica-
cies are rarely fed to pets. Conceited man is all too apt to think
that what is good for him must also be good for his best animal
friend. He will compromise on a nice clean bone, but beyond
that he draws the line.

Another reason for the lap-dog's constipation is that its owner
has remorselessly and cruelly conditioned it to evacuate in a
hurry—to order and at fixed times only. This means that faeces
have to stay far too long in the short, fast-moving carnivorous
gut, whereby all the water they contain is absorbed, making
them hard and dry. It is easy for man to condition his own
relatively sluggish, omnivorous gut, but to be able to do this
with a carnivorous intestine is indeed a triumph of the art of
domestication, which is the art of making animals do things
contrary to the purposes of their evolution.

The term *habitual constipation* implies an abnormal tendency
to retain faecal matter. Let it be said from the outset that no
such condition exists. Faeces may be blocked by mechanical
obstructions, such as intestinal kinks due to adhesions, constricting growths or by rare congenital malformations such as Hirsch-
sprung's Megacolon or embryonic failures in anal development,
but these serious disorders are neither habitual nor functional.
In the absence of organic lesions there is no such thing as an
abnormal accumulation of faeces in the colon or in the sigmoid,

nor does stool ever pile up behind locally or diencephalically induced spasms. On the contrary, habitual constipation is almost without exception due to an abnormal emptiness of the lower gut.

Only the cortex enjoys the privilege of occasionally being able to produce the one condition which may legitimately be called functional constipation. The cortex has some direct control over the anal ring-muscles and can prevent their relaxation in an otherwise normal defecation. In this case the sigmoid drives the faecal cylinder into the rectum but fails to expel it through the anus. Stool thus accumulates in the rectum, which is normally empty. The rectal wall is able to continue the absorption of water, and so such stool, blocked in the rectum, may eventually become almost stone hard.

The failure of the anal ring-muscles to open is not a normal diencephalic reaction to fear. It is a cortical measure of defence or protest, like throwing up one's arms in defence or protest, an action with which the diencephalon has little to do. The cortical mechanism that causes anal closure during an otherwise normal evacuation is either just below or above the threshold of consciousness. For example, the anus may close because of disgust for a dirty toilet in a train or because the bathroom door will not lock and there is a fear of embarrassment. Sometimes an anxiety concerning constipation may, paradoxically, be the cause. In this case the patient has usually taken a purge some days previously and has thereby emptied most of his colon. For the next three to four days there has been no evacuation, because the time required for new faeces to form in the sigmoid has been insufficient. The patient registers this delay with horror and consternation, believing that his constipation is now worse than ever. Each day he has been to the toilet, torn between hope and despair. He imagines that all the food he has eaten is rotting in his gut and that his only salvation will be an even stronger purge or, better still, an enema. In this state of frantic tension in the toilet his anus cannot relax.

Meanwhile, his colon has been functioning perfectly. It has finally overcome the abnormal emptiness produced by the purge and is in the process of putting matters right again. Possibly on the fourth or fifth day the sigmoid is full and goes normally into action, but by this time the cortex is in a shocking dither, believing that after four long days spontaneous evacuation has become impossible. In this state of anxious frustration the cortex does exactly the opposite of what it should do. Instead of relaxing the anus so that defecation can run its normal course, the cortex clenches the anal muscles and then tries to increase the pressure by calling up all its auxiliary forces—the lungs, the diaphragm and the powerful muscles of the abdominal wall. Contracted anal ring-muscles are almost as strong as a clenched fist. Against this obstruction the sigmoidal motor is helpless, even with the aid of puffing, groaning and straining till the face turns purple. Modern man's cortex seems unable to grasp that unless it lets go of the anus, such antics are a mere waste of time and energy.

The abnormal clenching of the anus is sometimes due to deeper psychological motives which often reach back into childhood. For instance, a cortical refusal to defecate may be an infantile expression of protest against authority, or it may be caused by an excessive revulsion to faeces which some parents unwisely arouse in their children. In all these cases the stool remains imprisoned in the rectum, giving the patient the most uncomfortable sensation of 'sitting on a cricket-ball'. Unless this very distinct sensation is continually present, the rectum is always empty. It is important to know this, because a spasm of the anus produces the feeling of 'a lump' even when the rectum is empty. The mechanism is the same as in the *boule hysterique* of the oesophagus, but as long as the rectum is empty there is never the feeling of actually sitting on a ball. In doubt, a digital examination reveals the difference at once. Sometimes faeces that have been in the rectum for several days have to be broken up mechanically before they can be evacuated.

The lower intestinal disorder which is known as habitual constipation is caused by a mechanism which is entirely different from the one which leads to rectal congestion with faeces. There is neither a block nor an abnormal retention of faecal matter; on the contrary, this so-called constipation is without exception due to a lack of faecal matter—i.e., an abnormal emptiness of colon and sigmoid. The cortex understands only those bodily mechanisms over which it has direct control. It can have no first-hand knowledge of what is going on in the colon and sigmoid because these organs are entirely out of its reach. Yet the cortex, with its usual presumption, does not hesitate to reason about what is happening in the lower intestine. Such reasoning is based on a false analogy inasmuch as the cortex starts out from the quite unwarranted supposition that what can happen at the anus can also happen higher up.

Though it may know nothing about the process of digestion and assimilation, the cortex arbitrarily sets up a standard of elimination. Whenever evacuation fails to come up to this corti-cal standard, the conclusion is reached that faecal matter has stayed behind. To bolster up its case the cortex cheerfully accepts further bodily evidence, which it then proceeds to falsify. For instance, the feeling of dissatisfaction which remains after a forced and premature evacuation is taken as evidence of stool having been left inside, though this sensation is exclusively due to the sigmoidal motor not having been able to function normally.

When the colon is empty, it is partially contracted and par-tially distended with gas (Fig. 7B). The gas causes bloating, which never occurs when the colon is full, but the untutored cortex always attributes bloating to overfilling with faeces. As the true intestinal condition is exactly the reverse of what the cortex thinks, habitual constipation can never be cured by any of those measures which are the outcome of faulty cortical reasoning; indeed, it is only made worse. Yet the modern cortex is so ridiculously opinionated where the inner working of the body is concerned that it cannot admit its own error; it con-tinues to blame the intestine, which is, in fact, behaving nor-mally. The cortex will go to any length in trying to interpret the situation; it will blame food, doctors, growths, intoxications, adhesions, drugs (other than purges and laxatives), a heritage from dyspeptic parents. The modern cortex is astoundingly resourceful in finding scapegoats for its own inadequacy.

The original excessive emptying of the colon which starts the psychosomatic vicious cycle may have been caused by an attack of diarrhoea due to an infection, food-poisoning, a casual purge or a diencephalic reaction to terror. A period of starva-tion, perhaps on account of illness, may have the same effect, particularly when the treating physician insists on producing an artificial evacuation when there is nothing that needs to be evacuated. Once the colon has been emptied, the cortex hardly ever gives it time enough to get full again. Before the three to five days are up, the cortex intervenes in order to procure the evacuation which it considers long overdue. This re-empties the colon, and so the process is repeated again and again.

Habitual constipation can never be inherited, because it is caused by faulty reasoning and not by any bodily condition. Yet it may exist from earliest childhood when the adult in attendance commits the error of misinterpretation. The good mother is busy training her infant to evacuate punctually. Every time she succeeds she is delighted. With a smiling face she radiantly praises her offspring for its co-operation, the infant is happy and proud and this is all as it should be. But when motherly indoctrination fails, as it occasionally must, maternal apprehension and disappointment are vented upon the child. The mother may gently scold the infant and will in any case consider putting matters right with some artificial subterfuge. The child thus gets the feeling that it has done something very wrong and is unhappy about having upset its beloved mother. Unfortunately, it can do nothing about it and is quite unable to understand what all the bother is about. But gradually continued indoctrination teaches it that waste-matter must at all costs be eliminated daily. At first this is done to please Mama, but in later life, when the young cortex begins to do its own reasoning, the daily evacuation becomes a matter of hygiene. The early dread of Mother's frown changes to a dread of internal fouling.

An empty and therefore contracted large gut causes many distressing symptoms, such as bloating, spastic pain when the contractions are strong, loud rumblings and a false urge to evacuate. On the other hand, there are no known symptoms due to colonic or sigmoidal fullness. It has already been explained that a coated tongue, a bad breath or an unpleasant taste in the mouth are never caused by faecal retention. Similarly, liverishness, listlessness, facial spots or a bad complexion and indigestion generally may be associated with habitual constipation as different manifestations of fear and anxiety, but they are certainly not due to insufficient elimination.

These symptoms may be psychologically connected with the intestinal disorder, but there is no other relationship of cause and effect. The notion that delayed evacuation can give rise to these various symptoms exists only because the cortex always

tries to find explanations without taking its own reasoning process into account. If a man were to walk down a dark and silent
alley, he would hear his own footsteps. If he then came to the
conclusion that there was another man walking behind him because he is unable to believe that he is hearing his own tread,
we would consider him crazy. Yet this is exactly what the modern
cortex does once it starts reasoning about the dark interior of
the body. In any case, it is a scientifically proved fact that there
exists no such condition as intestinal auto-intoxication, and this
bogey should now definitely be banished into the realm of myths.

In an abnormally empty colon the circular muscles are forced
to contract. The normal function of these muscles is a gentle
play around a mass having a diameter of about 3 ins. When
this mass is no longer present, the empty pipe must close until,
in the course of some days of normal feeding, it again becomes
normally filled. If the colon is left to its own local devices, refilling is smoothly accomplished without the slightest discomfort. But obviously, the refilling can take place only if there is
no evacuation until a solid faecal cylinder is ready in the sigmoid. A cortex which has set up its own arbitrary standards of
elimination loses this insight. Cortical anxiety mounts with each
day that passes without an evacuation. A state of emergency is
declared to which the diencephalon responds normally by increasing the spasticity of the second half of the colon. As a
result gases become blocked in the ascending and the first half
of the transverse colon and cause the bloating which is then
erroneously ascribed to faecal retention. Meanwhile, all the
other intestinal reactions to fear go into operation in the upper
intestine. The appetite flags and less food is eaten, so that it
takes the colon even longer to resume its normal shape. The
pylorus and the sphincter of Oddi may shut down tightly with
all the discomfort which this entails.

Just before the sigmoid is about to function normally, the
cortex arrives at the conclusion that it is time to rush to the
body's help, as it has little or no faith in the body's ability to
manage its own affairs. Busybody that it is, the cortex now
decides to chastise the innocent sigmoid with what it considers
a salutary dose of medicine. A delighted pharmacist, knowing
that a permanent client is in the making, readily displays the
latest pharmaceutical triumphs. A careful choice of laxative is

made to suit the case as the cortex sees it. The results achieved in a colon that was almost ready to function by itself are gloriously satisfactory. Anxiety is relieved and so, as if by magic, all the dreadful symptoms vanish. 'Aha!' says the boastful cortex in its ignorance, 'So I was right after all.' But here, too, pride comes before the fall. The purge was much too strong. Instead of emptying only the sigmoid, which would have been a minor disaster, it has also emptied most of the colon; and so the whole senseless fussing starts over again.

Inexorably, the dosage of purges and laxatives must gradually be increased. As spontaneous evacuations seem to have ceased altogether, the occasional dose soon becomes a daily dose until a stage is reached in which even the most drastic purging will no longer produce results that satisfy the cortex, particularly not a cortex which thinks so furiously that it has no time to think about its thinking. This supposedly clever, reasoning brain is so stupid where its own body is concerned that it refuses to be diverted from the course it has set itself, come what may. It plods on and on, stone deaf to the body's loud protests against such insensate antics.

Finally, in desperation the cortex resorts to the daily enema. The water which is forced into the colon under pressure momentarily distends the spastic areas. For a brief spell the colon is full and can take on an almost normal shape. This at once releases the imprisoned gas. For the next twenty-four hours the patient is relieved of gaseous distension and suffers merely from the spastic discomfort which recurs as soon as the water is eliminated. But much of the anxiety is relieved because the patient now knows that he is 'clean inside'. This reduced anxiety lessens the upper intestinal symptoms, and so the patient feels better and gradually settles down to this fantastic *modus vivendi*.

But after a while a new trouble arises. Such patients usually impose severe and quite unnecessary dietary restrictions upon their unfortunate body. This and the fact that they are completely deprived of all the nutritional advantages of colonic digestion sooner or later leads to severe malnutrition with its many consequences, now no longer psychosomatic.

How much wiser and simpler is the treatment of delayed evacuation given in impoverished Indian villages where no medicines are available. It consists of treating the worried patient to a couple of enormous meals. This treatment is based on the correct assumption that the digestive tract is a pipe, open at both ends. If more is put into one end, it will force the contents out at the other end—and this is exactly what it does.

Spastic constipation cannot be diagnosed by taking X-rays. To make the colon radiologically visible it must be filled with a large quantity of heavy and indigestible barium salts. The voluminous material opens all the spastic areas, and so a functionally very abnormal colon may appear to be radiologically normal. The patient is usually dismissed with a report stating that no abnormality has been detected. Yet if the abdomen of such a patient is carefully percussed, palpated and auscultated before the X-ray examination or after the barium has been voided, very abnormal conditions are found. The whole descending colon and the sigmoid can be rolled like a hard rope under the palpating fingertips. These spastic parts are usually tender to pressure and have the diameter of a fountain-pen. A normally filled colon can hardly be felt through the abdominal wall because it is soft and plastic. In a normal sigmoid the somewhat harder, but still plastic, faecal cylinder can be palpated shortly before evacuation is due. At other times the sigmoid is as yielding as the colon. In a typical case of habitual constipation, percussion over the ascending and the first half of the transverse colon produces a loud, hollow, drum-like sound, because that area is distended with blocked gases, provided no purge or enema has been taken for a day or two. Over the second half of the lower intestinal tract the tapping finger elicits a dull, solid sound because it is empty and contains no gas. In such an abdomen, loud gurgling and squelching can often be heard as intestinal gas is squeezed through colonic strictures. Sounds of such intensity and frequency are never heard in a normal colon. Another objective finding is an abnormal amount of mucus on the stool. The faeces are nearly always abnormal in shape. They may be cylindrical, but their diameter, which should be at least one inch, is often not more than that of a pencil. In other cases that are more spastic, the stool may be evacuated in the form of small pellets, either singly or in a conglomerated mass.

Patients suffering from habitual constipation usually give a very typical and extraordinarily uniform history, but it does occasionally happen that an empty spastic colon is found in patients who are being examined for something entirely different. Such patients may be quite unaware that there is something wrong with their colon, because they have no conception what a normal stool is like. They believe that a little daily dose—'very mild, of course'—is a fine way to keep fit, that it 'helps the digestion' and is, like soap and water, a civilized form of hygiene.

A common occasion for the discovery of an abnormal colon of which the patient was not aware is when medical advice is sought for an inflammation of the urinary bladder. The most frequent cause of urinary infection is Bacillus coli, a normal inhabitant of the colon. The wall of a normal colon cannot be penetrated by this germ, but when the wall is spastically congested and inflamed this bacillus can find its way out of the colon or sigmoid into the urinary tract, where it sets up the bacterial infection known as B. coli cystitis. Until quite recently such infections could be cleared up rapidly with antibiotics. Today the indiscriminate use of these potent drugs has produced highly resistant strains of B. coli, so that it is now in most cases necessary to return to the older and slower methods of treatment such as urinary antiseptics, autovaccines, etc., that were used before the antibiotic era. Unfortunate though this is, it has the advantage that the treatment of the colon has been brought back into the limelight. Unless the underlying spasticity and abnormal emptiness of the colon is cured, B. coli cystitis almost invariably relapses even after the first infection has been completely eradicated as bacteria continue to wander out of the colon into the bladder. Once the colonic disorder is cured, cystitis never relapses, provided the original infection of the bladder has been dealt with. As the spastic colon is a purely psychosomatic condition and as B. coli cystitis hardly ever occurs without it, this urinary disease can be said to be of psychosomatic origin. B. coli cystitis is a good example of faulty cortical reasoning causing a serious bacterial infection.

Habitual constipation in which there is an abnormal retention of faeces due to an excessive relaxation of the intestinal musculature does not appear to exist as a psychosomatic condition; at least the author has not seen a single case in thirty years. The operative mechanism is always a spasm and never a muscular relaxation. The so-called sluggish bowel is actually an over-active bowel. Therefore, the treatment of habitual constipation is always the same. It is quick and relatively simple once the underlying mechanisms are clearly understood. The object of treatment is to convert a colon as shown in Fig. 7B into one as shown in Fig. 7A, and to keep it always full.

The Role of Water

An experienced hunter is generally able to identify an animal by its droppings. In each species the size, shape and smell of the excreta are extraordinarily constant and characteristic. Only the colour of the faeces may be slightly altered when highly coloured foods are eaten. Otherwise the nature of the food and drink have surprisingly little influence on the appearance of the normal stool. This uniformity within the animal species applies also to man. The faeces of an Australian aboriginal, an Eskimo a South Indian Brahmin and a Parisian gourmet are indistinguishable to the eye and the nose, in spite of the extreme difference in the feeding habits of these races.

One reason for this uniformity is that food residue furnishes only a part of normal faeces. In all healthy humans the bacterial flora of the colon is very constant, and the chemical and cellular waste-matter which the body eliminates with the stool is the same in all races. There is hardly any item of normal human nutrition which can change the appearance of the stool. When modern man endows any ingredient of his diet with such properties, he is giving credence to yet another of his many dietary fables. What he observes is usually either a conditioned reflex or the result of his apprehensiveness regarding certain foods.

There is, however, one exception to this general rule—when an adult drinks milk in large quantities. When a milk diet is continued for several days, the stool usually becomes hard and dry. That this does not happen in infants is because the infant drinks human or humanized milk. In the stomach human milk forms a fine, flocculent precipitate which is easily and rapidly digested, the process requiring no additional water. Non-humanized milk of animal origin, on the other hand, forms an almost insoluble, solid mass of casein in the human stomach. The digestion of this mass takes very much longer and requires a large amount of additional water.

Milk produces hard stools not because of any intrinsic pro-

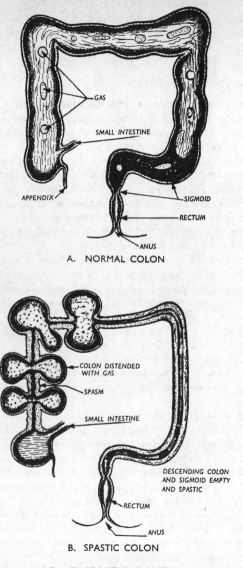

A. NORMAL COLON

B. SPASTIC COLON

Fig. 7. SPASTIC COLITIS

perty, but only on account of an erroneous modern cortical conclusion. The cortex does not know that cow's milk behaves like a solid in the human intestine. Proud of its achievements of domestication, it rashly presumes that cow's milk and mother's milk are more or less the same. The cortex registers the drinking of a glass of milk as fluid intake and therefore resists the body's demand for more water. It represses the natural thirst, which calls for at least the same amount of water. The cortex thinks it knows better and believes that so much fluid at a time cannot possibly be healthy.

The result is that the body has to supply the additional water needed to digest the cow's milk by increasing the secretion of digestive juices. The body is hard put to spare so much water and avidly withdraws it as soon as the digestion of the milk is finished in the sigmoid. It is this excessive withdrawal of water from the sigmoid that makes the stool hard and dry. If every glass of milk were topped with an equal or greater quantity of water, a hardening of the stool would not occur.

The orthodox Hindu drinks milk all his life. Being a strict vegetarian, milk is his only source of animal protein, which for man is indispensable, but he takes very good care to associate the drinking of milk with an ample intake of water after every meal. The African Masai, the greatest herdsman of that continent, never drinks the milk of his cows. He considers it unfit for human consumption, possibly because he is often faced with a shortage of the ample supply of potable water which the milk-drinker needs. Instead he drinks the raw blood of his cattle, which he taps from their jugular vein, thus making excellent nutritional use of both bulls and cows without having to slaughter them and without interfering with the natural nourishment of the calves. The digestion of raw blood requires very little additional water, and blood remains available when the milk of his cows dries up in time of drought.

Faeces become hard when the body is short of water, but they never become loose on account of excessive fluid intake. It is, therefore, impossible to provoke diarrhoea by drinking. In health the consistency of the contents of the small intestine and the colon is always the same, regardless of how much liquid is swallowed. An excess of fluids is rapidly absorbed and excreted through the kidneys. A lack of fluids is immediately made up by an increased secretion of diluted digestive juices, the additional water being drawn from the body's reserves. These automatic regulations keep the consistency of the middle and lower intestinal contents always constant. If the body as a whole is short of water, it absorbs every drop it can get from the sigmoid, where water is no longer required for the digestive process. Only as a last resort does the body burden the kidneys by making them secrete a more concentrated urine and thus save water.

Anxious persons usually drink insufficient water and suffer from the consequences. The reason is that fear abolishes thirst just as it abolishes hunger. But this the cortex of modern man has completely forgotten. Moreover, modern fears are often subconscious, because the cortex is too proud to admit them. The modern cortex must by its very nature reason about everything, and so it goes to work erecting formidable taboos around the act of drinking.

One notion of which the cortex is particularly proud is that drinking during meals dilutes the digestive secretions of the stomach. Yet it is easy to demonstrate radiologically that it does nothing of the sort. When a draught of water is taken into a stomach partially filled with solid food, the water runs rapidly along the upper curvature of the stomach, which makes way for it, while the rest of the stomach is tightly clamped round the solid contents. As soon as water—or any liquid other than milk —reaches the pylorus, it is allowed to pass into the duodenum and the small intestine, where it is rapidly absorbed. Only if liquids are taken in small sips at a time do they seep into the contents of the stomach. That is why hydrochloric acid given medicinally during meals must always be taken in small sips if it is to become effectively mixed with the food.

Another cortical tenet is that water bloats the stomach. The sensation of bloating can only be produced when the pylorus is tightly closed in a diencephalic reaction to fear and when there is an excess of swallowed air imprisoned in the stomach. When that happens there is no feeling of thirst, as the anxiety has wiped it out, though more water may be urgently required by the body. Yet in this state of alarm a person sometimes drinks water as a matter of habit or because he thereby hopes to make his stomach more comfortable. The water cannot get out of the stomach, owing to the pyloric cramp, and increases the pressure of the gastric air-bubble, causing the discomfort known as bloating. The cortex immediately jumps to the conclusion that water produces indigestion and should therefore be avoided as much as possible. After a while the fear of drinking too much water or of drinking at the wrong time is often sufficient to produce a pyloric spasm. The cortex interprets this as proof of the indigestibility of water and comes to this utterly false conclusion because it will not admit that it is frightened.

Another common notion is that excessive fluid intake increases body weight, though in fact the body is quite incapable of retaining even an ounce of water more than it requires. In lay circles the suggestion is sometimes heard that water changes to fat. If this were true it would be an alchemistic transmutation that even the chemically so resourceful body cannot possibly perform. Perhaps these ideas stem from the observation that obese persons drink plentifully because they perspire from a larger surface, breathe harder and may have diabetes. Moreover, a restriction of fluid intake is commonly advised as a method of weight-reduction. As the body dries out it gets gratifyingly lighter, but no abnormal fat is thereby removed.

The intestinal mechanisms of herbivorous animals require copious, though infrequent, drinking when the animal is not feeding; but this is not so in man's entirely different omnivorous intestine. Man can drink at any time before, during, after, or between his meals, because he was never intended by his early evolution to gorge himself at regular intervals. He is physiologically a nibbler of tidbits and can drink when he pleases. In any case, the knotty problem of drinking in relation to meals hardly existed before the Neolithic invention of pottery. Only when man could have water at hand every time he crouched down to eat did his cortex begin to bother about whether this was good for him or not. Many of the restrictions which man imposes upon his drinking probably stem from watching the behaviour of herbivorous animals, without knowing that their habits are not applicable to his own omnivorous body.

The amount of water required by the body depends chiefly on climate and physical exertion. There are no hard and fast rules, except that it is almost impossible for a healthy person to drink too much water. The body loses water in many ways. Most of the water is bound chemically and osmotically by processes of growth, replacement and metabolism. Water is exhaled in fine droplets in the breath and it is continually lost in perspiration, though this becomes noticeable only when the secretion of sweat exceeds the rate of its evaporation. Water is lost in urine and faeces and there are many minor losses, such as the evaporation or shedding of tears, the evaporation or discharge of nasal secretion, the ejection of semen, menstrual bleeding, sebacious and other secretions, spitting, vomiting, etc. All this water must be replaced from the digestive tract, which is the body's main reservoir of readily available water, and this is another reason why the colon should always be kept filled to capacity.

The inability to drink in the presence of danger was once a vitally important evolutionary achievement. In modern man this useful reflex has changed into a meaningless reaction which interferes with his health. The change has come about partly because civilization has eliminated most of the threats for which the reflex was designed, partly because modern man's fears are so often subconscious and partly because the aberrant reasoning of the cortex completely misinterprets this once useful mechanism.

Diarrhoea

This study is not concerned with diarrhoeas caused by chemical or bacterial toxins, the so-called food-poisonings, nor with those due to severe malnutrition or infections with bacteria or protozoa, such as amoebae. A diarrhoea which can be proved beyond doubt to be exclusively due to any of these causes is not psychosomatic. Unfortunately, purely psychosomatic diarrhoeas are all too frequently believed to be due to such causes and then fail to respond when the presumed cause is eliminated.

Psychosomatic diarrhoea is far more common than any other diarrhoea in modern man. It is caused by two mechanisms only. One mechanism produces acute and the other chronic diarrhoea. An attack of acute diarrhoea can be diencephalically produced in a healthy normal gut by fright, terror or panic. The evolutionary background of this mechanism has already been explained. It is the sudden liquefaction of the sigmoidal contents by the outpouring of a thin and watery mucus from the glands of the wall of the sigmoid. At the same time there is a violent contraction of the circular muscles of the sigmoid which forces out the liquid faeces, often under considerable pressure. The mechanism of this contraction is quite different from that of a normal evacuation (Fig. 6); it is more like the tight clenching of a fist round an open tube of tooth-paste.

Owing to the cortical control over the anus, the actual discharge of faeces can often be prevented for a while. What follows depends on the nature of the fright. If the fear is due to some environmental event reported by the senses and therefore fully conscious, and if it passes over soon, the sigmoid and the rectum relax. They can then re-absorb the excess fluid after the spastic pressure has been relieved, the feeling of impending diarrhoea vanishes and the next evacuation may be perfectly normal. If, on the other hand, the diencephalic fear-reaction is caused by a subconscious emotion which does not quickly subside, there is no relaxation and no re-absorption of water. Frank diarrhoea results and continues until the fear is overcome.

In habitual constipation there is a colonic and sigmoidal spasm of the circular musculature simply because the pipe is abnormally empty. The contraction is a normal response to an abnormal condition. It is in a sense a passive adjustment. But if the intensity of the spasm goes beyond what is necessary to keep the empty pipe closed and becomes active, habitual constipation changes into chronic diarrhoea. Thus, contradictory as it may seem, chronic psychosomatic diarrhoea is basically a more severe form of habitual constipation. The main difference between the two conditions is that habitual constipation is the result of faulty reasoning, while chronic diarrhoea is caused by a fear which is held back at the threshold of consciousness. Such repressed fear is not amenable to reasoning. It cannot be cortically resolved and therefore keeps the diencephalon in a constant state of emergency. The unrelieved dread changes the quick spasm of the sigmoid which is a normal reaction to terror into a permanent cramp. This permanent, active cramp is the mechanism which causes chronic psychosomatic diarrhoea.

In habitual constipation the colonic spasm is relaxed as soon as a normal filling of the colon makes this necessary; but when there is an active spasm produced by unrelieved fear, a normal filling of the lower intestine can no longer take place. The second half of the colon and the sigmoid lose their capacity to retain a normal amount of matter and their contents are hurried along much faster than they ought to be. Nourishment in the process of digestion can no longer dawdle leisurely through the bacterial garden of the colon but is evacuated before digestion and assimilation have had enough time to run their course. Thus the important point is that increased lower intestinal spasticity does not lead to increased constipation but, on the contrary, to diarrhoea.

Unless a psychotherapeutic manoeuvre opens the way for a subconscious fear to break through the terribly strict cortical censorship of modern urban man, the cortex cannot reason about the fear which is causing the diarrhoea. But the cortex is free to reason about the symptom of diarrhoea. This it does in its usual pedantic manner. For instance, it knows from experience that the application of heat may somewhat ease a spastic pain; so it jumps to the opposite, quite unwarranted, conclusion that external cold—which can, of course, never reach the colon—produces a painful contraction. Once the cortex has found this felicitous explanation, it clutches frantically at the superstition that a chill can produce diarrhoea; and that is then the beginning of that rather disgusting habit, the belly-band, still commonly used in Mediterranean and tropical countries. A belly-band is a sweat-poultice applied to the abdomen; as the evaporation from the huge surface of the wool or flannel is much greater than from the smooth skin, and as the belly-band induces abnormal sweating, it makes the skin of the abdomen cold and moist, exactly the opposite of what it is intended to do.

As the belly-band does not seem to improve the diarrhoea, the cortex next goes to work on the diet. Here it is soon faced with the baffling discovery that in this field nothing makes sense. After a pleasant evening spent with friends in a reckless orgy of dietary transgressions, there is often a marked improvement in the stools instead of the deterioration which the patient expects. The explanation is that the festivity has temporarily reduced the anxiety, while the fear of intestinal retribution is fully conscious and cortically legitimate. The cortex can reason about such a fear and say, for instance, 'I don't care if I suffer for it; it was worth it.' Such conscious reasoning immediately relieves the state of diencephalic emergency, the colon relaxes and the diarrhoea stops, only to begin again as soon as meticulous dieting is resumed—no wonder the anxiously observant cortex becomes confused.

That chronic psychosomatic diarrhoea is closely related to habitual constipation is also suggested by the fact that the same treatment cures both conditions. In both cases the object is to get the colon normally filled and to counteract the spasticity. In the protective security of the hospital, of nursing and medical attention, and by the removal of the patient from his usual environment, the subconscious fear diminishes to such an extent that it is nearly always possible to get the colon and the sigmoid to relax and to retain the residue of several days of forced feeding. If then the original fear is psychotherapeutically uncovered or at least brought into a conscious relationship with the diarrhoea, the cure is permanent, provided the patient correctly interprets any future onset of diarrhoea. Chills, food and infections should be the last things he suspects. His first thought must always be to reflect on what emotion went before. After a little practice in retrospection the unpleasant emotion that started an attack of diarrhoea is almost invariably discovered, and very often it is something which the cortex is inclined to discard as being too insignificant. Such cortical judgment should be treated with the utmost scepticism, because even a banal annoyance may reach down into psychological depths of which the conscious cortex has no inkling. Intestinal reactions to fear may be hair-triggered, but they never go off unless something has just previously touched the trigger. If the right connection of cause and effect is immediately established, an attack of psychosomatic diarrhoea never becomes chronic.

Sometimes a chronic diarrhoea which started as a reaction to subconscious fear continues long after the original fear has subsided. In this case the diarrhoea itself produces the panic which may be fully or only partially conscious. Such patients dread the impelling urge to evacuate and are constantly tortured by the appalling prospect of being caught short. To avoid this they force themselves to evacuate as much as possible just before they go to a concert, a play, a party, or a meeting. In some cases the mere thought of a lavatory being out of reach is so terrifying that it produces a profuse watery evacuation. For such a patient the proximity of a toilet into which he can unobtrusively disappear becomes the dominating feature of all his doings, often to the extent that he is forced to abandon most of his normal activities. Yet even such cases can be cured in less than two weeks by a treatment based on the correct psychosomatic interpretation of the condition.

A relatively mild and simple illustrative case is that of a prominent businessman who stated at the first consultation that he was in perfect health but wished to discuss a rather absurd thing that was happening to him during the last three months. With much embarrassment he explained that he had been forced to give up golf, of which he was very fond. The reason for this decision was the fact that every time he approached the fifth green he was assailed by violent and uncontrollable diarrhoea. When he was asked how all this had started, he looked taken aback and rather puzzled. After a little thought he declared that he could not remember the first time it had occurred. He then changed the subject and cheerfully explained that as long as he kept away from the golf course his stools were perfectly normal. Smiling, he commented, 'Idiotic, isn't it?' He was told that he could be cured only if he was able to remember all the circumstances surrounding the first time that he had had such an attack and was sent home to think about it.

The next day he returned and produced the following story in a less light-hearted mood. It had all started when one morning he had been dissatisfied with his evacuation and had casually swallowed one of his wife's pills which he found in the bathroom cupboard. In the midst of a very busy morning in his office, a lady of his acquaintance had telephoned to ask him if he cared to join her in a golf match in the afternoon. He had felt flattered and had readily accepted. The little pill swallowed in the bathroom had been forgotten, until suddenly it began to take effect at the approach to the fifth green. In a flurry of embarrassment he had made some silly excuse and dashed away to crouch behind a clump of bushes. When he returned to the game, his high-spirited companion had kept up a string of merry references to his vanishing act during the rest of the match. He now remembered that her frivolous remarks had needled him to the core, though he could not recollect her actual words.

Two days later he had played a round with a business friend and was again forced to beat an undignified retreat from the fifth green. He had returned to his friend saying that his lunch had not agreed with him and that he had been sick. He had abandoned the game and driven home. About ten days passed before he played again. He claimed to have forgotten the whole unpleasant incident until it happened again when he reached the fifth green. Now he was furious and decided to set about getting over this nonsense. In this he failed hopelessly and finally gave up playing. That was difficult because everyone knew that he was a keen golfer and explanations were demanded. He had sought plausible excuses and had been forced to invent ficti-tious board meetings, a sprained ankle, a threatening cold and the like. Occasionally he had been tempted to accept an invita-tion to play, but then he had felt an increasing urge to go to stool, which vanished as soon as he cancelled the appointment.

In this case the first attack of diarrhoea was caused by a laxa-tive and was therefore not psychosomatic. But all subsequent attacks were due to the panic evoked by the repressed memory of the first incident and its devastating effect upon his modesty and his pride. As soon as this mechanism was explained and accepted, he was advised to play another golf course a few miles away in a different town and then to play a single round on his usual course and report. Nothing happened on either occasion, and he was able to resume his matches as before.

Rarely is a case so simple and so straightforward, and it is only rarely possible to help a patient suffering from psycho-somatic diarrhoea without a short period of hospitalization during which the colon is artificially relaxed and deliberately filled under favourable psychological conditions.

In chronic diarrhoea there is always an inflammation of the colonic and sigmoidal lining. This is the result of the spasm of the intestinal musculature which impedes the reflux of blood in the veins and leads to congestion (Fig. 4). But in the colon and in the sigmoid the spasm can become maximal just as this may happen in the stomach and the duodenum. In this case the arteries that feed the inner surface of the tube are strangled, causing death and destruction of the cellular lining of the gut. The result is a disease known as ulcerative colitis. In ulcerative colitis the often extremely frequent evacuations—twenty to thirty a day are not uncommon—consist of blood, mucus, dead bits of tissue and very little faecal matter. No bacterial, protozoal or other causative agent is ever found.

Before the spastic nature of ulcerative colitis was understood, it was a most puzzling disease. Like the peptic ulcers, ulcerative colitis is peculiarly resistant to any medicinal approach. Here, too, the internist became inclined to abandon his patient to the radical, though mutilating, skill of his surgical colleague, who elegantly removed the offending gut. Just like the peptic ulcers, ulcerative colitis can have a very sudden onset; it may persist for years, often with apparently unaccountable remissions and exacerbations, but it can also heal in a few days. It is very tempting to speculate that in this disease too a subconscious guilt, rather than an anxiety, is involved.

Sometimes ulcerative colitis disappears after a long engagement is broken off. In that case the disease was caused by a consciously inadmissible dislike of a prospective marriage partner or a strong preference for another person which was not frankly admitted. A hated profession in which failure cannot be consciously faced because of parental insistence or a strong feeling of duty towards the family may produce ulcerative colitis. In such cases the ulcers may heal rapidly when the profession is finally changed. Ulcerative colitis is frequently seen among homesick political refugees, tortured by the feeling that they might have done more to save their relatives who stayed behind and suffered the bestialities of concentration camps.

Ulcerative colitis will heal only if changed circumstances or psychotherapy remove the underlying emotional conflict. Unfortunately, psychotherapy, even in the most experienced hands, is not successful in every case because patients suffering from this disease notoriously put up a fierce resistance against the uncovering of their often guilty conscience. Moreover, the dangerous and dramatic symptoms of this disorder make many clinical psychiatrists loath to carry the whole therapeutic burden. In their minds there is often a lingering suspicion that the condition is not purely psychosomatic. The spastic interpretation of ulcerative colitis should give the psychiatrist a more confident, energetic and clearly directed approach to the problem. At least it gives him the certainty that there is always something worth looking for and that he will be amply, even spectacularly, rewarded if he succeeds in getting the patient to see and accept the psychosomatic mechanism which is the cause of his suffering.

The psychotherapy of ulcerative colitis takes much longer and is far more difficult than that of the peptic ulcers. The guilt seems to lie deeper and is more severely repressed. It frequently concerns religion, ethics, morality and ingrained conventions and is less commonly the direct result of a thwarted sex instinct. It is as if the conflict lies on a cortical rather than on an instinct level and it does not usually conform to any of the well-known psychopathological patterns. It is therefore incredibly naïve to discredit the psychosomatic nature of ulcerative colitis simply on the grounds that patients asked if they are worried or under emotional stress say 'No'.

The Anus

There are four common psychosomatic disorders which affect the anus. One has already been discussed under the heading of constipation. It is the blocking of faeces in the rectum by a spastic closure of the large ring-muscles. A second minor anal disorder which can nevertheless cause considerable suffering is an anal burning or itching sensation in the absence of thread-worms or any visible alteration of the skin. Sometimes this condition responds to anti-allergic medication, particularly the local application of cortisone and its modern derivatives. It seems to be associated with an increased spasm of a small superficial ring-muscle which lies just under the surface where the anal mucuous membrane joins the outer skin (Fig. 8A). Though the psychosomatic mechanism which produces this cramp is as yet unclear, clinical experience suggests that it may be the somatic expression of a fear of rectal cancer and that sexual problems are frequently involved. The condition usually clears up for a while after reassurance and a placebo but frequently recurs, because the underlying psychic mechanism is still too obscure to be dealt with by psychotherapy directed to a definite psychic situation.

A third psychosomatic disorder is the anal fissure, tear or split. This too is due to a spastic contraction of the small superficial anal ring-muscle which is largely independent of the powerful, thick ring-muscles which are situated higher up and lie much deeper below the surface (Fig. 8A).

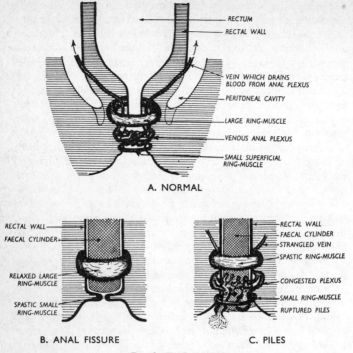

Fig. 8. THE ANUS

Under normal conditions this delicate ring-muscle follows the movements of the larger ones and so closes and opens as required by the passage of faeces. For reasons which must be central nervous but are as yet not amenable to evolutionary or psychological interpretation, this little ring-muscle can remain contracted when the other anal ring-muscles relax to make way for the solid faecal cylinder bearing down in the normal process of evacuation. The situation is then as shown in Fig. 8B. If now the stool is forced out, the skin which cannot give way owing to the spasm splits and the delicate fibres of the ring-muscle are torn apart. The mechanism is similar to that which causes the perineum to split in childbirth.

Anal fissures take long to heal because they are painful. The pain keeps the torn ring-muscle in spasm, which draws the split surfaces apart rather than together. Moreover, the spasm inter- feres with the blood-supply and this delays healing. Surgeons have made the surprising discovery that when in anaesthesia they violently dilate the anus, often making the tear worse, it thereafter heals very rapidly. To those who are not easily en- thralled by the surgical approach to psychosomatic problems this may seem drastic and almost brutal, but it is very effective because the forceful stretching of the small and delicate ring- muscle tears it in so many places that it can no longer go into spasm. The walls of the split are therefore able to approach each other and the tear heals before the ring-muscle has had time to repair the surgical damage and resume its normal function. Anal itching and burning occurs only between evacuations. The passage of stool relieves the sensation for a while, because defe- cation is accompanied by a relaxation of the superficial ring- muscle. The anal fissure, on the other hand, can occur only during the forced evacuation of a formed stool.

A fourth anal disorder which may be produced psychoso- matically is piles. Under the lining of the anus there lies a net- work of thick contorted veins, a so-called venous plexus. Blood is fed into the lower anal region by arteries which run inside the large ring-muscles. Parallel to these hard-walled arteries run soft veins which drain the blood away. When the anal ring- muscle is abnormally contracted over a solid faecal mass as it passes the anus in evacuation, only the veins are compressed (Fig. 8c). Such an abnormal contraction of the large ring-muscle is part of the mechanism of excessive and anxious straining. In this condition blood continues to flow into the venous plexus as the artery is able to resist strangulation, but venous blood can no longer flow back because the vein is compressed between the faecal matter and the spastic muscle. The veins of the anal plexus are therefore forced to dilate and often burst. When such dilated veins burst, the patient suffers from bleeding piles. If the engorged veins do not burst the body strengthens them with the formation of connective tissue, and this leads to the large hollow masses which protrude at every evacuation.

Even large haemorrhoidal masses can regress remarkably once the abnormal spasticity of the anal ring-muscle has been dealt with, but there do exist cases in which the process has gone so far that surgical intervention is advisable. Unfortunately, many surgeons are inclined to give their patients the impression that the operation has cured something, whereas all it does is to remove a disconcerting symptom of faulty evacuation. Unless there is a careful post-operative training and re-education in the normal mechanics of evacuation, new piles are bound to develop sooner or later. This is all the more likely to happen if the surgeon advises laxatives, mineral oils, etc., as a preventive measure, instead of explaining that a full sigmoid and formed bulky stools passed spontaneously are by far the best prophylactic because they prevent anal spasms. Surgeons who miss the psychosomatic point expose themselves to the lay criticism that the operation was neither radically nor properly performed.

Piles which protrude after evacuation usually slip back into the anus of their own accord, but sometimes they have to be pushed back manually. In these cases it is always a spasm of the small superficial ring-muscle, not of the large ring-muscle, which prevents the protruding piles from deflating and slipping back. If the mechanism is explained to such patients, they can learn to avoid this spasm and then have less trouble and discomfort.

Piles that occur during pregnancy are not due to intestinal mechanisms and will therefore be discussed in the next chapter, which deals with circulatory disorders.

In the two foregoing chapters a number of intestinal disorders has been interpreted as arising out of normal bodily reactions to central nervous stimuli. Modern man has made diseases out of these reactions, because they have ceased to serve a vital purpose. The cortex no longer takes them for what they are. The dangers from which they saved man's ancestors have been eliminated by the elaborate cortical defences which we call culture and civilization. Culture is a cortical artifact to which the body has no physiological relationship. The body continues to function as if these artifacts did not exist, and this the modern cortex is unwilling to admit. Whenever the body reacts according to its ancient organization in response to the new fears which civilization has created, it prepares for flight. But the new fears are such that escape is useless. They are cortically generated and can only be resolved by cortical reasoning. This the cortex will not do, because these fears are not admitted into the light of conscious contemplation. They are repressed because the cortex is ashamed of them; it dreads them because they are out of its control. As such fears are not fully conscious, the body's reactions to them appear to be entirely uncalled for and they are therefore interpreted as disorder or disease. Modern urban man has forgotten that these reactions were once the priceless evolutionary achievements to which he owes his existence. His cortex now only thinks in terms of its stupendous success in the creation of artifacts. It has lost touch with its past biological evolution and is led hopelessly astray when it tries to treat the body as if it too were a cortical artifact.

Man will only be able to overcome his psychosomatic suffering if he humbly acknowledges that he is still an animal as far as the working of his body is concerned. He needs more cortical humility and less cortical braggadocio if he wants to live healthily within his civilization.

6

Disorders of the Heart and of
the Blood Vessels

THE CIRCULATORY system transports blood to and from every part of the body. It consists of a central pump—the heart—and two kinds of tubing—arteries, which feed all living cells, and veins, which drain them. In addition to this basic circuit there are several other circuits, such as that which pumps blood in and out of the lungs. In the lungs the venous blood discharges gaseous waste-matter, chiefly carbon dioxide, which it has collected from the tissue-cells. The venous blood is then re-charged with oxygen from the air inhaled and thereby changed into arterial blood and returned to the heart, from where it is pumped back into the tissues.

Another type of circuit is called a *portal system* and consists of a vein which is finely branched at both ends, rather like the trunk of a tree with roots and branches. A very large portal system collects food from the intestinal tract and distributes it at its other end throughout the liver. A minute portal system connects the diencephalon with the anterior lobe of the pituitary gland. Other highly specialized circuits exist—in the kidneys and in the spleen, for instance.

There are basic functional and structural differences between arteries and veins (Fig. 9). Arteries have thick, tough walls in which strong muscular fibres are embedded. These muscles can constrict or dilate the artery, and in the arteries the blood is under pressure which rises and falls according to the heartbeat. When the left heart-chamber contracts, it forcefully drives out the arterial blood and the pressure in the arteries rises, but when the heart-chamber relaxes between two beats the pressure drops. It is this rhythmic rise and fall of arterial pressure which is felt

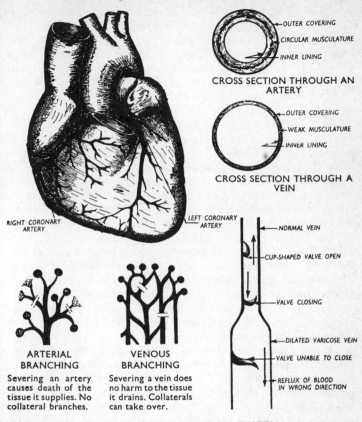

OUTER COVERING
CIRCULAR MUSCULATURE
INNER LINING

CROSS SECTION THROUGH AN ARTERY

OUTER COVERING
WEAK MUSCULATURE
INNER LINING

CROSS SECTION THROUGH A VEIN

RIGHT CORONARY ARTERY

LEFT CORONARY ARTERY

NORMAL VEIN
CUP-SHAPED VALVE OPEN
VALVE CLOSING
DILATED VARICOSE VEIN
VALVE UNABLE TO CLOSE
REFLUX OF BLOOD IN WRONG DIRECTION

ARTERIAL BRANCHING

Severing an artery causes death of the tissue it supplies. No collateral branches.

VENOUS BRANCHING

Severing a vein does no harm to the tissue it drains. Collaterals can take over.

Fig. 9. THE CIRCULATORY SYSTEM

as the pulse. One duty of the muscles in the arterial wall is to minimize constriction and expansion of the arteries due to variations in pressure and thereby ensure a less jerky flow. But that is not the only function of the muscles in the arterial wall.

In a sudden emergency man's body is instantly prepared for flight. The heart and the body muscles, the brain, the kidneys and many other organs—though not the intestinal tract—require an immediate increase in their arterial blood supply. A dilatation of the arteries would lower the blood pressure until the heart increases the volume of blood which it pumps into the arteries. But waiting for the heart to pick up would take far too long for safety in a life-and-death emergency. The blood supply to certain organs, particularly the heart-muscle itself, must be instantly increased in an emergency, and the diencephalon brings this about by a sudden narrowing of all the peripheral arteries.

The constriction of an artery does not increase the volume of the blood, but it raises its pressure, just as treading on a hose-pipe increases the force of the jet. The body uses this mechanism as an immediate reaction to fear, until the heart can gradually increase its output and feed a larger volume of blood into the arteries. This may be compared to further opening the tap which feeds water into a hose-pipe. As long as the artery remains constricted the pressure continues to be high, but as soon as the increased volume of blood fulfills the requirements of the fleeing body's musculature, the arteries are again free to relax. This lowers the pressure, but now the volume of blood fed into the organs is sufficient to cope with the exertions of flight.

The secondary relaxation of the arteries after the circulation has adjusted itself to a suddenly increased demand produces the phenomenon known as 'second wind'. In the second wind the blood pressure returns to a normal level. A second wind can occur only if the additional blood supply is actually being utilized in muscular effort. But when, as in modern man, a flight-reaction to fear and danger does not take place, the blood pressure remains high as long as the emergency lasts because there is no physical demand from all the body for more blood and because what is suddenly injected by the first contraction is not consumed.

In this case the diencephalon continues to react as if the immobility of modern man were due to an insufficient preparation for flight. It therefore prolongs its initial emergency re-action of arterial constriction. The diencephalon is completely unaware that the cortex inhibits the normal flight-reaction, and so it is only when flight actually takes place that the diencephalon is able to call off its initial emergency reaction and relax the arteries now filled with an adequate supply of blood.

Large arteries split up into ever finer ones until the branches become microscopically small arterioles and end in so-called capillaries. Capillaries carry blood to individual cells. The capillary endings are devoid of circular muscles and dilate under increased pressure. Thus a constriction of the larger arteries and arterioles produces a dilatation of the arterial capillary system. Thereby the tissue cells are flooded with blood, even though the volume of the blood supply has not increased.

In the tissues the arterial blood is deprived of foodstuffs, hormones, enzymes, vitamins and above all oxygen. The tissue cells then reload the blood with waste-matter and carbon dioxide, changing the bright-red arterial blood into the darker venous blood. The venous blood now enters a different capillary network which gathers it into ever larger veins and carries it back to the right heart-chamber, from where it is pumped into the lungs, changed into arterial blood, returned to the left heart-chamber and pumped back into the tissues.

Veins are constructed quite differently from arteries (Fig. 9). In the veins the blood is not under pressure, because the heart sucks venous blood into its right chamber—veins do not need a hard and rigid wall. On the other hand, it is a long distance from the toes to the heart and the weight of a column of blood nearly five feet high would dilate the thin-walled veins unless there were some mechanical provision to decrease the effect of this weight.

The human body has two such provisions. The first is that long veins such as those which drain the legs are surrounded by muscles. The muscles give the wall of the veins support; and when these muscles rhythmically contract and relax, as in walking or running, they exert a slight pumping action on the veins that lie between them. This is particularly important because the veins of the recently up-ended human body are not yet fully adjusted to the erect posture and are even less adjusted to urban man's cortically imposed restrictions on the use of his legs in running.

The second device which prevents veins from dilating under the weight of the blood they hold is a remarkable evolutionary achievement. Inside all large veins there are little folds of skin which act as valves (Fig. 9). These valves, spaced at regular intervals, are like small cups, with their opening facing the heart. At one part the rim of the cup is attached to the lining of the vein, while the rest of the rim is free. When venous blood is sucked up into the heart, the current folds the skin-cup against the wall of the vein so that the blood can pass freely. But when the heart is not sucking but pumping the venous blood into the lung, the blood in the veins tries to flow back in the wrong direction. This opens the cups and presses their rim all round the wall of the vein. In this way the cup prevents a reflux. Thus the wall of the vein only has to withstand the weight of the short column of blood between two valves. In very small animals there is no need for such a device, but in large ones the blood would not be able to circulate without it.

Another important difference between veins and arteries is their mode of branching (Fig. 9). Arteries branch like a tree. If a branch is cut, all the tissues beyond the cut die because there are no large collateral connections from one branch to another. Only at the capillary level do the areas supplied by individual arteries overlap. Arterial capillaries can eventually widen and conduct blood to the areas that have been cut off from the main supply, but this takes far too long for the tissues to survive. The dead tissue can only be replaced in the course of some weeks by new cells fed by new arteries which slowly grow out of what were once capillary connections.

Veins, on the other hand, have many large collateral connections; their branching is more like that of a net. When a vein is severed, other veins can in most cases instantly take over its circulatory function. There is thus no venous congestion, unless all the veins of the area are severed or blocked by compression.

The human heart is a complex and remarkably efficient pump. It really consists of two pumps which are joined into a single organ. The heart derives its power from the rhythmic contraction and relaxation of a unique type of musculature found nowhere else in the body. The heart-muscle is strong and quick-acting, like the large muscles of the body. But it also resembles the small muscles of the inner organs in that it can work without rest for a lifetime. The heart-muscle is ultimately under diencephalic control, but its rhythmic functioning is managed by local nerve-centres of its own. As in the intestine, the diencephalon takes over only when an instinct or an emotion creates an emergency.

The heart-muscle is nourished and supplied with oxygen by

the coronary arteries (Fig. 9). Two coronary arteries girdle the middle of the heart, and their many branches reach every part of the organ. The heart can respond quickly and adequately to an emergency only so long as the coronary arteries are able to contract and dilate according to the blood requirements of the heart-muscle.

High Blood Pressure

In the foregoing section it has been explained that the normal circulatory reaction to fear is an instantaneous constriction of the arteries and that the contraction of the muscles in the arterial wall is brought about by the diencephalon. The diencephalon has two ways of evoking this response to an emergency. One is to send a nervous impulse directly to the arterial muscle-fibres. This direct nervous reaction takes only a fraction of a second to go into operation. It maintains the constriction until the second mechanism, which is hormonal, gets under way.

Situated just above the kidneys are two small glands called suprarenal or adrenal glands. These glands play a vitally important role in the hormonal regulations of the body, of which more will be said in a later chapter. The adrenals consist of two functionally quite different parts, the outer adrenal rind or cortex, which is hormonally controlled, and an inner core known as the adrenal marrow or medulla, which is controlled by the autonomic nervous system. The function of the adrenal medulla is to produce a hormone called adrenalin.

When the diencephalon sends out an emergency signal through the autonomic nervous system, the adrenal medulla is made to discharge a gush of adrenalin into the blood-stream. As soon as adrenalin floods the body, the diencephalon can call off its emergency signal to the organs concerned because adrenalin alone can produce all the normal bodily reactions to fear without further central nervous intervention.

The mechanism is something like starting a car. The initial diencephalic impulse is like pressing the button of the self-starter. This makes the engine behave as if it were running of its own accord, though actually the motor can run by itself only after the self-starter has initiated the flow of combustible gases from the carburettor. The combustible gases may be compared to the flow of adrenalin; as soon as they take over the engine runs of its own accord, there is no further need for the self-starter and the car can move. Just as in a car the powerful motor of the self-starter consumes an enormous amount of energy from the batteries, so the diencephalic emergency reaction uses up a great deal of nervous energy which is diverted to this purpose. In the car the headlights dim when the self-starter is running. In the same way the many diencephalic activities suffer momentarily from the concentration of energy in the emergency reaction. It would be highly uneconomical and even deleterious if this extreme nervous effort had to be continued as long as the emergency lasts. It is therefore very important that the adrenalin should take over as soon as possible, but it takes a few seconds before the adrenalin can go fully into action. This delay would be fatal in a sudden threat, and that is why the instantaneous nervous reaction must precede it.

As soon as adrenalin takes over, the diencephalon is free to resume its normal activities in full. In the foregoing section it was said that this diencephalic relaxation does not take place in modern urban man as he no longer escapes from danger by running away, and that this is so because adrenalin can take over fully from the diencephalon only if actual flight is resorted to. It was explained that unless the body is actually running the diencephalon remains in a state of emergency and can only interpret immobility in the presence of danger as being due to an insufficient preparation of the body for flight. The diencephalon knows nothing of the cortical artifacts which have rendered physical escape unnecessary, and so it keeps on trying to make the body run. Reverting once more to the simile of the car, modern man's behaviour is like that of an inexperienced driver who does not realize that the engine is running by itself. He keeps his finger pressed down on the self-starter and then wonders what is producing all the unpleasant noise.

If the fear to which the diencephalon is reacting is fully conscious and can be eliminated by reasoning, as when the caged lion roars and rushes at the bars, the cortex can inform the diencephalon that there is no real emergency. In this case the diencephalon relaxes, though the reaction to adrenalin continues for a while in the form of palpitation, a rise in blood pressure and blood sugar, increased muscular tension, faster respiration, etc. But if the fear is subconscious there is no such diencephalic release, because the fear is not eliminated by running away or by reasoning. The arterial musculature remains contracted and fresh charges of adrenalin are poured into the blood.

In a fleeing animal a single gush of adrenalin is usually enough to carry it through to safety. In modern man one flooding with adrenalin can see a boxer through a round or a sprinter through his course, but it cannot provide for long-drawn fears and anxieties from which no physical escape takes place. In prolonged anxiety one flooding follows another, because the diencephalon does not stop trying to make man run away from danger, regardless of whether the danger is real or not.

It is possibly this process which initiates the disorder known as arterial hypertension or high blood pressure so common in modern man. In other words, high blood pressure may result from fear to which the normal bodily reaction of flight is cortically blocked. If the fear is conscious the cortex may see no reason to run, as for instance when a man is threatened with financial disaster. If the fear is subconscious it cannot be resolved by reasoning, but as far as the diencephalic reaction is concerned the nature of the fear is of no consequence. The diencephalon always reacts with the same emergency measures. As soon as the reasoning cortex becomes aware of these bodily reactions for which it is unable to find an explanation, it interprets them as a disorder. The threat of disease further increases the fear, and a psychosomatic vicious cycle thus becomes established.

There exist cases of high blood pressure which are not directly due to psychic factors, such as when a new-growth of the adrenal medulla leads to an excessive secretion of adrenalin or when severe kidney disease interferes with arterial circulation. Such comparatively rare cases obviously lie outside the scope of this study, which is concerned only with psychosomatic high blood pressure, often called *essential hypertension*.

If this interpretation of essential hypertension is tenable, four ways of treating the condition seem possible: (1) Psychotherapy directed towards relieving the anxiety; (2) Dampening the diencephalic response to fear; (3) Interrupting the nervous conduction from the diencepahlon to the wall of the arteries; and (4) Suppressing the inner secretory function of the adrenal medulla.

The psychotherapeutic approach to high blood pressure has been somewhat neglected, and for this there are one bad and several good reasons. A good reason is that hypertension is generally a disorder of middle-age. In many cases the uncovering of the subconscious anxiety might tempt the patient to make too drastic a change in the established pattern of his life. He might feel called upon to relinquish his profession, sharply lower his standard of living or divorce his wife. It is usually impossible to give a middle-aged person a fully gratifying compensation for such incisive changes, and unless this is done he is worse off than before. The conscientious psychiatrist, therefore, bewares of producing any such vocational or domestic cataclysms. He wisely prefers to let the sleeping dog lie, even if it does growl in its sleep, particularly as the patient is not usually aware of any emotional conflict. Another good reason to forego psychotherapy is that modern drugs can achieve, at little cost and in a matter of days, symptomatic results that would take months to obtain by psychotherapy. A third good reason is that as long as dangerous complications such as a stroke can be avoided, advancing age tends to improve the psychic situation.

The bad reason for neglecting psychotherapy is that its results may appear to be disappointing. No amount of psychotherapy can bring the blood pressure down lower than the state of the patient's arteries permits, and this may be considerably above the normal range. The patient then feels that he has wasted a good deal of time and money, and the psychiatrist is apt to be discouraged. The object of psychotherapy is to maintain the prevailing condition and merely to prevent its getting worse. Once that is agreed upon, a number of patients can be helped psychotherapeutically if the nature of their anxiety is such that it can be eliminated without too great an upheaval. Where that is too risky the role of the clinical psychiatrist must be confined to helping the patient establish a reasonable emotional attitude towards his condition and to putting the prognosis into a correct perspective.

Physicians who have watched anxious patients over many years are familiar with the young man who comes for a routine physical check which he requires for a new job or a life-insurance policy. The job may be a turning-point in his career, and he is then extremely anxious about the outcome of the examination.

Such apprehensiveness can produce a rise in blood pressure. The physician reassures the patient and suggests another examination when the emotional atmosphere is calmer. But once the spectre of high blood pressure has been raised, some patients cannot calm down and their blood pressure rises before every subsequent examination. Such patients often plague their doctor with continual requests for measuring their blood pressure. They make entries in a diary, and an utterly insignificant fluctuation of 10 mm. mercury pressure makes all the difference between hopeful elation and abysmal depression.

In the old days when patients were not in the habit of checking on their family doctor, they were not given any figures. To-day anxious patients cross-check with other doctors on every possible occasion and so they are usually given the exact readings. As the years go by, the continued anxiety gradually produces a fixed hypertension. The impression is unavoidable that this might not have happened had the blood pressure not been measured in the first instance or if at that time the case had been skilfully handled psychotherapeutically.

The second approach to the problem of essential hypertension is to dampen the anxiety at a diencephalic level. The damping can also be done at a cortical level, but to be really effective this requires measures which interfere with many other cortical processes. They make the patient drowsy and dull-witted. Alcohol and the modern tranquilizers may be useful in dealing with a brief conscious anxiety. Bromide seems to be more satisfactory in alleviating a subconscious anxiety of longer duration, but none of these drugs is suitable for the treatment of established hypertension as they cannot be used in effective doses for the necessary length of time.

About fifteen years ago a drug called reserpin was introduced. It was obtained from a plant known as Serpina Rauwolfia, the snake plant, which then only grew on the Indian slopes of the Himalayas. This plant had from time immemorial been used by Himalayan villagers to calm maniacal patients. Indian cardiologists were the first to show that the drug was eminently suitable for the treatment of high blood pressure. Reserpin appears to dampen the diencephalic reaction to fear. It is non-habit-forming and can be taken continuously for years. It does not interfere with intellectual processes and is usually dramatically effective. This is another link in the chain of evidence pointing to the diencephalic origin of essential hypertension.

A third method of treating high blood pressure is to block the nerve-paths along which the diencephalic impulse to contract is conveyed to the arterial wall. If the lower reaches of this conduction are completely interrupted, the muscles in the arterial wall are paralyzed and the artery becomes fully relaxed. Such denervated muscles cannot even respond to adrenalin because this hormone requires an intact nervous conduction from the local nerve-centres to the muscle-fibres in order to operate.

An artery can be surgically deprived of its nerves by stripping them off its outer covering. Until recently this operation was frequently practised upon the large arteries in advanced cases and was known as *sympathectomy*. To-day the popularity of this operation is waning, partly because the control of high blood pressure with reserpin is so effective and partly because new drugs, the so-called *ganglioplegics*, can interrupt nervous conduction without surgical intervention. The use of these drugs in the treatment of severe hypertension is spreading rapidly.

A fourth method would be the suppression of the secretion of adrenalin from the adrenal medulla. This approach has not yet found clinical application in the treatment of essential hypertension, but it is conceivable that it has a future. There exists one natural condition in which fear does not produce an outpouring of adrenalin and that condition is pregnancy. When a woman suffering from high blood pressure becomes pregnant, her blood pressure drops—often to normal—and stays there as long as the pregnancy lasts. After delivery the blood pressure gradually tends to rise again. Obviously it is of greatest clinical interest to know the exact mechanism of this lowering of the blood pressure during pregnancy.

It has been explained that in the biologically timid human female pregnancy brings about a profound change in the diencephalic reaction to fear. All the normal reflexes which prepare the body for flight are greatly diminished or even abolished, and the flooding of the body with adrenalin as a reaction to danger does not occur. If it were known exactly how pregnancy brings about this diencephalic change, there might be some hope of inducing a similar change in the non-pregnant body of either sex as a method of treating high blood pressure.

In pregnancy the mother's body is flooded with a powerful hormone known as chorionic gonadotrophin. This hormone is produced in the placenta and is eventually eliminated in the mother's urine. After confinement the hormone is no longer present and it is never found in the absence of placental tissue.

As chorionic gonadrotrophin is a hormone which exists only in pregnancy and as pregnancy is the only condition in which the normal diencephalic reactions to fear are abolished, it seemed worth while to investigate the possibility of a connection between the two phenomena. When human chorionic gonadotrophin (HCG) was injected into patients suffering from high blood pressure it was found that this had no effect in patients of normal weight. However, when the same treatment was given to overweight patients in daily doses of 125 international units and the diet was at the same time restricted to 500 calories daily this rapidly lowered the blood pressure far more effectively than a restricted diet alone. It seems that in a non-pregnant patient HCG cannot produce the effects seen in pregnancy unless there is a simultaneous withdrawal of nourishment from the body. In pregnancy the foetus does this; however, reducing the food intake so drastically that the body is forced to yield its reserves also seems to have the effect of activating HCG.

Thus in obese persons who can afford to lose about a pound per day which they do under this regimen high blood pressure can be reduced rapidly and normal readings are often reached in about two weeks. The treatment is not as drastic as it sounds because under the influence of HCG which mobilizes only abnormal fat deposits such patients can go about their usual occupation without feeling hungry. This mechanism will be fully discussed in the chapter on obesity.

At present HCG + Diet is not a rational treatment for essential hypertension. It can only be practised in overweight patients, because as soon as the body's surplus fat-reserves are consumed the HCG loses its effect, the patient becomes hungry and he can no longer stay on the 500-calorie diet. He thereby loses what might be called his phantom foetus and the pregnancy-like condition ceases, in spite of continued administration of chorionic gonadotrophin in any quantity. The HCG + Diet treatment can be continued only as long as the patient can afford to lose about 300–400 grams of weight daily. Even if the patient is still obese, HCG + Diet cannot be continued longer than six weeks because by that time the non-pregnant body learns to inactivate the HCG. However, after a pause of about six weeks the body's ability to neutralize HCG is lost and another course can be given. Thus, paradoxically, the fatter a hypertensive patient is the more benefit he can obtain from the HCG + Diet treatment.

Obviously HCG does not remove the underlying anxiety; it merely represses the diencephalic reactions to fear. As soon as the HCG treatment comes to an end the diencephalon again reacts to the basic anxiety in the normal way and the blood pressure gradually rises, unless the patient happens to be one of those cases in which psychotherapy can safely remove the anxiety. However, there is the advantage that after a treatment with HCG the blood pressure rarely rises to its former level and is much easier to control with small doses of reserpin if these are given the moment the blood pressure shows renewed signs of rising.

Even though the HCG method is not wholly satisfactory as a general approach to the problems of high blood pressure, it does seem to throw a new light on the mechanisms involved, and it remains to be seen whether out of this knowledge better methods can be developed.

Arteriosclerosis

In man and all timid animals fear leads to a contraction of the muscles in the arterial wall. At the onset of alarm the reaction is produced by a direct nervous impulse from the diencephalon which also increases the secretion of adrenalin from the suprarenal glands and in a second phase the adrenalin takes over from the diencephalon.

In modern man fears and anxieties may last for a few days, a few weeks or months. In this case the continued contraction of the arteries will do no permanent harm to the extraordinarily adaptable circulatory system. But when, as is so often the case, a state of subconscious dread persists for years, a permanent change in the arterial wall may take place. This change is found only in man[1] and consists in a hardening of the arterial wall, a process known as arteriosclerosis.

Arteriosclerosis begins as a deposit of a fatty substance, known as cholesterol, just below the inner arterial lining. These deposits act like a foreign body and evoke a tissue-reaction in the arterial wall. The tissue-reaction consists in the formation of excess connective tissue—a kind of scar is produced. In the course of years this connective tissue becomes harder and finally calcifies, so that in very advanced cases a calcified artery may be as hard and brittle as a raw macaroni. This whole process is a normal tissue-reaction to a lesion and exactly the same as occurs when a tubercular lesion of the lung-tissue eventually heals. So far all is clear. What is not yet fully understood is the mechanism which leads to the deposit of cholesterol in the arterial wall in the first instance.

It has recently been shown that cholesterol, always present in the circulating blood, is normally absorbed in small quantities through the arterial wall much as food is absorbed through the intestinal lining. The arterial wall is built of living tissue, and this tissue must have its own little arteries which feed it and its own little veins which drain it. They are known as the *vasa vasorum*, the blood vessels of the blood vessels. As in the intestinal tract, these small blood vessels reach the artery which they supply from the outside and pass through the muscular layer to the inner arterial lining. It may be assumed that such small veins carry away the cholesterol as it is absorbed. It would then follow that a constriction of the muscles in the wall of the artery can strangle these veins, thus making it impossible for them to dispose of the cholesterol as it is absorbed through the inner lining of the artery. If this be so, the cholesterol must accumulate just below the inner surface of the artery. When the arterial spasm which occurs in response to a brief fear is relaxed, the abnormal accumulation of cholesterol is rapidly removed because free venous drainage is restored. But when, as in modern man, the arterial spasm continues for months and years, a connective tissue-reaction imprisons the cholesterol deposit before

---

[1] Very occasional cases have been found among the highly intelligent baboons, who live in an organized community, and it sometimes occurs in captive apes. In the case of baboons the social structure produces emotional stress, as does captivity in apes.

it is carried away. Once caught in a mesh of connective tissue the cholesterol deposit can no longer be removed, even if the arterial muscles relax their stranglehold on the small veins, and so the tissue-reaction continues its normal course towards calcification.

An area of the arterial lining which is clogged with cholesterol is probably unable to absorb more cholesterol in the normal way. Thus the extent of the arterial surface which performs the function of absorbing cholesterol from the blood gradually becomes less and less. The lack of absorption might then contribute to the rise in the level of blood cholesterol commonly associated with progressive arteriosclerosis.

If these views are correct, they would suggest a psychosomatic factor in arteriosclerosis. Moreover, it would follow that a high blood-cholesterol never produces arteriosclerosis. On the contrary, it would be the arteriosclerosis which contributes to the high blood-cholesterol.

The sequence of events would then be as follows: a subconscious fear produces an abnormally protracted diencephalic reaction to this fear consisting of a continued nervous and adrenalinic contraction of the arterial musculature. The constriction of the muscles in the arterial wall causes a venous block in the disposal of cholesterol normally absorbed through the arterial lining. This leads to the formation of cholesterol deposits in the arterial wall. A normal tissue-reaction to the cholesterol deposits is evoked causing a loss of arterial surface able to withdraw cholesterol from the blood flowing in the arteries. There follows a rise in blood-cholesterol and a hardening of the arteries due to calcification of the cholesterol deposits.

The general trend of modern research into the problem of arteriosclerosis is directed towards discovering dietary ways of reducing an abnormally high blood-cholesterol. So far no indisputably satisfactory results have been achieved. If the foregoing deductions are correct, very meagre results can be expected from this approach. Should ways and means of substantially and innocuously reducing the level of circulating cholesterol be found, the arteriosclerotic process might be slowed down a little; but if this has to be achieved by permanent and severe dietary restriction, it would defeat its own purpose. Any patient told that he must, in order to escape early death from a stroke or a coronary thrombosis, strictly control his diet for the rest of his days, is faced with a predicament which enormously increases his anxiety.

Nowadays there do exist a few people who get satisfaction and pride out of treating themselves the way man treats his domestic animals. They take a perverse delight in suppressing all instinctive choice in their behaviour. Their reward is a slightly improved report from the clinical laboratory, but the price they pay for their cortical control is the danger of tumbling into one of many other psychosomatic pitfalls. It is just because wild animals yield to their instincts and have no censorship at the threshold of consciousness that they never suffer from high blood pressure, arteriosclerosis or too much cholesterol in the circulating blood. These morbid conditions are particularly apt to arise in a body equipped with a post-Neolithic cortex. If pre-Neolithic Man had suffered from arteriosclerosis one would expect a calcified artery occasionally to be found among his remains, and the author is not aware of any such find ever having been made.

Arteriosclerosis is often regarded as a steadily progressive disease; yet this is not necessarily so. Once a cholesterol deposit in the arterial wall has evoked a connective tissue-reaction, this reaction will inevitably proceed towards calcification. But this does not mean that new deposits continue to be formed. Once the underlying fear ceases, the arteriosclerotic process also ceases to progress. The already affected areas will continue to get harder, but no new deposits of cholesterol will be laid down.

That explains why calcified arteries are often found in old people who have a normal blood pressure. They are the ones who are at peace with themselves and their world. Yet at some time in their lives they have gone through a prolonged period of fear and anxiety. During this period they laid down deposits of cholesterol in their arteries. The fear then subsided at a time when their arteries were as yet elastic and could still dilate. In the course of years the old deposits harden and calcify, but this process does not constrict the arteries, nor does it interfere with longevity.

When an elderly person has arteriosclerosis without high blood pressure, it means that his arteries were still elastic when the period of anxiety came to an end. The arteries were thus able to resume a normal diameter before hardening had gone very far. But when a person continues to have high blood pressure after the anxiety has subsided, this indicates that his arteries had already hardened while he was still under the influence of fear. The period of anxiety must have lasted a very long time—maybe several decades—so that his arteries became permanently set while they were still contracted. In these cases the high blood pressure is mechanical and no longer diencephalically induced. To such a fixed hydrodynamic condition the circulation can adjust itself remarkably well. The best treatment for this type of high blood pressure is 'intelligent neglect'.

In pregnancy there is an interesting change in the nature of the circulating cholesterol. Normally the blood contains cholesterol in two forms, esterified (i.e. chemically bound) cholesterol and free cholesterol, and there is about three times more esterified than free cholesterol. In pregnancy—and in pregnancy only—this proportion is reversed. The cholesterol which passes through the arterial wall is the esterified fraction of which there is far less during pregnancy so that a pregnant woman is to a certain extent protected from developing arteriosclerosis as long as her pregnancy lasts.

Here again it seems that the placental hormone HCG is responsible for the reversal of the normal ratio of free to esterified cholesterol. The same reversal of the cholesterol ratio occurs where patients are treated with HCG + Diet as has been described in the section dealing with high blood pressure, suggesting that here too HCG + Diet produces a pregnancy-like condition and this may eventually prove to be an effective way of dealing with a high blood-cholesterol, a condition in which diencephalic regulations appear to play an important part.

The Coronary Arteries

Two coronary arteries (Fig. 9) supply blood to all parts of the heart. Their strong and efficient musculature adjusts their diameter to the oxygen requirements of the heart. In an emergency the heart-muscle's consumption of oxygen is so enormous that the coronary arteries must be able to supply as much as a litre of blood per minute. Like all arteries, the coronaries contract when more pressure is required and dilate when more volume is necessary; but in this respect their position is unique because they control the heart, which in turn controls them.

The heart can only work faster if the coronaries provide it with more oxygen, but the coronaries cannot provide more oxygen unless the heart pumps more blood through them.

Under normal conditions this interdependence is regulated by hormones and the heart's own local nerve centres and needs no central nervous supervision. Whenever the heart is required to work harder suddenly, the coronary arteries in an emergency are filled with blood which is pressed out of the normal alarm reaction. The coronary arteries can therefore dilate at once with a drop in blood pressure occurring in them. This increases the amount of blood which is fed into the capillaries of the heart-muscle. The capillary flooding permits the heart to pick up and feed still more blood into the coronaries so that they can continue to dilate without diminishing the capillary blood supply, and this mechanism takes place at the beginning of every exertion.

When an instinct such as fear, or an emotion such as anxiety, calls for an increased cardiac output in preparation for flight, the diencephalon supersedes the local regulations and produces a powerful coronary dilatation instead of a constriction as it does in the other arteries of the blood concerned in running. In the case of the coronaries it is particularly important that the diencephalon can do this along direct nervous channels without having to wait for the second wind; otherwise an animal would not be able suddenly to break into headlong flight at the first sign of danger.

No wild animal suffers from coronary disease, though the hearts of higher mammals very closely resemble the human heart. Coronary disease is uncommon among primitive races, but in modern urban man it is taking more lives than almost any other ailment. This cannot be due to the wear and tear of muscular exertion. Collectively no human beings have ever exerted their bodies less than do contemporary city-dwellers. The majority work at desks or benches and move almost exclusively by mechanical transport. But a mere lack of muscular activity cannot be responsible either; otherwise coronary disease would be common among cripples, invalids, prisoners, etc., which it is not.

Particularly prone to coronary disease are such professional groups as senior executives in industry, managers in general, bankers, brokers, doctors; that is, persons who carry a heavy load of responsibility and must face the daily threat of disasters over which they have no control. Many of these men live in a constant state of tension, worry and anxiety, and it seems to be this cortical state which more than any other single factor causes coronary disease. Though this has often been stated to be so, few physiological connections between fear and coronary disease have as yet been established; and until this is done on a much wider scale than hitherto, the psychological approach to the problem will remain in the background. It will be grudgingly admitted that psychic factors may play a role, but with that admission the subject is brushed aside as unworthy of or unamenable to serious physiological investigation.

It seems rather unlikely that man's food is to any significant extent involved in the causation of coronary disease. Looking back over the history of Western man's feeding habits, one finds many times and places in which gluttony was common. Coronary disease should then have been rampant, according to current views on the hazards of nutrition, yet there is no historical evidence to suggest that coronary disease was as common in such periods as it is to-day. In an effort to establish a relationship between diet and coronary disease a vast amount of research of a highly complex biochemical nature is being conducted. Yet the much more obvious psychosomatic interpretation is not considered worthy of urgent investigation. It is shied away from as being unscientific, because for such investigations laboratory animals are useless.

This attitude will have to change. Diseases which exist only in man will never be elucidated fully by the study of laboratory animals which have no censorship of the threshold of consciousness. In the investigation of the relationship between diet and coronary disease, the uselessness of laboratory animals for the study of diseases in which a psychosomatic element is involved has been realized to the extent that at the time of writing the rat has given way to the African Bantu tribesman, whose diet is now being scrutinized because he rarely suffers from coronary disease. More fruitful results might be forthcoming if the Bantu mind rather than the Bantu menu were up for consideration.

The coronaries are subject to arteriosclerosis just like any other artery in the human body. A limited period of anxiety during the course of a person's life may lead to a hardening of the coronaries in a normal state of dilatation. Such arteries are unable to respond satisfactorily to a sudden emergency, but they can well cope with the minor exigencies of a quiet life.

Highly calcified coronary arteries are often found in old people who have never suffered from clinically manifest coronary disease and have died of other causes. Frequently, however, the coronaries harden while they are contracted and are thus permanently narrowed. In this case the heart is insufficiently supplied with oxygen, and it gradually undergoes a process of degeneration which leads to a weakening of the heart-muscle. Such patients are unable to perform a sustained effort. They can initiate an effort because the peripheral arteries which feed the skeletal muscles can still contract, but the coronary arteries can no longer dilate to admit more blood into the heart as it picks up under the influence of adrenalin.

The result is that the heart-muscle suffers from a sudden severe lack of oxygen, and this lack of oxygen may be the cause of the excruciating constricting pain which is known as angina pectoris. If angina pectoris were caused by a sudden constriction of a coronary artery, one would expect an attack to occur at the beginning of an exertion and not, as it usually does, halfway up the stairs or after a few hundred yards of walking. It seems probable that the attack of angina is not caused by a sudden constriction of a coronary artery, but rather by its failure to dilate.

An attack of angina pectoris can be relieved by standing still for a short time. This reduces the activity of the heart so far that the limited flow of oxygen which the narrow coronaries can supply is once more sufficient, and the pain is thus relieved. The pain of angina pectoris can also be rapidly relieved by nitroglycerin and its derivatives. Whatever nitroglycerin may do to the healthy coronaries of laboratory animals, it seems doubtful whether it can significantly dilate a hard, arteriosclerotic human coronary. It is more likely that its mode of action in angina pectoris is to dilate the capillary system in the heart and elsewhere. It thereby momentarily improves the blood supply to the cells of the heart and drains blood out of the whole arterial system of the body into the capillaries, thus lessening the cells' demand on the heart for more blood.

A true attack of angina pectoris is not in itself a psychosomatic phenomenon. It is due to an exertion, not an emotion, though the arteriosclerotic background of this condition is decidedly of psychosomatic origin. A milder, angina-like pain can be produced in a healthy coronary artery by fear. Such an attack is called pseudo-angina and is always psychosomatic.

A coronary disease which is claiming a rapidly increasing number of victims is the occlusion of the main-stem or a branch of the coronary arteries. The occlusion is usually produced by the formation of a blood-clot inside the artery and is known as a coronary thrombosis. The occlusion of any part of a coronary artery stops the supply of oxygen to those heart-cells which depend on the occluded branch. Without oxygen the cells die, and such an area of dead tissue in the wall of the heart is called an infarction.

Unlike veins, arteries have no large collateral branches, and the coronaries are no exception. Thus if the main-stem of a coronary artery becomes occluded, the heart ceases to function and death is almost instantaneous; but if the destroyed area is not too large and only a coronary branch is affected, fine collateral communications gradually enlarge. In the course of some weeks they can repair the damage by bringing new living connective cells into the infarct. A scar forms and the new blood vessels finally take over the function of the branch that was blocked. That is why patients who survive a coronary thrombosis can often be returned to their usual occupation after two to three months.

The coronaries differ from other arteries in that adrenalin dilates them. This must necessarily be so, because in an emergency which may be fear, rage, sex, exertion, overeating or sudden exposure to cold they must quickly supply the heart with a greater volume of blood. It is probably never an impulse to contract which causes a coronary thrombosis, but rather the failure of the coronaries to dilate.

A failure to dilate may have two different causes. One is that an old arteriosclerotic process in which the arteries harden in a contracted state may render the necessary dilatation mechanically impossible. This is usually the case in elderly patients. In younger persons in whom the coronaries have not yet hardened, the dilatation is prevented by a spasm which the diencephalon maintains when flight is not cortically conceded. In either case the coronaries cannot accommodate the sudden onrush of blood which is being fed into them.

In an emergency the pressure in the narrowed coronaries rises very suddenly and there is a stagnation of blood. It is conceivable that a sudden rise in pressure may damage the inner lining of a sclerotic or contracted artery. Damage to the interior lining of an artery always leads to the formation of a small protective clot. Under normal conditions such a small clot is rapidly absorbed by the body's repair mechanisms and nothing further happens. Similarly, when blood stagnates in an artery it is more liable to clot, but this too is not particularly dangerous as long as the blood's tendency to coagulate is normal and the duration of the stagnation short.

Unfortunately, in modern man the diencephalon prolongs the peripheral arterial constriction because modern man sits still with his fears, dreads, worries and apprehensions and often debars them from conscious awareness. He can neither reason about them nor run away from them as his evolution intended him to do. He firmly believes the cortical fiction that primitive fears no longer bother him, that they have all gone the way of the woolly mammoth and the sabre-toothed tiger. He thinks he has smothered his old animal instincts as he has smothered the instincts of his domestic animals and that his cortex can do no wrong. The result is a prolongation of what was originally intended to be merely an initial diencephalically induced arterial spasm.

Arteriosclerotic hardening provides conditions favourable for the formation of a blood clot in the coronary arteries because it prevents the normal dilatation under the influence of adrenalin, but under otherwise normal conditions it appears rather unlikely that this would lead to the rapid formation of a thrombus large enough to occlude the whole artery. Yet under such circumstances the rapid formation of a large clot would become immediately plausible if it could be shown that fear and related emotions increase blood coagulation. There is evidence to suggest that this may actually be the case. In animals such a mechanism would be so extremely useful that any tendency of this kind would almost certainly have been developed by natural selection. If the blood of an animal wounded in fight or flight coagulated faster than normal, this would prevent a dangerous loss of blood in mortal combat or in running for life. A mechanism of this sort would be of such enormous advantage for survival that it is hard to believe that evolution should have missed the chance to develop it.

All the body's diencephalic reactions to fear are the same as those produced by a sudden exposure to cold, and stepping out of a heated house into a cold, wintry morning has been known to precipitate a coronary attack. It is also known that exposure to cold sharply increases the coagulability of the blood, and it is therefore possible to assume that fear does the same. This is another reason to believe that when sudden cold produces a coronary infarction the attack is not due to a coronary constriction, but rather to a failure to dilate sufficiently combined with a sharp rise in the clotting ability of the blood.

Thrombosis, coronary or otherwise, is extremely rare during pregnancy in spite of the great additional burden on the circulatory system. This lends support to the view that in the absence of the usual reactions to fear the blood's readiness to clot is held within normal limits. At confinement the mother's body is suddenly deprived of chorionic gonadotrophin, all the flight reflexes are re-established, and this may be the reason why thrombo-phlebitis occurs so comomnly after delivery. It is also interesting that neither during nor shortly after the treatment of thousands of cases of obesity with the HCG + Diet method, which puts the body into a pregnancy-like condition, the author has never seen a thrombosis occur, though a large number of his cases seemed predisposed and a fair number had already survived a coronary thrombosis.

Many surgeons have noted that the patient who is very frightened of operation or anaesthesia is particularly liable to develop a post-operative thrombosis. The modern method of allowing a patient to leave his bed very soon after a major surgical operation has reduced the incidence of post-operative thrombosis. This is explained as resulting from improved circulation, but it seems quite possible that the most important factor is the strong assurance that all is well which early ambulation gives the patient.

Recently a rather surprising discovery was made. It was found that a severe bleeding from any part of the body can be stopped in a very short time by the intravenous injection of a large dose of a female sex hormone and that, more surprising still, the method works equally well in men and women. This has an interesting bearing on a possible relationship between fear and blood coagulation.

The diencephalon chemically regulates the function of the anterior lobe of the pituitary gland through a minute portal system which connects the two organs. One of the many functions of the anterior pituitary gland is the secretion of two hormones which stimulate the sex-glands into producing two other hormones. This is so in the ovary and in the testicle.

The two ovarian hormones which are thus produced are known as folliculin and lutein. Between two menstrual periods folliculin predominates, until the egg ripens and is expelled from the little cyst-like ovarian follicle in which it grows. What remains of this ovarian follicle changes into a small gland called the corpus luteum. If no pregnancy ensues, the corpus luteum is absorbed and folliculin again takes over as the controlling hormone until the next ovulation. But if the egg is fertilized and becomes embedded in the wall of the uterus, the corpus luteum persists and plays the dominant role throughout the period of gestation. During pregnancy there is thus a comparatively high level of lutein in the body.

Put into relationship with the lower tendency to form a thrombus during pregnancy, this could mean that lutein decreases coagulability. In fact, the mestrual flow of not easily coagulable blood is brought about by the corpus luteum, and the cessation of the menstruation is probably caused by the increase in folliculin which occurs after the corpus luteum has ceased to function. Menstrual bleeding ceases because blood-clots are formed in the open uterine veins, while during the menstrual flow such clots do not form. A similar mechanism probably makes it possible to stop any bleeding with a massive dose of folliculin injected intravenously.

Ultimately the diencephalon controls the follicular and luteal phases in the female body, and it is well known how closely the menstrual phases are linked to fear, which may suppress or prolong the menstrual flow. Along this path it may, therefore, become possible to strengthen the as yet flimsy bridge which connects fear and the coagulability of the blood. If this could be done it would be an important advance in the understanding of the psychic factors involved in coronary thrombosis.

There already exist a number of drugs that have powerful anti-coagulant properties, and the importance of their use in the treatment and prophylaxis of coronary thrombosis is now generally recognized. As long as the coagulability of the blood is kept below normal but high enough to prevent haemorrhages, it is very unlikely that a patient undergoing such treatment will suffer a coronary thrombosis, regardless of the state of his arteries. He would still be prone to attacks of angina but would not be likely to suffer infarction.

The trouble with anti-coagulants, particularly when used prophylactically, is that such treatment requires constant and careful clinical supervision because the coagulability of the blood is apt to show sudden fluctuations. These fluctuations are common in anxious patients, and the only way to account for them satisfactorily is to consider them psychologically induced. Thus it may happen that when anti-coagulants have brought down the danger of an excessive tendency to clot, a sudden re-lease from anxiety may still further decrease the clotting time. The combination of the medicinal and the diencephalic de-crease in clotting-ability may make this so low that the slightest lesion anywhere in the body may produce a severe haemorrhage.

On the other hand, the insurgence of a sudden emotional stress may raise coagulability so high that the dose of anti-coagulant is insufficient to keep coagulability within safe limits. When anti-coagulants are used under circumstances which do not permit a very close watch on the coagulability, a psycholo-gical watch over the patient should be maintained; and if this, too, is impossible, the nervous patient should be given sedation with a clear explanation why this is advisable.

Until prophylactic methods, safer and simpler than anti-coagulants, are found there certainly seems to be room for a more intense psychotherapeutic approach to the problem of coronary occlusion. So far psychotherapy has been largely confined to admonitions such as 'relax, take it easy, lay off', etc. More often than not these veiled threats increase the sub-conscious anxiety, particularly as few patients are able to follow such advice and then feel that they are beckoning disaster.

We cannot tell a frightened patient to run for his life, but there can be no doubt that mild, regular, open-air exercise is very helpful as long as the patient feels he is enjoying himself. It is useless to tell a tired, worried businessman to walk twice round the block, just as brooding strolls in the park are not relaxing. There must be enthusiasm and the need to concentrate on something. Among many other activities regular, passionate golf is an excellent prophylactic against coronary disease, but it is worse than futile to persuade a patient to take up some game or hobby which he detests, as he is apt to look upon a prescribed activity as a waste of time which might be more usefully spent in his office. Though this attitude of the patient is physiologically wrong, his psychological attitude may eventually prove his contention justified—he will be safer in his office than on the playing fields. It all depends on his enthusiasms. A good deal of psychiatric insight is necessary to weigh the pros and cons of such advice which is often given all too jauntily.

Other Circulatory Disorders

Evolutionary considerations play an important role in the causation of some other ailments of the human circulatory system. Among them one of the most important and dangerous is known as a stroke, a cerebral vascular accident or apoplexy. There are four common kinds of apoplexy. Three forms are due to the occlusion of a cerebral artery and the resulting damage to that brain-tissue which the artery serves. The occlusion may be due to a diencephalically induced spasm, to the formation of a clot at the site of the spasm or to an embolus, i.e., a small blood-clot shot into the artery from some other part of the body, from where the circulating blood picks it up. Most of what has been said about coronary occlusions also applies to the similar lesions in the brain and need not be repeated.

The fourth and most dangerous form of cerebral accident is the rupture of an artery inside the brain. When this happens the blood which is under high arterial pressure is forced into the soft surrounding brain-tissue and wreaks havoc in these extremely delicate structures. The damage goes far beyond that which the mere occlusion of the same artery would produce.

The occlusion of a cerebral artery may occur in a person with a low or normal blood pressure, but a rupture takes place only when the blood pressure is abnormally high, and even then only when it is suddenly raised still further through emotional stress.

It seems unlikely that a normal cerebral artery ever bursts. Long before the dramatic event the arterial wall has undergone a slow process of weakening. The wall of the sector which may later burst has been previously thinned out and dilated locally in what is known as an aneurism. In the absence of new-growths or infective lesions, such as are occasionally produced by syphilis, the local dilatation of the artery is possibly caused by a diencephalic constriction just above the aneurismatically enlarged area. If such spasms are frequent, the arterial wall gradually gives way and thereby loses the muscular strength with which it resists a sudden rise in pressure.

An apoplectic cerebral haemorrhage most frequently occurs in one particular artery of the brain, and this fact invites evolutionary speculation. The artery concerned is the one that feeds those areas of the cortex which regulate the movement of the body. That is why a haemorrhage in one cerebral hemisphere may lead to a complete paralysis of one half of the body. Again this type of cerebral haemorrhage exists only in man, and it is very tempting to suggest that the diencephalon in a state of emergency produces an excessive spasm in just this artery because modern man does not use his body for flight or physical violence when he is frightened.

There are, however, further reasons why this particular cerebral artery is so exceptionally liable to form an aneurism with local dilatation and a weakening of the arterial wall, a phenomenon uncommon in other arteries of the body and unknown in the coronaries. From an evolutionary point of view, the large and finely branched arteries of the cerebral hemispheres are the youngest. More than any arterial system in the human body they have had to undergo a spectacular development to cope with the rapid growth of the brain. Moreover, the recent acquisition of the fully erect posture has made staggering hydrodynamic demands on the arterial circulation in the brain because the heart must now pump the blood a long way against the force of gravity. The comparatively brief time which has elapsed since these drastic changes took place in man's ancestors is not nearly long enough for a perfect evolutionary adaptation to have been reached.

Man's early evolution was directed, among other things, to the cortical control of his bodily movements, and of these flight was by far the most important for his survival. It is thus not surprising that the motor centres of his cortex are furnished with a lavish supply of blood through large arterial channels. Modern sedentary, non-athletic man makes far less use of his cortical motor centres than did his pre-Neolithic ancestors. The hurried-ly evolved arterial supply to this part of his cortex is already idling before its full adaptation has been accomplished. Its evolu-tion stopped halfway, because the unnatural life of contemporary urban man no longer calls for further physiological improve-ment. This cortically induced arrest of an evolutionary trend probably contributes to the high incidence of cerebral haemorr-hage in modern man, as it is a general evolutionary rule that organs not taxed to the utmost are particularly prone to dis-orders.

Another circulatory disorder, fairly common in modern man, is recurring attacks of heart-racing, technically known as *paroxys-mal tachycardia*. In patients suffering from this disease the heart will for no apparent reason suddenly start beating at a rate of 150–200 beats per minute; yet between attacks it shows no abnormality whatever.

Paroxysmal tachycardia is caused by excessive nervous and possibly adrenal stimulation. The nature of paroxysmal tachy-cardia strongly suggests that a psychosomatic mechanism under-lies the attack. Yet when such patients are questioned after an attack they almost invariably deny any foregoing emotional stress. However, if psychiatric investigation is skilfully pursued, it is usually possible to reveal a deep-seated and severely re-pressed anxiety of which the sufferer had no previous inkling. Apparently paroxysmal tachycardia only occurs when there is not the slightest conscious awareness of an emotional conflict and when this subconscious conflict is suddenly made to flare up by some event which the patient in no way suspects of having upset him. Whenever the clinical psychiatrist is able to bring the psychic mechanism to a conscious level, the attacks cease. It seems as if the diencephalon, in the absence of a normal bodily response to the subconscious fear which it registers, is forced to go to extremes in its preparation for flight by enor-mously increasing the pulse-rate.

It was mentioned in the first part of this book that the dilata-tion of the facial arteries in blushing as a reaction to shame, and their contraction in pallor as a reaction to fear, have an obscure evolutionary origin as regards their significance. However, after the foregoing it can now be suggested that both phenomena have the same origin in fear. A mild fear produces a mild arterial contraction which suddenly raises the pressure in the arterioles, flushing the facial capillaries. A greater fear, on the other hand, produces a tighter constriction which blocks the flow of blood to the skin and renders it pale, just as cold will produce a ruddy colour of the face while freezing makes the skin white. Yet why blushing should be largely confined to the face and more common in children and young women is not thereby explained.

A minor circulatory tribulation from which many anxious persons suffer is cold feet. Even in common language the expression 'he got cold feet' is often used as a synonym for fear. Here again it is a case of the diencephalon prolonging what was originally intended to be only an initial arterial contraction in response to fear. The contraction was designed to produce an instantaneous capillary flooding of the feet with arterial blood in preparation for flight. But if instead of running the anxious person lies still in bed with all his fears and dreads, the diencephalon continues to constrict the arteries. Cold feet are commonly believed to be due to 'bad circulation', which of course they are, but it is never realized that the circulation would be quite normal if the arterial contraction were relaxed by putting the harassed diencephalon at ease by running away or by correct reasoning. In this connection it is interesting to note that in hypnosis the circulation in the feet can very easily be changed from poor to ample and vice versa by appropriate suggestions.

So far only arterial disorders have been discussed, but veins, too, suffer from disorders which have an evolutionary background, though hydrodynamically the veins are an evolutionary masterpiece. The most important venous disorder is their varicose dilatation in the leg. The reason man suffers from varicose veins is that he was too suddenly up-ended. In birds bipedal gait and long-leggedness took many millions of years to evolve, as did the long legs of the giraffe. In these animals the leg-veins are perfectly adjusted to their arduous circulatory duties and never give trouble, but in man they have not yet reached such perfection.

Though the large veins are embedded in musculature which gives them support and though they are provided with valves, this is not always sufficient because in urban man the muscles are not constantly in use. The body sometimes tries to help with a cramp in the calf-muscles—the so-called Charlie-horse—and yawning probably serves the same purpose; but the hydro-dynamic situation of the superficial veins of the leg is particu-larly difficult, because these veins have no muscular support. The superficial veins are therefore the ones that are most likely to give way under the weight of the blood-column which they carry. When a vein dilates, a point is very soon reached at which the valves can no longer close (Fig. 9). From that moment on dilatation increases steadily, because the uninter-rupted column of blood which the wall of the vein has to support gets higher and heavier.

It is common knowledge that varicose veins frequently make their first appearance during pregnancy. In pregnancy there is in addition to the weight of the column of blood a compression of the large pelvic veins. In quadrupeds the weight of the preg-nant womb bears down on the abdominal wall, but after man acquired the erect posture all this weight was transferred to the bottom of the pelvis. Human pelvic veins are not yet adjusted to withstand this weight; it compresses them, and this impedes the flow of venous blood coming up from the legs. It is this pelvic congestion which leads to the dilatation of the veins of the legs during pregnancy.

For exactly the same reason piles frequently occur during pregnancy. The mechanism is entirely different from that which otherwise causes piles. As has been explained in the foregoing chapter, this is purely psychosomatic, whereas the piles of preg-nancy occur for evolutionary reasons only—the psyche plays no role in their causation.

A few aspects of the most important diseases of the circulatory system have been reviewed under evolutionary and psychoso-matic aspects. An attempt has been made to throw a thin life-line across the chasm which still separates the psychological from the physiological approach to these disorders. Thus the foregoing speculations can do little more than suggest the great possibilities of a closer working hand in hand.

On both sides of the gorge there is feverish activity and great strides have been made. Yet most workers have turned their back on the yawning gap and are straining away from it. Each is achieving admirable results on his own side, but the basic problem of decreasing the incidence and the mortality of circulatory disease has not been resolved. While each side admits that the other is doing useful work, it is typical of the presumptuous human cortex that where it sees no way out of a difficulty it turns its back to it, pretends that the problem does not exist and ignores it.

It is to be feared that little real progress can be made until physiologists and psychiatrists enter into an enthusiastic and cordial collaboration. This presents certain difficulties because physiology is old, sedate and mature, while psychiatry is young, speaks a language of its own and is, in its juvenile exuberance, inclined to be less severely disciplined in its scientific comportment.

The present situation is rather like that of a grumpy, shy old bachelor having fallen secretly in love with a rather attractive, young and frisky maiden whose behaviour shocks him. Psychiatry, on the other hand, is awed by her secret lover's moral standards and does not know how to break down his overpowering dignity. Perhaps the time is now at hand to bring the unhappy couple together by a little match-making. Perhaps the evolutionary bridge may lead them into each other's arms.

7

Disorders of the Thyroid Gland and the Nature of Obesity

Metabolism

THE WORD *metabolism* means change. The term is used to cover all the chemical transformations by which food is turned into energy or living tissue and also the processes whereby tissues are broken down into simpler compounds which the body then excretes as waste-matter. The basal metabolic rate (BMR) is an indicator of the speed with which such transformations take place, and it can be measured by the rate at which these chemical operations consume oxygen when the body is at rest.

Man suffers from innumerable metabolic disorders, which may be hereditary, toxic, degenerative, nutritional or infective. In some metabolic disorders psychosomatic factors play an important part, because in them the psyche starts the morbid metabolic process or activates a latent disposition. In the latter case the disposition is inherited, but the psychic factor makes the latent trait change into overt disease. This is a very important point, because a patient sharing a metabolic disorder of this type with other members of his family is apt to ascribe his illness to heredity only and completely ignore his own psychic contribution. The psychic factor is therefore often overlooked when diseases such as obesity, diabetes or gout occur in several members of the same family.

In this and the following chapter three metabolic disorders in which the brain is deeply involved will be discussed. The first is hyperthyroidism, a condition in which the thyroid gland is overactive. The second is obesity, which is a disorder of the utilization and storage of fats. The third is diabetes, in which the metabolism of carbohydrates is abnormal.

The Over-Active Thyroid

The thyroid is a gland which produces an extremely potent hormone known as *thyroxine*. The most outstanding function of thyroxine is to increase the metabolic turnover. Metabolism is essentially a process of consuming oxygen and may be likened to a chemical fire. The more oxygen a fire consumes the brighter it burns. Thyroxine keeps the metabolic fires burning at a steady rate, and it is so powerful that the action of one milligram produces about 1,000 calories of heat or energy in the body. One milligram of thyroxine is roughly the amount a normal thyroid produces daily.

In the absence of thyroxine, all the chemical activities of the body are markedly reduced. It is as if the air pumped into a blast-furnace were shut off. If this happens in childhood, further development is sharply braked and a previously healthy child turns into the ugly, dwarfish idiot known as a cretin. A cretin can, however, be transformed back into a normal human being by artificially supplying its body with thyroxine in the form of desiccated animal thyroid. There are no psychosomatic mechanisms involved in cretinism. The condition can be reproduced in animals by removing their thyroid gland, and it occurs spontaneously if the gland fails to develop normally.

The opposite condition is an abnormal increase in the secretion of thyroxine, owing to a permanent over-activity of the thyroid gland. An excess of thyroxine accelerates all metabolic processes far beyond normal and, regardless of how much is eaten weight is lost, provided the patient is not suffering from obesity.

Associated with a rise in the basal metabolic rate, an abnormally active thyroid evokes a number of other bodily reactions. The output of the heart is substantially increased in order to transport sufficient oxygen to the over-active tissues, and the beat becomes faster. There may be a rise in blood pressure, and the capillaries are flooded with blood; breathing is deeper and faster. The blood sugar may rise so high that sugar appears in the urine. The muscles are tense and the hands tremble. Such patients are in a continuous state of extreme nervous excitability, and a sudden noise makes them 'jump out of their skin'. Diarrhoea and excessive urination are usually present.

To the reader this combination of symptoms will already have a familiar ring. He will recognize all the normal diencephalic reactions to fear by which the body prepares for flight. Seen from this angle, one other symptom very commonly associated with an over-active thyroid is particularly impressive. It is the protrusion of the eye-balls and the retraction of the eyelids, known as exophthalmus. Exophthalmus gives the patient's eyes an expression of being torn wide open in stark terror.

It cannot be a coincidence that an excess of thyroxine provides exactly those bodily conditions which would be best suited to cope with an extreme physical emergency. It might be argued that, as adrenalin already produces such reactions, there would be no need for the thyroid to do the same thing. There are two answers to this contention. The first answer is that nature hardly ever relies on one mechanism only to achieve its ends; it always works with an enormous margin of safety. Just as adrenalin can take over from direct diencephalic intervention, so thyroxine can in some respects replace adrenalin.

The second answer is that, though the action of thyroxine resembles that of adrenalin, there are several important differences. Adrenalin acts in a few seconds and is thus able to deal with sudden dangers. Thyroxine takes twenty-four or more hours before it evokes a measurable response. The reason for this delay is that thyroxine as secreted by the thyroid gland cannot act directly on the metabolism of the tissue-cells. Thyroxine has to undergo complex chemical changes which are brought about by enzymes before it becomes active. The end-product of this chemical is a compound known as triiodotironine, and it is this substance which directly increases the metabolic activity in the body's cells.

Adrenalin brings about a slight increase in the basal metabolic rate, but this is insignificant when compared with the much more powerful effect of thyroxine. The secretion of adrenalin from the adrenal medulla would exhaust the cells which are responding to it if its action were continued for a long time. This exhaustion never takes place under the influence of thyroxine. Thyroxine is thus eminently suitable to sustain a frightened animal exposed to a threat of long duration which requires continuous exertion, as when the cold of a severe winter calls for more caloric energy to keep up the body-temperature or when drought enforces long treks in search of food and water.

If an increase in the secretion of thyroxine is a normal reaction to prolonged fear, there must be a mechanism by which the diencephalon controls the activity of the thyroid gland. Such a mechanism does indeed exist. It has already been explained that the diencephalon controls the anterior lobe of the pituitary gland through chemical substances which are carried to the gland in a minute portal blood system. The anterior pituitary lobe is thus diencephalically induced to secrete a hormone which controls thyroid activity, just as other anterior pituitary hormones control the sex-glands and the adrenals. There is thus no physiological objection to assuming that a diencephalic state of alarm can evoke an increase in the secretion of thyroxine.

It is a clinical fact, now widely recognized, that a period of severe emotional stress always precedes the onset of the disease—exclusively human—known as hyperthyroidism, Graves' disease or exophthalmic goitre. The exophthalmic protrusion of the eyeballs and the retraction of the eyelids is not the direct result of too much thyroxine, as it may occur or progress after the basal metabolic rate has been normalized by the surgical removal of a large part of the thyroid gland. On the other hand, these ocular symptoms never appear unless hyperthyroidism has gone before. The exact mechanism which causes exophthalmus is as yet unknown, but it seems probable that it lies at a high level which may be cortical, diencephalic or pituitary. Future research into this problem should take into account that the identical facial expression occurs as a normal reflex to sudden horror, though in this case the reaction is only momentary.

All the other bodily reactions which are associated with hyperthyroidism are the result of an excess of thyroxine and were originally designed to sustain an extreme physical and mental exertion in the presence of danger. The fact that animals make full use of all these admirable provisions by actually indulging in flight or fight is the reason why they never suffer from an over-active thyroid as a morbid condition.

Modern man's body reacts to fear just like that of other mammals, but his cortex and its artifacts prevent him from making use of these reactions. This produces a situation which may be compared to a boiler-house and an engine room. When, as in an animal, the engineer (the cortex) and the stoker (the diencephalon) are in close communication, the stoker regulates his furnace and the steam-pressure strictly in accordance with the engineer's requirements. When the engineer needs more power (for escape), he informs the stoker who immediately stokes up (increases thyroid activity); and when the engine (the body) is shut off (no need for escape), the stoker is told and at once dampens his fire.

In modern man's unfortunate position, the engineer (the cortex) tells the stoker (the diencephalon) that his engine (the body) requires the highest possible steam-pressure to cope with an emergency. The stoker stokes for all he is worth, but the engineer fails to speed up his engine and also fails to inform the stoker of this fact. If the stoker discovers that the engine is not running faster, he thinks that this is due to insufficient steam-pressure; so he stokes some more. The result is that sooner or later the boiler (the thyroid) bursts (psychosomatic disease). The engineer hears the bang, rushes over and starts berating the poor stoker. The engineer is a bossy and conceited type; so when the stoker shouts back at him the foolish engineer puts the blame on constructional faults in the boiler and in the engine (disease), but he will never admit his own mistake, which was not to let the stoker know what he was doing.

An emotion which is basically fear, and is often subconscious, initiates the over-activity of the thyroid. The resulting excess of thyroxine makes the senses and the cortex more alert, a mechanism which is obviously of greatest advantage to a threatened animal. In man this increased vivacity serves no useful purpose, because the cortex sees nothing to which the increased alertness can be applied. All this stimulation does is to increase the initial fear, and this makes the thyroid work harder still. A vicious cycle is thus established and may explain why hyperthyroidism can be so rapidly progressive.

In the early stages of this process simple sedation—preferably with bromides—and associated psychotherapy are usually sufficient to bring thyroid activity back to normal. But if the vicious cycle continues to spin for weeks and months, the demand for more and more thyroxine cannot be met by the normal thyroid gland. One might have hoped that once the thyroid is working to capacity there would be no further progress of the disorder. This, alas, is not the case. From the evolutionary standpoint, a supply of thyroxine sufficient to meet any emergency was of such vital importance that the thyroid gland acquired an almost unlimited ability to increase its output of thyroxine by enlarging its size. As the human cortex keeps up the state of emergency indefinitely, the thyroid continues to grow more secreting tissue; it begins to bulge at the neck and is then known as a goitre.[1]

Once the thyroid starts enlarging, the metabolic disorder which it causes is no longer reversible. Successful psychotherapy may still arrest further progress, but even if diencephalic impulses are called off the enlarged thyroid will never return to normal of its own accord.

When a large part of the overgrown gland is removed surgically, the production of thyroxine is drastically curtailed. The basal metabolic rate returns to normal, and all the symptoms of hyperthyroidism, except the bulging eyes, are relieved. But it should still be a routine procedure for all operated patients to be given the benefit of psychotherapy, a precaution which is all too frequently neglected in the excitement over the spectacular post-operative improvement. It is quite conceivable that psychotherapeutic neglect after the operation is one reason why an exophthalmus often gets worse, even though the basal metabolic rate has been rendered normal.

Recently, the ever busy pharmaceutical industry has developed drugs which have a dampening effect on thyroid activity. They are very effective and a little dangerous, but they are certainly not a fully satisfactory answer to the problem of hyperthyroidism.

It is still widely believed that the abnormal growth of the thyroid gland, the goitre, produces the metabolic disorder of hyperthyroidism. Yet it would seem that a goitre which produces too much thyroxine is always a secondary response to an increased demand for this hormone, which is in turn invariably due to a psychosomatic mechanism. It follows that everything depends on the early detection of hyperthyroidism before the condition has become irreversible.

Hyperthyroidism rarely arises in persons past middle age, but

---

[1] There are several other types of goitre which have nothing to do with an increased demand for thyroxine. Such goitres never cause hyperthyroidism.

until then the basal metabolic rate should be regularly checked. If it is found to be higher than $+12$, the case should be carefully watched and any tendency of the BMR to rise still further should be taken as a warning that the patient is under an emotional stress which must be dealt with seriously and at once. If that is expertly done by a clinical psychiatrist, hyperthyroidism will not become an established disease. This does not mean that such early cases should be hurriedly referred to a psychoanalyst, as that is liable to precipitate new terrors. The patient must stay under the treatment of his physician. The clinical psychiatrist should join the physician in an informal consultation, and together the two doctors should frankly explain the position to the patient. The first session with the psychiatrist is then arranged.

In these cases there is no need to go through orthodox psycho-analytical procedures. The aim is merely to uncover the present cause for anxiety, and the psychotherapeutic approach should be oriented only towards this goal. The interview should have a physiological rather than a psychological undertone. An experienced psychiatrist rarely requires more than six sittings to achieve a satisfactory clinical result, because the fears that evoke hyperthyroidism are not as a rule severely repressed and have arisen only a short time before the onset of symptoms. As in the case of the peptic ulcers, it is hardly ever necessary to rake over the whole personality structure of the patient.

Obesity

The ability to accumulate fat is a normal and necessary function of the body. Fat has the highest caloric value of all nutrients and is, therefore, ideal for the storage of food-reserves in the smallest possible space. When ample food is eaten the body stores away any surplus not required at the moment of eating or during the period of assimilation from the digestive tract. Such stored fat is always readily available for sustenance whenever the food-intake falls below the body's requirements. A well-fed, healthy body can function perfectly for a certain period subsisting only on its normal reserves of fat.

Apart from being a nutritional reserve, fat has another important function in the body. It acts as a kind of upholstery or packing-material for the inner organs which it cushions. Fat-tissue is strong, yet soft and resilient. In the sole of the human foot the pad of fat which lies between the bones and the skin carries the whole weight of the body and still remains springy. Fat which is a structural part of the body is called essential fat. Essential fat surrounds the coronary and other arteries; it softly beds the kidneys and the eyeballs; it keeps the intestines in their place and performs many other important functions.

Additional fat which is merely laid down as a nutritional reserve is normal, but not essential. In wild animals the accumulation of non-essential fat is severely restricted and never exceeds the normal limit. Even in hibernating animals the great autumnal accumulation of fat is a normal process and has none of the abnormal features associated with human obesity.

Obesity exists only in man and a very few domestic animals in which this abnormality has been developed by controlled breeding. In man, too, the tendency to accumulate abnormal fat is always inherited, though the trait may skip any number of generations. Persons who do not have this inherited tendency can eat as much as they please; they never suffer from obesity.

Potential obesity is so common in modern man because he has developed the trait by sexual selection. In early Neolithic times man began to own property and to assure his nutrition through agriculture and animal husbandry. A fat body thus became associated with wealth and leisure, as it still is in many parts of the world. The males of most modern races prefer a plump mate to a skinny one; the girl with heavy hips, large thighs and breasts has generally had a better chance in the marriage-market, because overweight was taken to indicate that her family was rich and would provide her with a substantial dowry. It implied that she liked good food and would know how to prepare it and that she was healthy and amorous. It was also taken for granted that such a girl could easily bear many strong children and suckle them well. None of these notions are necessarily true, but they play a definite role in post-Neolithic mating.

Potentially or overtly obese parents may pass the trait on to their progeny, but this does not mean that a person who has inherited a tendency to accumulate abnormal fat must necessarily do so. When the trait is inherited from the ancestry of both parents, it will be very marked and may manifest itself in childhood; but when the trait is carried by one parent, it may reveal itself only in later life or not at all.

As every case of obesity can now be cured and as the disease can always be prevented, heritage alone cannot account for its insurgence. What is inherited is merely a greater or lesser tendency to become overweight. In order to understand the nature of this inherited disposition, it is first necessary to analyse the metabolic abnormality which underlies the disease.

In obesity the normal mechanism of fat-storage and utilization is grossly disturbed. The disorder can best be explained with the help of a simile, in which fat is compared with money. The essential fat which is part of the normal structure of the body may be compared to a man's possessions, his land, his house, its furnishings, etc. The normal non-essential fat, stored for a nutritional emergency, is like surplus income which he deposits with his bank in a current account. From this current account he can immediately withdraw nutritional funds whenever the need arises, instead of paying in 'ready cash' that comes in as food assimilated from the intestinal tract. This is the way the healthy body manages its fat; and as long as the arrangement continues, the weight never rises above normal. Animals and persons who have no inherited disposition to become obese keep their current fat-account within reasonable and manageable limits. As soon as their reserves are sufficient to cope with any likely emergency, they cease to feel hungry, eat only enough to cover their daily caloric expenses with intestinal 'cash' and make no further deposits.

Animals eat only when they are hungry. They never eat more than they require to still the hunger of the moment, and Paleolithic Man probably did the same. The Neolithic institution of meal-times changed this. By his evolutionary nature man eats a little every now and then, and this provides him with ready 'cash' throughout the day; but when his cortex forced him to confine his eating to a few meals and to fast for twelve hours or more, he could no longer eat only to appease his hunger. Modern man has to eat more than his body requires at the moment in order to provide for the long interval between two meals.

As long as man ate raw and unrefined food, digestion was a slow process, furnishing a steady flow of nourishment from the intestine. This kept the body in 'cash' for long periods. Modern man's habit of eating cooked—particularly boiled—food, sugar, finely-milled white flour, etc., enables him to assimilate much faster. This means that he runs out of cash sooner and is obliged to fall back on his current account a few hours after eating his meal, thus putting a further strain on his fat-bank's ability to manage the turnover. If then, for one of many possible reasons, the total intake of food is greater than the needs of his body, the deposits in the current account grow larger and this calls for a still greater banking capacity.

The management of the body's fat-bank appears to be located in one of the nerve-centres of the diencephalon. There is some experimental evidence to support this view. If in healthy animals a tiny diencephalic centre is mechanically destroyed—for instance, by a needle inserted through the skull—the animal develops an enormous appetite and begins to accumulate abnormal fat. It develops a disease which is in many respects identical with human obesity.

The diencephalic fat-banking centre has a certain capacity to manage hoarding and a high turnover. When the limit of this capacity is reached in animals or persons who have no inherited tendency to become obese, the diencephalon automatically curbs the appetite and no further weight is gained. But this mechanism does not operate in persons predisposed by heredity to accumulate abnormal fat. In them the diencephalon has lost its ability to regulate the appetite strictly in accordance with nutritional needs after the current account has reached its normal limit. The result of continued accumulation of fat is that the size of the deposits and the work involved in dealing with 'cheques' come to exceed the diencephalon's banking capacity. Some way out has to be found.

The diencephalon solves the problem by performing the same transaction as a bank manager might suggest to a rich client. The work involved in managing an excessively large current account can be substantially reduced by cutting the account down to a reasonable sum and transferring the surplus to a fixed deposit which does not require constant supervision. Money can always be paid into a fixed deposit, but it cannot be withdrawn at short notice. It is a transaction of this kind which the diencephalon is forced to make when it loses control over nutritional income.

The opening of a fixed fat-deposit which is no longer available for metabolic purposes is the beginning of the disease known as obesity. In initiating the disorder hereditary factors are involved in two ways. In mild forms of obesity only the ability to curb the appetite automatically at the right moment is lost, but in severe and early forms it seems that, in addition, the diencephalon's banking capacity is less than normal. In the latter case the diencephalon is forced to resort to the device of creating a fixed deposit at a very early stage in the process of building up a large current account. Thus, paradoxical though it may sound, a person with a strong hereditary trait can begin to suffer from obesity before his weight exceeds the normal limit. Such cases are quite common in medical practice. Dressed, the patient looks perfectly normal, but on careful examination he shows all the typical signs of congenital obesity. His body-fat is abnormally distributed, and he distinctly feels that there is something wrong with him. In the consulting room such patients are often given short shrift; their plea for help is brushed aside as a faddish weight-fixation. Yet unless they are helped at once, these patients are almost certain to develop obesity in the usual sense at some later date.

Similarly, a person may be distinctly overweight without suffering from clinical obesity. Such persons are heavily built and have larger normal fat-reserves than others. The difference from real obesity is that their weight is stationary. They may be able to gain a few pounds by gross over-eating, but they can just as quickly take them off by eating a little less. This a patient suffering from obesity can never do.

As the weight of the obese body increases, caloric requirements for the maintenance of body-temperature and muscular activity rise sharply. Translated into the more familiar language of banking, this means that larger sums must be withdrawn from the now limited current account. Thus, when an obese patient tries to control his diet, a point may be reached in which the current account and the essential fat are exhausted while the fixed deposit continues to swell.

When the obese patient eats a large meal he thereby supplies all the immediate wants of his body and replenishes his small current account, while all the surplus goes into the fixed deposit. Unfortunately, however, the enormous demands of his huge body deplete the restricted current account long before the next meal is due. As he cannot touch the fixed deposit, he becomes ravenously hungry a few hours after he has gorged himself and is forced to eat again, with the same unhappy result.

This mechanism is the cause of the 'gluttony' of which the obese are commonly accused. It is also the reason why the obese have such a desperate longing for sweets and sometimes alcohol, because sugar and alcohol are very rapidly assimilated and thus bring the quickest possible relief to a patient tortured by hunger. It is therefore grossly unfair to accuse the obese of gluttony, and such calumny may play havoc with their psyche. What they suffer is real, primitive, gnawing hunger, which makes them feel faint if it is not rapidly appeased. When such patients are continually and often authoritatively told that this is not true, that the hunger pangs of which they complain are imaginary or an excuse for a lack of self-discipline, they may rightly conclude that their condition is not understood. But all too often they come to believe that they are weaklings, subject to uncontrollable delusions or disgusting urges. This is liable to make them so depressed that they throw all medical advice to the winds, eat as much as they need to feel tolerably comfortable and, of course, continue to gain weight rapidly. In such cases even the modern drugs which decrease the appetite have little effect. They act at a cortico-diencephalic level by decreasing the perception of hunger, but here we are dealing with what amounts to starvation and not greed. If this real hunger is suppressed by drugs, the result is a further depletion of essential fat. The continued over-eating of an advanced case of obesity is thus never the cause of the condition; it is the result.

As long as no fixed deposit has been established, a person can control his weight by eating less or by increasing his metabolic rate with exercise or by taking thyroid, the latter being a particularly undesirable and often dangerous method, unless expertly controlled. Once a fixed deposit has been opened, these measures are no longer effective. Strictly enforced, they merely deprive the body of essential fat and are liable to produce all the symptoms of malnutrition and hyperthyroidism, in spite of the huge amounts of fat inaccessibly stowed away in vaults to which there is no key.

Several contributory factors other than heredity may lead to obesity, though the manifest disease is always due to the same mechanism: the abnormal storage of fat in fixed deposits.

Throughout the years many theories on the causes of obesity have been propounded. They have come, had their heyday and disappeared. The oldest is that obesity is directly due to over-eating. This theory is again enjoying a certain popularity among students of the problem; but its protagonists feel a little uneasy and lack enthusiasm, because they know that their approach is essentially a nihilistic reaction to a long series of theoretic disappointments. There is certainly no generally valid, simple and direct relationship between excessive caloric intake and the insurgence of obesity. There are many obese patients who gain weight on a diet which would be grossly deficient in a healthy person of normal weight. It is true that over-eating may eventually lead to obesity, but it can do this only in persons who are by heredity predisposed to become fat. It is for the same reason that the established disease cannot be cured by dieting. Dieting may, at a terrible bodily and mental cost, bring about a reduction in weight; but it will never correct the under-lying metabolic disorder, as is clearly shown by the fact that weight is rapidly regained as soon as the diet is brought back to a normal level.

Much has been written about the psychosomatic aspects of obesity. Cortico-diencephalic mechanisms certainly play a most important part in creating conditions which may eventually lead to obesity. They may also make the disease progress more rapidly than it would without them. For instance, a person may over-eat on account of loneliness. At a certain point this simple form of instinct-gratification may change from a bleak comfort into the real disease of obesity. Once that critical point has been passed, no amount of company will correct the disorder.

There is a form of eating which is called compulsive. Compulsive eating has nothing to do with the very real physiological hunger from which most obese patients suffer, though the two conditions are all too often confused. The compulsive eater frankly admits that hunger is not the cause of his sudden, irrepressible need to stuff himself with anything edible he can lay hands on. He will cram into his mouth the left-overs on other people's plates, stale bread, cold greasy food, almost anything; he can easily polish off two pounds of chocolates at a session; he has no time for the niceties of using knife, fork or spoon—he uses his hands to devour food with a primeval ferocity which is terrifying to watch.

Compulsive eating is due to a cortical suppression of the sex-instinct. In the compulsive eater sexual instinct-demands bounce back to the diencephalon from a tight cortical censorship. They continue to accumulate at the diencephalic level until some outlet must be found. To relieve the pressure of the sex-instinct the diencephalon uses the device of drawing off a turbulent sex-demand through other instinct-channels which are less severely repressed. The outlet may be through the instinct of fear, in which case the patient feels an upsurge of irrational terror, or the diencephalon may unload through an orgy of eating or drinking. That the diencephalon so often relieves sex-pressure through an attack of compulsive eating is because eating produces an infantile oral gratification which is essentially sexual.

The psychotherapy of compulsive eating may prevent obesity if it is successfully undertaken early enough. It may slow down the rate at which weight is gained in established obesity, but psychotherapy can never cure the underlying metabolic disorder. The situation may be compared to that of a child playing with a sharp knife. If the knife is snatched away in time the child will not cut its fingers. If a finger is already cut the removal of the knife will prevent further injury, but it will not heal the wound that has already been inflicted. In the treatment of established obesity, successful psychotherapy and many other common forms of treatment play the same part as taking away the knife after the damage has been done. The vicarious instinct-gratification which expresses itself in compulsive eating is the result of the severe cortical censorship which modern Western civilization has imposed upon sex. It is, therefore, a psychosomatic phenomenon of quite recent origin.

A very much older mechanism calls for an increase in caloric intake under the influence of a constant threat. Among timid, flight-conditioned animals there may occur a persistent state of emergency, as when a balanced fauna is suddenly upset by an increase in large carnivora. In this case the hunted will have to do more running than usual. It has been explained that in all timid animals sudden danger wipes out hunger and the ability to eat. But this is so only as long as the actual danger lasts. As soon as safety is reached, the appetite returns to normal and the reserves that were used up in flight are rapidly replaced. But when the peril is long-drawn, such as in cold weather or increased pressure from pursuing flesh-eaters, those animals survive which are sufficiently intelligent to anticipate the night-frost or the frequent need to run for their lives by stocking up their reserves while danger is not imminent. The trait is thus developed by natural selection, because those animals that possess it have a better chance of survival.

The trait which makes an animal eat in anticipation of danger has nothing to do with the human trait which predisposes modern man to obesity, though man has inherited both traits from his ancestors. In animals excessive feeding in anticipation of abnormal requirements never leads to obesity. For this there are three reasons. The first is that animals have no predisposition to become obese. The second is that the mechanism stops as soon as normal conditions are re-established, and the third is that they actually consume the nutritional excess in flight or the maintenance of body-temperature.

Contemporary man's situation is quite different. In the first place, he may be predisposed to develop obesity, in which case any form of over-eating may lead to the establishment of a fixed deposit. Secondly, his fears, dreads and anxieties are usually debarred from resolution by reasoning, because cortical censorship keeps them below the threshold of consciousness. Such subconscious fears are particularly liable to become involved in a cortico-diencephalic vicious cycle in which fear produces bodily reactions and these produce more fear, further increasing diencephalic responses. The spinning of this cycle often continues after the initiating experience is long forgotten. Lastly, modern man rarely uses the caloric provisions his body is making for physical flight or exposure to cold. The result is that his preparations against stress continue to pile up until his diencephalon is forced to limit his current account, open a fixed deposit and thereby initiate the disease of obesity.

It was man's post-Neolithic reasoning about the choice of a mate which developed a hereditary tendency to obesity in his progeny by sexual selection. It is the cortical censorship at the threshold of consciousness which perpetuates his fears and the artifacts of civilization which prevent him from reacting to danger the way his evolution intended him to do. Thus, here too, modern man has used his cortex to turn a wonderfully useful evolutionary adaptation into a psychosomatic disorder which eventually leads him into organic disease.

In predisposed persons, outer circumstances may sometimes lead to obesity. When a normally nourished person undergoes a long period of severe privation—such as in war, in concentration camps or in chronic intestinal disease—the diencephalon gradually adjusts the fat-bank to a very small turnover. When such a person is then all at once enabled to eat all the food he wants, he is liable to develop obesity, because his diencephalon is unable to manage the enormous sudden influx.

When a physically very active person suddenly takes to a sedentary life or is in other ways immobilized, he will retain his former eating habits if, by heredity, he lacks the mechanism which automatically adjusts food-intake to requirement. Owing to the decrease in his caloric output in muscular energy, he gains weight and may overshoot the capacity of his diencephalon to manage the swelling current fat-account. He is then forced to establish fixed fat-deposits and continues to gain weight, in spite of any dietary restrictions he may subsequently try to observe.

Finally, climatic conditions may be responsible for the insurgence of obesity in a predisposed person. When someone who has spent all his life in a cold or temperate climate moves to the tropics, he uses up little or no energy to maintain his body-temperature. He is also likely to lead a physically less active life, which further reduces his caloric requirements. When no hereditary factor is involved, his appetite will automatically adjust itself to the new conditions. But if this mechanism does not operate, he continues the feeding habits acquired in a cold climate and eats far too much. The point at which the normal accumulation of fat-reserves changes into obesity is thus easily reached.

There was a time when in quick succession various glands were suspected of causing obesity. The first to be accused were the sex-glands. It was reasoned that, as genital underdevelopment and malfunction are often associated with obesity, ovarian or testicular deficiency might be the cause of overweight, particularly since obesity frequently occurs after castration. The middle-age spread in men, and in women the increase in weight after childbirth or in the menopause, seemed to confirm this view. But when the sex-hormones were isolated and highly potent preparations became available, it was proved that they had no effect whatever on obesity and so the whole theoretical structure collapsed.

However, the fact remains that sex-deficiencies are frequently, though not necessarily, associated with obesity. Organic sexual deficiencies such as underdevelopment of the genital organs, some menstrual disorders and female sterility, are secondary consequences of a primarily diencephalic disorder when associated with obesity. The mechanism which causes sexual deficiencies in obesity is probably the following sequence of events: At first there is an inherited diencephalic inability to cope with a rapidly growing current fat-account; other diencephalic nerve centres suffer under the strain in which the fat-bank is involved, and among these nerve centres is the one which stimulates the anterior lobe of the pituitary gland. Insufficient secretion of those pituitary hormones which directly stimulate the sex-glands prevents the sex-glands from developing or functioning normally. It is thus the diencephalic strain imposed by obesity which causes the pituitary deficiency affecting the sex-glands and neither the deficiency of the sex-glands nor of the anterior pituitary which causes the obesity.

In castration the mechanism is different. Here the sequence is as follows: The sudden removal of the sex-glands produces an enormous demand for more pituitary sex-hormones. This is due to a so-called feed-back mechanism through which the sex-glands normally advise the diencephalon of their need for more or less stimulation. When there is much sex-hormone in circulation, the diencephalon decreases the pituitary stimulation of the sex-glands; and when there is little sex-hormone in circulation, the diencephalon increases anterior pituitary activity. Then when in castration all the sex-hormone disappears, the diencephalon brings heavy pressure to bear on the anterior pituitary in a vain effort to correct the situation by pouring out as much of its sex-gland-controlling hormones as it can. The diencephalon can comply with this sudden extreme demand only at the expense of its many other functions; and the fat-banking capacity is one of the first to suffer, as this function is less important than many others for life and the propagation of the species. A sudden decrease in the diencephalon's ability to manage the current fat-account forces it to establish a fixed deposit, and from then on abnormal fat continues to accumulate. If after castration there is no other reason to over-eat, the artificial administration of large doses of sex-hormones started immediately after the operation prevents the onset of obesity; though once it is established the condition cannot be cured by giving sex-hormones.

A similar mechanism is to some extent responsible for the gain in weight after the menopause, though here the process is very slow, giving the diencephalon much more time to adjust itself. Sex-hormones should never be used to control a tendency to obesity in the menopause, as they merely delay a normal process and make a belated adjustment to the lack of ovarian hormone more troublesome.

Finally, there is another mechanism involved in the relationship between sex and obesity. This mechanism is cortical. The sex-instinct is by no means dependent on the presence or functioning of the sex-glands. Castration, genital underdevelopment, the menopause, advancing age and sexual abstinence do not eliminate the sex-instinct. When the diencephalic sex-instinct becomes severely repressed at a cortical level, as often happens after middle age, it is reflected from the cortex back to the diencephalon. The diencephalon may then be forced to resort to the culinary outlet as in compulsive eating. It is thus not the diminished sex-urge which increases the appetite, but rather the cortical blocking of sexual outlets. It is common knowledge that when a rakishly promiscuous bachelor settles down to respectable married life he is liable to put on excessive weight. Obviously marriage has not decreased his sex-urge nor the functioning of his sex-glands. What has happened is that his former sexual appetites have become severely censored and repressed. It is the cortical block, suddenly imposed, which increases the interest in food.

When it was discovered that the thyroid gland controls the basal metabolic rate, the problem of obesity seemed solved. It was thought that increasing metabolism by administering thyroid gland would rapidly deplete abnormal fat deposits. Giving an obese patient thyroid unfortunately does nothing of the sort. Normal non-essential and even essential fat can be removed by increasing thyroid activity because such fat is not in a fixed deposit; but once fat is stored in deposits which no longer take part in the metabolic turnover of the body, thyroxine cannot touch it.

Obese patients may have a low, normal or high basal metabolic rate, but this has no bearing on their disordered fat-metabolism. In those relatively few cases of obesity in which the BMR is very low, raising thyroid activity brings about a small loss of weight. This is due to the elimination of the mucoid substance known as myxoedema which accumulates in the tissues when thyroid activity is grossly deficient, but the loss is not due to the removal of any fat from the abnormal deposits. Such results as are still being claimed for the thyroid treatment of obesity are usually due to associated dieting and not to the thyroid hormone. The removal of the thyroid gland produces cretinism, but it never leads to obesity. It is high time that thyroid preparations ceased to be used in the treatment of obesity, in which they do no good and may do serious harm.

Considering the almost unbelievable complexity of the pituitary gland, it is not surprising that it should have been one of the chief suspects in the case. A vast number of different pituitary extracts and isolated pituitary hormones have been prepared. None of them proved to be of any value in the treatment of obesity.

That the pituitary control of the sex-glands is not directly concerned in causing obesity has already been explained, but the anterior pituitary control of the thyroid gland has been blamed for causing obesity. From what has been said about the thyroid, it is obvious that this is not so. Insufficient stimulation from the pituitary may lead to thyroid deficiency, but never to the accumulation of abnormal fat.

The pituitary gland was about to be exonerated when it was discovered that certain new-growths or tumours in the gland produced a condition known as Cushing's disease, which in some respects closely resembles a severe case of obesity. In Cushing's disease there is a rapid increase in weight and the face becomes round—the so-called 'moon-face'. Long purple lines appear just under the surface of the skin where it is most distended by rapidly accumulated fat. These lines, known as striae, are the same as often appear on the abdomen during pregnancy. They are caused by the splitting of the lower layers of the skin, which cannot adjust themselves to the sudden stretching. Marked sexual deficiencies are always present in Cushing's disease.

The pituitary new-growth which causes Cushing's disease produces an enormous increase in the pituitary hormone which regulates the rind of the adrenal glands. This pituitary hormone is known as the adreno-cortico-trophic hormone or, for short, ACTH. When the anterior pituitary produces too much ACTH, the adrenal rind is overworked. The over-activity of the adrenal rind leads to those symptoms which are characteristic of Cushing's disease but rarely occur in ordinary obesity, such as an increase in the hairiness of the body, a de-calcification of the bones and other abnormalities. In Cushing's disease there are thus two sets of symptoms—those which are typical of obesity and those which are the direct result of over-stimulation of the adrenal rind.

The mechanism by which an ACTH-secreting pituitary tumour upsets the diencephalon's management of the fat-account is possibly the following: Normally the diencephalon stimulates the anterior pituitary into producing an adequate amount of ACTH. When a tumour begins to flood the body with far more ACTH than required, the diencephalon receives frantic messages through the hormonal feed-back begging it to stop any further stimulation of the anterior pituitary. Even though the diencephalon responds at once, the developing tumour keeps on feeding more ACTH into the body. The inability to check the anterior pituitary eventually creates such a commotion in the harassed diencephalon that it shuts down many of its other functions which are not directly involved. The diencephalon's fat-banking centre lies quite close to the nerve-centre which controls the anterior pituitary. In the diencephalic turmoil the current account is hurriedly closed, a fixed deposit is established and from then on all superfluous fat goes into this deposit. A patient suffering from Cushing's disease has a voracious appetite and rapidly gains weight, because his diencephalic capacity to manage the fat turnover has been drastically decreased. As in obesity, the excess weight is deposited around the shoulders, hips, thighs, abdomen and in the face.

When ACTH was first isolated, it was discovered that it had

the surprising effect of rapidly relieving pain in all rheumatic conditions. Almost as soon as ACTH was injected, bed-ridden victims of chronic arthritis could move their crippled limbs freely. ACTH was hailed as a new wonder-drug, which indeed it is. However, this early enthusiasm was damped when it appeared that the continued use of effective doses of ACTH produced the same symptoms as were already familiar from Cushing's disease.

The sudden flooding of the body with injected ACTH— normally secreted continuously in small amounts which are strictly in accordance with requirements—is inexplicable and violently alarming to the diencephalon, there being no evolutionary precedent for such an extraordinary emergency. A sudden excess of ACTH so confuses the diencephalon that it calls off not only its normal stimulation of the pituitary gland, but also the working of the current fat-account. As always, this leads to the accumulation of abnormal fat, locked away in a fixed deposit. Fortunately, this artificially induced obesity is reversible in the early stages, as the diencephalic banking capacity has been only temporarily reduced. If no more ACTH is injected, diencephalic equilibrium is re-established and the fixed deposit goes back into the current account, unless the gain in weight has been so great as to exceed the normal diencephalic capacity, in which case the obesity is no longer spontaneously reversible.

Thus Cushing's syndrome can be produced either by a pituitary tumour which secretes an excess of ACTH or when too much ACTH is injected as a method of relieving the pain of arthritis. But there is still a third condition which leads to the same disorder and that is a hormone-secreting tumour of the adrenal cortex. In this case the diencephalon is maximally employed in shutting off any further secretion of the adrenal cortex-stimulating hormone ACTH from the anterior pituitary and again this excessive strain on one diencephalic function can only be sustained at the cost of other functions among which the fat-bank is the first to suffer.

In ordinary obesity there is no excessive secretion of ACTH and no over-stimulation of the adrenal rind. In fact, the clinical evidence points the other way. There seems to be a depression of the diencephalic-anterior-pituitary-adrenal mechanism. It follows that neither the pituitary nor the adrenals can be directly involved in causing ordinary obesity. The view that obesity, with the two exceptions just discussed, never arises from a disorder of any endocrine system and that no inner-secretory gland can be blamed, is slowly gaining ground.

The prevention of obesity obviously consists in keeping the weight within the diencephalon's capacity to manage the current fat-account. The trouble is that this capacity is an unknown quantity. All that can be said is that when no signs of obesity have appeared before puberty, the diencephalon is certainly able to manage a body-weight which is close to the normal statistical average for a given height, age, bone-structure and muscular development. If a person with a normal diencephalic capacity later becomes obese, this is always due to the addition of cortical or circumstantial factors, never to heredity alone.

When unmistakable signs of obesity occur before puberty, it invariably indicates a strong hereditary factor and possibly a diencephalic banking-capacity which is congenitally below normal. At birth there is no way of telling to what extent a child has inherited the trait, and it may be several years before this becomes possible. A child must be considered particularly prone to obesity if it is born into a family in which there have been cases of pre-adolescent obesity in the last few generations on either parent's side or if one parent is obese. Such children should be very carefully watched from birth. A determined effort must be made to keep them just a little below the average normal weight for their height and age.

Parents must be made to understand that a slightly underweight healthy child is preferable to one which is even a little chubby. Chubbiness may be perfectly normal and even delightful in a child that has inherited no tendency, or only a slight one, to become obese in later life, but in a child that has inherited a strong trait it may be the beginning of childhood obesity; at an early age one cannot tell the difference. Stout parents who pride themselves on their plump babies are in danger of allowing their cortical presumptions to make their children victims of obesity and all the misery which this entails. It is thus the parental cortex which may cause a latent disposition to develop into the obesity of childhood, because it foolishly presumes that the more food they stuff down their infant's throat the stronger and healthier the child will become.

As the child gets older, an inherited diencephalic deficiency can be recognized even before there is any abnormal accumulation of deposited fat. In the male child genital development may begin to lag, particularly as regards the scrotum, into which one or both testicles may fail to descend. In both sexes the legs may become slightly knock-kneed, there may be a little pad of fat on the inside of the knee-joint and two deep dimples may persist above the buttocks on either side of the sacral bone. When the second teeth break through, such children always have disproportionately large first upper incisors. At puberty there may be some delay in the appearance of axillary, pubic and—in boys—facial hair. In girls the onset of menstruation and mammary development may be late.

If any of these symptoms are present, it means that the weight must be watched without fuss, alarm or anxiety. The child must be taught to take a hygienic interest in its weight, much as it is taught to wash its hands and brush its teeth. This is best done in confidence with one parent or an older brother or sister. No drastic dietary restrictions need be openly imposed. It is not important what the child eats, and it should never be deprived of anything other children eat. What is important is that the weight be controlled frequently and that necessary reductions in food be made in the servings at meals, eliciting the child's co-operation as much as possible. The whole matter must remain a topic rigorously debarred from the table and the family circle. It must never be allowed to become the source of nicknames, jests or teasing. If at puberty the child shows none of the signs which indicate diencephalic deficiency, all precautions can be dropped; its diencephalon may be presumed to be normal, and it will never suffer from the obesity in which a congenital factor plays the dominant role.

The situation is totally different once the child's weight has increased beyond the normal average. In this case a child that has a diencephalic deficiency is already suffering from obesity. Its appetite will have become voracious and uncontrollable. The first fine striation caused by a splitting of the lower layers of the skin may already be visible on the hips. In boys the breasts become large and almost female, and in girls they swell with fat before the glandular tissue has had time to develop and they may already show striation of the skin.

Such children are often physically sluggish and lazy, though their intelligence is frequently above average. Their often remarkable scholastic ability is probably due to the fact that their cortex is less hampered by the primitive and stormy instincts of fear, rage and awakening sex. All these instincts are subdued in obese children, owing to the fierce domination of a single instinct, which is hunger. When the obesity is cured, these children become more active and less docile, while their exceptionally good school-reports may level off to a normal average.

The treatment of obesity will never be effective as long as it is directed towards the causes of the disease. All such measures have their justification in prevention, but they are never curative. The situation may be compared with a house on fire. There are thousands of ways in which the conflagration may have started, but these are of no consequence in dealing with the fire, which must be put out regardless of what caused it by extinguishing the flames. Obesity is a perfectly clear clinical entity and is a symptom of always the same abnormal diencephalic mechanism. To be effective, treatment must be aimed at this diencephalic mechanism and at nothing else. The object can thus be stated very clearly. It is to get the fixed fat-deposit back into the current account. At first sight this seems a hopeless undertaking. There is no way of changing a hereditary trait, and the diencephalon's fat-banking capacity is already over-strained. Yet there are two ways out of the quandary.

It is an interesting observation that people who have been fighting a losing battle with obesity for many years are easily able to utilize their abnormal fat-deposits when their life is in real danger through a combination of mortal fear and famine. A starvation diet voluntarily adopted in the midst of plenty does not have this effect. The addition of terror and the complete impossibility of obtaining food are necessary. Moreover, there must be no end in sight. The mechanism does not operate when the patient knows that on a given date he can get all the food he wants. Evidently under the influence of conscious terror the diencephalon is able to enlarge its banking capacity to such an extent that it can start drawing on the fixed deposits long before the normal deposits are exhausted in severe malnutrition. In the absence of stark horror the diencephalon seems to be unable to do this, as starvation without mortal terror is not effective in the same way. The mechanism is merely mentioned as a matter of interest. For obvious reasons it furnishes no practical approach to the problem of obesity. Fortunately, the second way out is more promising.

In placentals—i.e., mammals which retain their young up to a high degree of maturity inside the female body—the growth of the foetus calls for an enormous metabolic turnover. Evolution provides for this exigency by vastly increasing the diencephalon's banking capacity during pregnancy. In humans this ancient mechanism is so powerful that it can even overcome hereditary deficiencies. The hormone that brings about this astounding change is again chorionic gonadotrophin.[1]

In a woman suffering from advanced obesity the current fat-account may be assumed to be almost exhausted. When such a woman becomes pregnant, the growing foetus makes huge demands on her reserves, demands which could not possibly be met out of her depleted current account. Yet the foetus never suffers. In fact, obese women usually have large and heavy babies, because all their reserves, be they current or fixed, are placed at the unrestricted disposal of the foetus. During pregnancy an obese woman can be kept on a starvation diet without suffering from hunger, and when then her baby is born it is just as big and plump as ever. That obese women so rarely make use of pregnancy as their one great chance to reduce abnormal fat is the fault of their pedantic cortex, which comes up with 'now there are two mouths to feed' and such-like physiological drivel.

During pregnancy all fixed deposits are unlocked and can be freely drawn upon to keep the current account at any level that may be required. A woman may gain weight during pregnancy, but she never becomes obese in the clinical sense of the term. This happens only after delivery, when her diencephalon is

[1] The designation 'chorionic' is correct, because the hormone is manufactured in the chorion of the placenta; but the term 'gonadotrophin' is most misleading, because the hormone has no direct action on the 'gonads' or sex-glands. Where this seems to be the case—as in immature rats or adolescents—the effect is due to a diencephalic stimulation of the anterior pituitary gland, which increases the output of those sex-gland-controlling pituitary hormones (the follicle- and the corpus luteum-stimulating hormones known as F.S.H. and L.S.H. and their male equivalents) which alone can correctly be called 'gonadotrophic'. Human chorionic gonadotrophin has no effect on normally developed and normally functioning sex-glands. It could more appropriately be called 'chorionic diencephalotrophin'.

suddenly deprived of the action of chorionic gonadotrophin. It has been pointed out repeatedly that in pregnancy the normal bodily reactions to fear do not occur in the human female, and the primitive urge to eat more in anticipation of a crisis is abolished. Over-eating in pregnancy is thus always due to higher, conscious cortical pretensions and never to primitive evolutionary mechanisms. Over-eating in pregnancy can easily be controlled by educating and reasoning with the prospective mother, if she and her family are at all amenable to instruction.

In the last chapter the pregnancy-like condition which can be artificially induced in any overweight person by HCG+Diet (HCG+D)—i.e., small daily doses of human chorionic gonadotrophin and a diet of 500 calories—was discussed. It was suggested as a means of temporarily relieving high blood pressure and arresting the progress of arteriosclerosis; the loss of weight which HCG+D brings about was treated as incidental. In the present context the loss of weight is the primary object, and the many other effects of HCG+D are welcome, but secondary, phenomena. As far as the diencephalon's banking capacity is concerned, HCG+D has exactly the same effect as pregnancy.

The method can be used in both sexes and at all ages with identical results. It works equally well in hideously advanced cases and in the earliest stages in which only a few pounds have begun to accumulate in a fixed deposit. The dose of HCG and the diet are the same in all cases, regardless of age, height and degree of overweight, and the daily loss of weight averages just under one pound in all patients. A course of treatment consists of not more than forty daily injections, because after that amount the non-pregnant body develops a resistance to the hormone which temporarily loses its effect. However, such courses can be repeated as often as may be necessary after an interval of at least six weeks.

During such treatment patients feel no hunger or weakness and are able to go about their usual occupations. The loss of weight is achieved only at the expense of the fixed deposits. The current account remains fully stocked throughout, as the normal, essential or structural fat and the normal non-essential fat reserves are not touched.

The normal fat, for instance that under the skin, is put back, the face becomes less flaccid, wrinkles disappear and the patient looks much younger and fresher. When the skin is healthy and well-nourished, it easily adjusts itself to the rapidly shrinking size of the body and does not become loose, flabby or baggy.

Abnormal fat deposits are never evenly distributed over the body in the early stages of obesity. They are largely confined to certain parts such as the waist, the thighs and the shoulder-girdle. As HCG+D removes fat only from these abnormal deposits, it produces a spectacular change in the configuration of the body. In a moderately advanced case it is not unusual for a single course of HCG+D to reduce the wasitline by six inches.

The severe restriction of the diet is of utmost importance. A gross caloric deficiency in intake is necessary to activate the chorionic gonadotrophin. In pregnancy the foetus takes over this role, while in HCG+D the diet acts diencephalically like a phantom foetus. Without the diet, HCG brings about no loss of weight in whatever dose it is given. However, small daily doses are not completely inactive. This is shown by the fact that when HCG is given without the diet to very obese patients who have lost much of their essential fat, the abnormal measurements show some improvement; the patients feel less tired and exhausted and less voraciously hungry. This is because, under the influence of HCG, their depleted current account is replenished from the fixed deposits. There is thus a redistribution of the fat but no loss of weight. As soon as the structural fat and the normal reserves have been restocked, no further change takes place, however much additional HCG is given. In early cases of obesity in which there is no depletion of the normal fat, this phenomenon does not occur. It is therefore the dietary deficit which enables the body to consume abnormal fat while it is in transit from the fixed deposits to the current account. On the other hand, no patient can be comfortable and go about his usual occupation for more than three to four days on 500 calories unless he is simultaneously given HCG.

The aim of the HCG+D method of treating obesity is to get rid of all the abnormally fixed fat-deposits. Once this is achieved, patients can eat all they want, because their diencephalon is now running a current account which is within its normal capacity. Patients who have reached their normal weight after treatment with HCG+D do not have to observe any dietary restriction whatever, but they must make it a rule to weigh themselves every day at the same time. If the scales show an increase of more than two pounds over the weight reached at the end of the treatment, they must skip one meal on that day. This immediately corrects the increase because there has been no time to establish a fixed deposit. If they delay this correction for more than forty-eight hours, a small fixed deposit becomes established and a relapse is inevitable. However, a relapse can always be corrected by another short course of HCG+D, but never by dieting alone.

Whether a patient relapses or not depends to some extent on the care with which he watches his weight, but it also depends on whether the disease was brought on by cortical mechanisms such as chronic anxiety, frustration or repressed instinct-gratification. Patients in whom obesity was brought on by hereditary factors, outer circumstances or a temporary emotional stress rarely relapse. It is the patient in whom an unresolved cortico-diencephalic antagonism persists who is liable to relapse. In such cases physician and psychiatrist are faced with the necessity of making a very careful decision—whether to recommend psychotherapy or short courses of HCG+D at regular intervals. Unless the psychological mechanism is particularly simple and easy to correct without the danger of a personality-upheaval, the latter course is usually to be preferred.

The continued increase in weight is the most obvious symptom of obesity, but many other symptoms are frequently associated with the disease. Outstanding among these are high blood pressure and other circulatory disorders, a certain type of diabetes, gout, rheumatism and a host of minor ailments such as severe headaches, spastic constipation, an often insuperable lethargy and inertia, menstrual disorders, vaginal discharge without infective agent, sterility, allergies, psoriasis, loss of hair, brittle fingernails, etc. Some of these conditions will be dealt with in their respective chapters because they are not necessarily associated with obesity and may occur in patients who have no weight-problem. Here it will only be mentioned that all these disorders have four features in common. First, they have no exact counterpart in wild animals. Second, diencephalic mechanisms are involved in all of them. Third, they are apt to improve dramatically in pregnancy. Fourth, they are quickly and often spectacularly relieved when the associated obesity is treated with HCG+D.

In many thousands of cases of obesity, the author has found the HCG+D method to be the most satisfactory way of treating overweight.

8

Diabetes

THE WORD *diabetes* is of Greek origin and means 'going through'. It was applied to conditions in which too much water 'went through' the body, as when excessive thirst is associated with an abnormally increased urinary output. In the days when no clinical laboratories existed, an important diagnostic test was the taste of the urine, in addition to its smell and appearance. We owe the discovery that there are two kinds of diabetes to the zeal of early physicians to whom repugnance was as nothing compared with the welfare of their patients. They found that in some cases of diabetes the urine tasted sweet, and so they called this condition *diabetes mellitus*, the 'honey-sweet going through'. In other cases the urine was clear and neither sweet nor salty; it tasted just like water. The humanistically inclined diagnosticians of the fourteenth century called this disorder *diabetes insipidus*, the 'tasteless going through'. These two designations are still in common use, though it is now known that diabetes mellitus has nothing to do with diabetes insipidus. Diabetes insipidus is indeed an abnormal 'going through'. It is the inability to retain water.

The posterior lobe of the pituitary gland secretes a hormone which inhibits the excessive urinary elimination of water. This hormone is called the *antidiuretic hormone*, and its secretion is controlled by the diencephalon. When there is a deficiency of the antidiuretic hormone. the kidneys eliminate far more water than they should. In this flood of urine the waste-products excreted by the kidney are enormously diluted, and hence the insipid taste. In diabetes insipidus several gallons of urine may be excreted in a day, and the patients are forced by terrible thirst to drink an equal amount of water to make up for the loss.

Here we are only concerned with diabetes mellitus, the passing of sugar in the urine, also known as *glycosuria*. Actually, the passing of sugar in the urine is a secondary phenomenon. The primary disturbance is an increase in the amount of sugar circulating in the blood-stream. In a healthy fasting person at rest, one litre of blood contains about one gram of glucose, but in a fasting diabetic one litre of blood may contain three to four grams. If the blood sugar of a diabetic patient rises still higher, there is danger of so-called diabetic coma, in which the patient loses consciousness and may die if the coma is not rapidly relieved. Should the blood sugar drop well below one gram of glucose per litre of blood, the patient also becomes unconscious, has violent convulsions and may die from lack of sugar in his blood in what is known as a *hypoglycaemic shock*. Fortunately, a hypoglycaemic shock can only be produced artificially by insulin and does not occur spontaneously.

The level of the fasting blood sugar is very finely adjusted and is normally kept within a narrow range. Sugar is the food of all the muscles of the body. It is the fuel which they burn up rapidly when at work. The consumption of circulating sugar in the form of glucose, therefore, varies enormously depending on whether the body is under physical exertion or at rest, and yet the fasting blood sugar remains remarkably constant. There must thus be a way in which the body is able to adjust the blood sugar to a fixed level despite variations in food, rest and exertion.

The constancy of the blood sugar level is ensured by the action of an extraordinary hormone. The pancreas (Fig. 4) has already been mentioned as the gland which produces most important enzymes for the digestion of proteins, fats and carbohydrates—i.e., sugars and starches. As far as its digestive functions are concerned, the pancreas is an exocrine gland, which means that it produces a liquid secretion. This is the pancreatic digestive juice which is piped into the duodenum. The pancreatic tissue which manufactures the digestive enzymes is easily recognized under the microscope, but scattered between this exocrine tissue clusters of entirely different cells are found. Under low magnification these clusters of cells lie like conspicuous islands surrounded by exocrine glandular tissue. Accordingly, the clusters were called 'Islands of Langerhans' after the scientist who first described them.

It was subsequently discovered that these islands are, in fact, endocrine glands—that is, glands whose cells secrete a hormone directly into the blood-stream which feeds them. The hormone produced by these islands was, with unusual endocrinological reserve, given the non-committal name of *insulin*. In this particular case the terminological restraint was unnecessary, as it was soon proved that insulin is the hormone which keeps the blood sugar at a constant level.

Why the vitally important control of blood sugar should, of all places, be localized in a lot of glandular fragments scattered in the pancreas was at first a physiological mystery. But further knowledge showed that there are important reasons why the Islands of Langerhans are distributed throughout the pancreas and nowhere else. The digestive function of the pancreas is evoked only by the presence of food and hydrochloric acid in the stomach. When the stomach is empty, the pancreas lies dormant. Roused to activity by the passage of food, it requires an increased blood supply to be able to perform its digestive duties in a sudden burst of activity. Among other things, pancreatic digestive duties are concerned with rapidly preparing carbohydrates for assimilation. The sudden influx of sugar from the intestinal tract has to be met by a corresponding increase in the secretion of insulin from the islands, which are thus able to take advantage of the additional supply of blood; the control of blood sugar could therefore have been localized nowhere more appropriately than in the pancreas. That the exocrine digestive function of the pancreas should be closely linked with its endocrine blood-sugar-controlling function seems inevitable once the connection is understood.

Further evidence for the role of the pancreas in diabetes was soon forthcoming. It was shown that the removal of the pancreas produced very severe diabetes in animals and that the postmortem study of the pancreas of diabetics revealed degenerative lesions in the Islands of Langerhans. When then Banting and Best succeeded in isolating pure insulin from the pancreas of animals and proved that it could replace human insulin, the nature of diabetes mellitus appeared to be clear. Diabetes could now be explained as being due to a lack of insulin in the patient's body. The lack of insulin could be ascribed to a degenerative process in the insular apparatus of the pancreas and this insulin deficiency could be corrected by the injection of animal insulin. Thousands of diabetic lives were saved as a result of these great discoveries.

For a while patients, practitioners and physiologists enjoyed a period of therapeutic exhilaration. A tidal wave of optimism swept scientific sceptics, grumblers and sticklers for facts off their feet—the evidence was too overwhelming; the old problem of diabetes seemed solved at last. Only when the treatment of diabetes became a routine were the scientific kill-joys once more able to rear their heads out of the calmer waters and begin to ask embarrassing questions.

One of the highly inopportune questions these scientific *enfants terribles* asked was how to explain the undeniable fact that in some cases of advanced diabetes the post-mortem findings revealed a perfectly normal pancreas with normally functioning Islands of Langerhans. They also asked why some cases of diabetes proved to be insulin-resistant and why, in such cases, no amount of insulin was able to render the blood sugar normal. They pointed out that in diabetic women pregnancy sometimes eliminated and sometimes worsened the diabetic status, and they wanted to know why. They made much of the fact that diabetes sometimes starts suddenly and then remains stationary for years, while in other cases it begins surreptitiously and then slowly gets worse. The *enfants terribles* clamoured for an explanation of the indisputable fact that an obese diabetic is far less liable than a lean one to suffer from coma, diabetic circulatory disturbances such as gangrene of the toes and diabetic changes in the retina of the eye. They stressed the observation that in some cases of diabetes the slightest change in diet had a precisely predictable effect on the fasting blood sugar, whereas in other cases dietary escapades produced no corresponding fluctuations in the fasting blood-sugar readings. Finally, they showed that in some diabetics a mild emotional stress produced wide variations in the fasting blood-sugar level, whereas in others a similar psychic jolt had little or no such effect.

The scientific trouble-makers kept harking over ground where even most medical journals trod with a wary step, until their bickering could no longer be ignored. Reluctantly, the older views on diabetes had to be put back into the theoretic boiling-pot in order to distill a more generally satisfactory brew. This laborious process seems about to be completed, and one can already see the rough structure of the outcome.

One feature of the new interpretation of diabetes which is

shaping up is that an abnormally high fasting blood sugar can no longer be regarded as an indication of a single clear-cut disease. A rise in fasting blood sugar must be looked upon as a symptom much as fever is a symptom and not a disease. Merely saying that a patient is suffering from diabetes is diagnostically almost as unsatisfactory as saying that he is running a temperature. In other words, different mechanisms are now suspected of being able to cause diabetes. These causes remained obscure as long as the fasting blood sugar was regarded as the supreme diagnostic criterion, but meanwhile, research has progressed so far that some of these mechanisms can be tentatively discussed.

The fact that diabetes is not necessarily caused by a hormonal deficiency of the pancreatic islands is beginning to be generally accepted. It has already been mentioned that in some cases of diabetes the Islands of Langerhans are found to be perfectly normal after death. It has also been known for a long time that when in healthy animals a small nerve-centre which lies close to the fat-banking centre in the diencephalon is mechanically destroyed, the animal becomes severely diabetic, though its pancreas has not been tampered with. There is thus good reason to suspect that in man a diencephalic disorder may cause diabetes.

In man's ancestors a sudden rise in blood sugar was a biologically necessary and normal reaction to fear, as it still is in all wild animals. It instantly provides the muscles with enough fuel in the form of sugar to sustain the maximal exertion of running away from danger. This rise in blood sugar cannot be accounted for by a drop in the secretion of insulin from the pancreatic islands. The flow of insulin is a slow and steady process, primarily tuned to cope with the influx of sugar assimilated from the intestinal tract. The Islands of Langerhans are quite unable to make any instantaneous adaptations, and in any case such a hormonal mechanism would be far too slow in an emergency. Even if insulin production could be sharply braked, the blood sugar would rise only as long as more sugar kept pouring in from the intestinal tract. In a hungry animal there would be no rise, and this would be extremely dangerous when survival depended on a large supply of muscular fuel. There must thus be some other mechanism by which the blood sugar can be instantly raised in an emergency.

The storehouse of readily available muscular fuel is the liver. The rate at which the liver issues this fuel is regulated by the small local centres of the liver's own nervous system. As long as life is peaceful and placid, these local nerve-centres are perfectly able to adjust supply to demand without central nervous interference. But in the slightest emergency the diencephalon at once assumes command over the lower regulatory centres of the liver. Through its fast-moving nervous communications the diencephalon calls for emergency-rations to be distributed at once. The liver responds by pouring glucose into the blood. Once the motor of headlong flight has been started up, the diencephalic impulse is withdrawn and further provisions are made by the adrenalin which has meanwhile reached its various destinations.

As soon as the danger is over, no further adrenalin is secreted; the liver settles back to a normal routine, and all the extra sugar has been avidly consumed by the musculature working to preserve life by flight. In a few moments normal conditions are re-established, without insulin having taken any part in the process.

In modern man all these normal reactions to fear run off, just as they do in wild animals. There is, however, one fundamental difference. As modern man no longer runs away from danger, he finds himself left with an abnormally high blood sugar once the fear has subsided. It is only then that his pancreas goes to work. The Islands of Langerhans, which have been quietly managing the storage of assimilated sugar, find that something has gone wrong. There is an inexplicable rise in blood sugar through no fault of theirs. The only way in which the insular apparatus can react to this extraordinary situation is to do what it would normally do in case of a sudden influx of assimilated sugar—it desperately produces more insulin.

In the absence of pancreatic stimulation by the passage of food, and lacking the additional blood supply which this would normally provoke in the pancreas, the job of the insular apparatus is particularly arduous. The removal of sugar which should have been consumed in flight is thus a strain to which the pancreas of an animal is never subjected and which exists only in modern man. However, with a maximal effort the islands do manage to get the blood sugar back to the normal range in a couple of hours or so, in spite of the fact that the institution of regular meals, the eating of sugar and refined starches already puts a heavy, unnatural burden on modern man's insular apparatus.

Fortunately, healthy human organs—even such hard-worked ones as the endocrine glands—are able to cope with such an emergency, for which they have had no evolutionary preparation. But if one emotional shock follows another and if a diencephalic state of emergency is prolonged for months, the liver continues to pour too much sugar that cannot be consumed into the blood. A point may thus be reached at which the maximal production of insulin is not sufficient to keep the blood sugar within the normal range, although there is as yet no damage to the insular apparatus. From that moment on the patient is suffering from diabetes. In this type of diabetes, however, there is no absolute, but only a relative, lack of insulin. It is not that the pancreas is producing less insulin than normal; on the contrary, it is producing more than ever. All that is happening is that the diencephalon is making the liver issue more and more glucose to muscles that are cortically forbidden to use it.

Every physician is familiar with the patient who seeks medical advice because something has recently 'shot his nerves to pieces'. On routine examination, an abnormally high fasting blood sugar is sometimes discovered. To the patient this is a profound, but entirely conscious, shock. He is hospitalized, investigated, dieted and treated with insulin. The sudden removal from his environment and the impact of a conscious disaster break the vicious cycle of the usually repressed dreads which caused his diencephalon to raise his blood sugar. In a week or two he is completely cured. His blood sugar stays normal on general hospital diet, and he needs no more insulin. At subsequent checks his sugar metabolism is found to be normal.

This happy outcome occurs only in patients who have suffered from high blood sugar for a very short time—say a week or two. But when emotionally induced diabetes is not discovered until several months after its beginning, hospitalization, diet and insulin may keep the diabetes in check but they will never cure it.

The reason for this unfortunate fact is possibly a diencephalic mechanism similar to that which occurs in obesity. It seems that once an elevated blood sugar has persisted for a certain length of time, the exhausted diencephalon is able to make a new adjustment by permanently establishing a fixed blood-sugar level well above normal. To this new high level the body is able to adjust itself. The insular apparatus in the pancreas then no longer tries desperately to bring the blood sugar below this new level; it merely works to maintain it. Similarly, the liver keeps its output of sugar at the new level without trying to increase it. To maintain this status, no further diencephalic impulses are required, and so the diencephalon is once again free to work normally and under less pressure. The whole mechanism is essentially a diencephalic labour-saving device, and it explains why the high blood sugar of such patients may stay stationary for many years.

These patients do not suffer from gangrene, diabetic coma and diabetic retinal disorders of the eye, complications which frequently arise when diabetes is due to an organic insular deficiency. In what may be called a diencephalic form of diabetes there has merely been a shift in the level at which the blood sugar is normally maintained.

The diencephalic origin of some cases of diabetes, commonly known as *stable*, could also explain why these do not respond to the injection of insulin, as do those cases which are due to a real pancreatic insulin deficiency and are known as *brittle*. In stable or diencephalic diabetes there is no lack of insulin, because all the insulin required to maintain the new high level is easily available. When in spite of this situation insulin is injected, often in large doses, in the vain hope that these will overcome insulin-resistance, it merely forces the liver to re-establish the newly acquired high sugar balance by pouring more glucose into the blood-stream. Injecting insulin in these cases also sets in motion all those mechanisms which are able to reduce the output of the body's own insulin. In diencephalically induced diabetes, injected insulin does not relieve any abnormal demand on the Islands of Langerhans. They are under no particular strain, as they have adopted the raised level of the blood sugar as normal.

The administration of insulin in diencephalic diabetes depresses the normal activity of the insular apparatus; when such treatment is continued for a long time, the insulin-enforced inactivity of the islands gradually leads to their degeneration.

In this process the islands may eventually become really deficient in absolute terms and are then unable to secrete a normal amount of insulin. At that point a diencephalic stable diabetes begins to change into a progressive pancreatic brittle diabetes in which the insular apparatus becomes increasingly exhausted and which is, therefore, more dangerous. It seems to follow that a diencephalic diabetes should never under any circumstances be treated with insulin, regardless of the level at which the blood sugar stands. Insulin should be strictly reserved for those cases in which there is a real and not merely a presumed pancreatic deficiency. Diencephalic diabetes calls for an entirely different management, particularly also as regards the diet.

The diencephalic form of diabetes is almost invariably associated with obesity, and this could hardly be otherwise. The continual and excessive withdrawal of glucose from the liver calls for rapid replacement, and this increases hunger and appetite, particularly for sweets from which the sugar is rapidly assimilated. If the patient knows that he is diabetic, sugars and starches are just the things he most scrupulously tries to avoid, and he is liable to make up for them with fats.

In dealing with obesity it has been explained that an excess eaten at mealtimes must pass through the fat-bank and that this may lead to the establishment of a fixed fat-deposit, and thus to obesity. Over-eating in diabetes may also be due to the same fear which is responsible for the rise in blood sugar.

In both obesity and diabetes, the onset of the metabolic disorder depends on the diencephalon's capacity to cope with the additional strain of a long continued state of emergency. As soon as the limit of diencephalic capacity is reached, a way out must be found. In the case of over-eating the diencephalon establishes a fixed deposit of fat, and in the case of excessive sugar-output from the liver it fixes the blood sugar at a new elevated level. In obesity and in diabetes the degree of diencephalic capacity seems to be an inherited trait, which may be strong or weak, depending on genetic factors. Whether there also exists an inherited primary pancreatic deficiency is not quite certain, but it is probable.

It is conceivable that a grossly over-worked diencephalic fat-banking centre diminishes the capacity of the neighbouring blood-sugar control, forcing it to fix a higher blood-sugar level at an early stage. In this case it is the obesity which causes the diabetes to become manifest. But the reverse mechanism, in which an overworked diencephalic sugar-centre exhausts the capacity of the fat-bank, is also possible. In this case it is the diabetes which causes the obesity.

With these concepts in mind, it is easy to understand why, in stable diencephalic diabetes, dietary fluctuations do not have a very marked effect on the fasting blood sugar. In these cases the insular apparatus is normal and is quite able to cope with variations in the flow of assimilated sugar from the intestine. The duty of the islands is merely to keep the blood sugar as close as possible to the newly fixed high level. In pancreatic or brittle diabetes, in which the normal production of insulin is reduced, the situation is entirely different. In the first place, there is no fixed level in a higher range. There is no reason to fix a new level, as no diencephalic emergency is concerned. There is also no excessive immission of sugar from the liver into the blood-stream. Pancreatic diabetes is, therefore, strictly dependent on the assimilation of food, and even a slight change in the intake of carbohydrates has an immediate repercussion on the fasting blood sugar.

In well-studied cases in which the pancreatic capacity for producing insulin is known, the blood-sugar-response to dietary changes is predictable with almost mathematical precision. Equally predictable is the response to a given amount of insulin. In the diencephalic type of diabetes such predictions are impossible, because the islands have plenty of reserve power and are not continually running at their maximum output.

A diencephalic diabetes disappears almost at once in pregnancy, because pregnancy abolishes the normal reactions to fear. There is no need for the liver to furnish more sugar to the muscles in flight, as flight is not a normal reaction in pregnancy. Moreover, diencephalic capacity is enormously enlarged during pregnancy; there is no further need for a blood-sugar range fixed at a higher level, and so it is abolished. In diencephalic diabetes the blood-sugar becomes normal within a few days of the onset of pregnancy—in fact, as soon as the pregnancy tests become positive. Thus when a pregnant woman is found to be diabetic, she is always suffering from the pancreatic form and her condition is inclined to deteriorate during gestation.

One reason for this deterioration may be that pancreatic diabetics are usually lean or underweight. In such women pregnancy demands additional food, putting a further strain on the insular apparatus. But there are almost certainly other endocrine mechanisms involved in the deterioration of diabetes in pregnancy, as it occurs even when the food-intake is not increased. The posterior lobe of the pituitary gland and the adrenals seem to play an important role in the phenomenon, but these mechanisms are not yet fully understood. When a pregnant woman suffers from diabetes, the foetus is fed with blood that contains too much sugar, it grows too fast, and its intra-uterine death is a common occurence in such cases.

It now becomes clear why a diencephalic diabetes is so extremely sensitive to emotional stress. When a patient suffering from the diencephalic form is kept at rest in hospital on an exactly fixed and carefully controlled diet and the fasting blood sugar is checked every day, the most surprising fluctuations are often observed. But when such patients are closely studied, watched and questioned by a clinical psychiatrist with whom a good rapport has been established, it is found that these fluctuations of the blood sugar are an exact reflection of the emotional ups or downs of the last twenty-four hours. We have gained the impression that when in such cases blood for the test is withdrawn by a technician whom the patient knows to be an expert with the needle, the blood sugar reading is lower than when the operation is performed by a technician at whose hands the patient has on previous occasions experienced clumsiness and pain of which he is frightened. The reason for this sensitivity of the blood-sugar level is that in a diencephalon which is already in a state of emergency any small additional stress produces an exaggerated rise in blood sugar. Similarly, psychotherapeutic or circumstantial release from anxiety brings about a sudden drop to the lowest level of the previously fixed blood-sugar range. In this process the pancreas is not concerned.

The brittle pancreatic diabetic, on the other hand, has a diencephalon which is peacefully going about its usual business. There is no state of psychic emergency. Compared with the speed of diencephalic mechanisms, the reactions of the insular apparatus are sluggish; they take no part in the lightning responses to danger. Insular action is largely determined by intestinal, rather than by diencephalic, happenings. The diencephalon of a pancreatic diabetic reacts in the usual normal way to strong emotional stimuli, but it is not nearly so sensitive nor so easily upset as it is in the diencephalic type of diabetes. It does not respond violently to minor emotional exigencies, as does the harassed diencephalon of the non-pancreatic diabetic.

Such views on diabetes are thus able to answer most of the criticisms levelled against the theories in which only the pancreatic factor was taken into practical clinical consideration.

It has been explained that the diencephalic form of diabetes may gradually change into the pancreatic form and that this process is hastened by the unwarranted use of insulin. In clinical practice, therefore, mixed forms are commonly seen. There is as yet no simple clinical test by which the two forms can be differentiated, and the estimation of the blood sugar is certainly no help. It is, however, of utmost practical importance to find some way of distinguishing one form from another and to know the extent to which one form prevails in a given case. There are a number of pointers in both directions, but they have no quantitative or absolute value. These pointers can best be summarized in the form of a table on p. 216.

Recently new drugs have been introduced into the treatment of diabetes. They have the advantage that they can be taken orally and do not have to be injected like insulin. It was very soon noticed that these drugs work best in obese diabetics and in those cases that have never had insulin. In cases which respond perfectly to insulin, they prove to be much less satisfactory. It was further discovered that their mode of action in controlling the blood sugar is entirely different from that of insulin. Further research indicated that the point of action of these drugs is the liver, where they decrease the immission of sugar into the blood-stream. Whether this action takes place in the liver-cells where sugar is stored in the form of *glycogen*, at the level of the liver's own nerve-centres, or in the diencephalon, has not yet been definitely established.

It follows that these drugs should be eminently suitable for the treatment of diencephalic diabetes and much less so for the treatment of the pancreatic form. If the pancreatic deficiency has been induced or made worse by the unwarranted use of high doses of insulin in originally diencephalic cases, the action of oral anti-diabetics is not wholly satisfactory. Watching the reaction of a diabetic to the new drugs can thus furnish some guidance to the prevalence of diencephalic or pancreatic mechanisms in that particular case.

FEATURES	DIENCEPHALIC OR STABLE FORM	PANCREATIC OR BRITTLE FORM
Time of onset	Usually later life	Usually early life
Mode of onset	Sudden	Very gradual
Cause of onset	Emotional stress	Uncertain
Tendency to progress	Little	Marked
Effect on body-weight	Increase (obesity)	Loss of weight
Response to insulin	Poor	Excellent
Response to oral anti-diabetics	Good	Unsatisfactory
Response to dietary changes	Little	Pronounced
Response to emotions	Marked	Little
Behaviour in pregnancy	Disappearance	Deterioration
Incidence of diabetic coma	Nil	High
Incidence of gangrene	Nil	High
Incidence of other circulatory disorders	Low	High
Incidence of diabetic retinal changes of the eye	Nil	High

Should the new drugs be found able to suppress the output of sugar from the liver well below normal requirements, this might lighten the pancreatic burden and thus have some beneficial effect even in pancreatic diabetes; but it is to be feared that if such action is pushed too far, irreversible damage to the liver-cells might eventually result. At the moment of writing this question still awaits clarification. In well-responding diencephalic cases no evidence of liver damage has so far been found, but it is obviously undesirable further to depress the immission of sugar from the liver when this is normal—as it almost certainly is in purely pancreatic diabetes, in which no diencephalic mechanism is directly involved.

It has been noted that in responsive cases large initial doses of the oral antidiabetic drugs are required to produce an immediate effect, but once a normal blood sugar has been established far smaller doses are able to maintain the blood sugar within the normal range. However, so great is the tenacity of a diencephalically fixed, elevated blood-sugar level that complete cures—in the sense that the patient can eat as he pleases and requires no further medication—have not yet been reported.

A complete cure will probably never be possible in those forms in which there is an organic deficiency of the insular apparatus. But the great discovery of insulin makes it possible to keep such patients in a perfectly normal metabolic equilibrium, and that is almost as good. Hitherto it was the diencephalic form for which little could be done, but the situation of such patients has been vastly improved by the new drugs. Yet it seemed disappointing that such a purely functional disorder as diencephalic diabetes could not be cured outright, and this led to a further study of the problem.

It has been said that for good evolutionary reasons pregnancy promptly relieves diencephalic diabetes during the period of gestation. It therefore seemed worthwhile to try the HCG+D method in these cases. The experiment appeared particularly indicated, as such diabetics are generally obese. It has long been known that a loss of overweight tends to improve the diabetic status. The trouble was that until the introduction of the HCG+D method it was extraordinarily difficult for an obese diabetic to lose weight before his diencephalic diabetes turned into a pancreatic one, in which case he would lose weight easily while his diabetes got worse. The actual deterioration of the pancreas is often masked by the temporary improvement of the blood sugar owing to dietary restriction. Thus when an obese patient has been struggling with his overweight for a long time and then suddenly finds that he is able to lose weight, this must always be viewed with concern, as it probably indicates the beginning of pancreatic deficiency. If weight could be reduced easily and without hardship or the danger of diabetic complications in the early stages before there is any deficiency of the insular apparatus, this would be of greatest value in the treatment of diencephalic cases.

The results of such experiments have been promising. Provided the insular apparatus is intact, the pregnancy-like condition which HCG+D induces brings the blood sugar down to normal in less than two weeks. The blood sugar comes down steadily day by day, and a drop from 3.5 grams of sugar per litre of blood to 1 gram per litre is usual.

Owing to the enormous fat-turnover in the body which takes place under HCG+D, one diabetic phenomenon had to be very carefully checked in the first experiments. In severe diabetes it often happens that fats cannot be normally metabolized. This gives rise to the formation of chemical compounds known as ketone-bodies, of which one is acetone. Ketone-bodies also appear in the blood during starvation and in the 'acidosis' of children. As diabetics are particularly liable to the formation of ketone-bodies, it was feared that the large fat-turnover and the starvation-diet of HCG+D might provoke this dangerous condition.

When non-diabetic obese patients are treated with HCG+D, it occasionally happens that some ketone-bodies are formed, particularly in patients who have previously been starving themselves; but this rise in ketone-bodies is never significant or dangerous and can be clinically ignored. Whether this would be so in obese diabetics was not known. Fortunately, it was found that when HCG+D was used in cases that were predominantly diencephalic, a clinically significant increase in ketone-bodies never occurred. In other words, the huge fat-turnover was managed by the body in the normal way.

It could be argued that putting any diabetic patient on a diet of 500 calories per day is bound to bring the blood sugar down.

When this was tried in obese diabetics without giving HCG, it was found that the blood sugar sometimes dropped to lower levels but it never became normal. The hunger of the patients increased intolerably, and in two to three days they began to feel very weak. They did not lose weight, and there was often an alarming increase in ketone-bodies. In no case could such treatment be continued for more than five days in hospitalized patients, by which time the condition of the patients made it imperative to interrupt the experiment. When HCG was added to the restricted diet, none of these symptoms occurred. In fact, there was a marked subjective and objective improvement in the patient's general condition which was felt and could be seen from day to day.

Further evidence that it was not only the diet but its association with HCG that produced the remarkably beneficial effect was furnished by the observation that though the diet remained unchanged throughout the treatment, the blood sugar decreased gradually and steadily. There was never the sudden drop in blood sugar which invariably occurs when a pancreatic diabetic is abruptly and severely restricted in his carbohydrate intake.

But not all cases of diabetes reacted to HCG+D in this way. In some patients the blood sugar came down gradually in a few days to a point which was still above the normal range and then stayed there, in spite of continued HCG+D and a further loss of superfluous fat. When this happened it was taken to indicate that the case was not purely diencephalic, but that there was already some pancreatic damage. A pancreatic factor is, of course, not influenced by HCG+D, nor can this method be used in purely pancreatic diabetes. The cases that retain some rise in blood sugar are the mixed forms in which, however, the diencephalic factor dominates the clinical picture. The point at which the blood sugar stays higher than normal though HCG+ D treatment is continued indicates the extent to which a pancreatic factor is involved.

Finally, there are some slightly overweight cases of diabetes in which HCG+D produces a rise in blood sugar in spite of the restricted diet. These patients continue to lose weight and feel perfectly well, but their diabetic status deteriorates. In such cases retinal diabetic changes which were present before treat-

ment are inclined to get worse if HCG+D is continued for more
than a week or so.

When HCG+D produces a rise in blood sugar, it is a clear
indication that the pancreatic factor dominates the clinical picture. If then insulin is added to the HCG+D it proves to be very
effective, but the dosage has to be steadily increased as long as
HCG+D is given. This is certainly not a satisfactory therapeutic procedure and should never be adopted.

These various responses of diabetes to HCG+D are a further
indication of how closely the induced pregnancy-like condition
resembles natural pregnancy. HCG+D dramatically improves
diencephalic and aggravates pancreatic diabetes just as does
pregnancy.

Under controlled conditions the HCG+D method of treating
obese diabetics furnishes a very reliable gauge for the degree to
which one form or the other is present in a given case. In
patients in whom there is as yet no pancreatic factor involved,
the HCG+D method is curative in the full sense of the word.
After HCG+D has rendered the weight of such patients normal,
they are no longer diabetic. They require no anti-diabetic medication and can eat as they please, provided weight is not regained. If for reasons set out in the preceding chapter the obesity
relapses, a further course of HCG+D always gets both weight
and blood sugar back to normal, provided no insulin has been
given in the meantime.

In modern urban man most cases of diabetes start diencephalically. Those that begin as a primary pancreatic deficiency
are usually juvenile forms. The causes of the latter condition are
not yet fully understood, but genetic factors possibly play an
important role. In primarily pancreatic cases there is never an
initiating emotional conflict, while in diencephalic cases the
precipitating emotional stress is usually found when expertly
looked for, though it is obviously insufficient to ask a patient
whether he is worried and then take 'no' for an answer.

In all overweight cases of diabetes that show diencephalic
features as set out in the table on page 216, HCG+D should
always be tried before insulin or oral anti-diabetic drugs are prescribed. If this were regularly done, the majority of diabetics could
be saved from developing the more dangerous and irreversible
pancreatic form and a high percentage could be cured outright.

Many of the complex mechanisms which animal experimentation has shown to be involved in the regulation of the blood sugar have here been purposely omitted. Many of these theoretical complexities are still controversial and have not as yet produced practical clinical results, whereas a better understanding of the psychosomatic factors concerned in diabetes has some eminently practical aspects.

Thus, once again the modern human cortex cannot be absolved from the blame for much diabetic suffering. If the cortex had not learned to suppress emotions at the threshold of consciousness, and if it had not surrounded man with artifacts which prevent him from reacting to danger and fear with flight, the diencephalic type of diabetes would not exist.

9

Disorders of the Bones and of the Muscles

WILD ANIMALS hardly ever suffer from rheumatic diseases. It is therefore pertinent to inquire why only man should be afflicted with these painful disorders. One reason is probably that man distinguishes himself from all other mammals by his erect posture. In the evolutionary time-scale his up-ending was a very recent event and cannot be compared with the two-leggedness of birds, who acquired this trait more than a hundred million years ago.

Man's upright posture developed out of sitting in the trees, and the first mammals that walked fully erect were the Ape-Men—the Pithecines—that evolved less than a million years ago. These early men lived in open country, their only means of escape was running, they could not elude an enemy by swinging in the boughs. Their ancestors, recently descended out of the trees, ambled over the ground as the apes still do to-day using their knuckles for support; they could stand on two feet, but they probably could not run on their feet alone. Over thousands of years the ability to run was slowly acquired by natural selection. Those individuals in whom mutations provided legs that were better adapted for running away from grass-fires and dangerous beasts survived, while the clumsier forms perished.

In the trees a distant threat could be discovered by swinging up into higher branches, but in the open plains a greater visual range could be achieved only by raising the head as far above the ground as possible. The added safety furnished by a head held high must have been an important factor in the vertical stretching of the human body.

The early mammalian evolution of man's ancestors did not

prepare him for this sudden up-ending, as the mammalian body was designed for four-legged life in the trees. The basic pattern of its structure was most unsuitable for the erect posture. To become erect the body had to undergo innumerable changes in its skeleton and its muscles and, with the possible exception of the lower arms and hands, there is neither bone nor muscle in man's body that does not show signs of recent adjustment to the new posture.

The head became more mobile and needed complicated muscles to support and move it in every direction; the neck became longer. In a four-legged animal the spine carries hardly any weight, but in man the whole weight of head, arms and trunk bears down upon the lower vertebrae, the hips, the knees and the feet. In quadrupeds there is no pressure on the soft discs that lie like cushions between the single vertebrae, but in man the pressure on these discs is enormous and so they had to become more firmly anchored, while their fibrous capsule needed to be greatly strengthened. Huge masses of back-muscles were required to hold the flexible spine erect and yet leave it mobile in the neck and the lumbar region. Man had to acquire muscular buttocks, thighs and calves to carry the unnaturally poised weight of his upright body. Great changes had to take place in his knee and hip joints; he needed a sturdy heel and a thick layer of strong, springy fat-tissue in the soles of his feet to manage the new distribution of his weight.

All these developments may have evolved for the single purpose of providing the greater safety which lay in the ability to run and to hold the head high above the ground. This new evolutionary trend proceeded rapidly and satisfactorily; had it continued it would have led to stronger, taller and faster men than we are to-day. Some negro tribes that live in open country such as the Masai have gone further in this direction than other men, but generally the new evolutionary trend lost much of its importance when culture started to provide entirely new methods of defence and safety.

Man's cultural achievements stopped the process of natural selection. The result is that in modern man the bodily adjustment to the erect posture is by no means complete. Man's skeleton and muscles have remained particularly vulnerable at all those points that were forced to undergo the most radical, and as yet not fully completed, changes. It is in these points that modern rheumatic disorders are especially liable to occur.

Bones can adjust themselves rapidly in form and strength to mechanical requirements; tendons and fibrous ligaments can do this only to some extent; cartilage, the gristle which covers the bones where they form joints, adjusts to pressure very poorly. The large skeletal muscles are unable of their own accord to make any adjustment to mechanical needs; they can only develop in response to a cortical demand and under cortical supervision in the process known as training.

Commercial body-builders—Atlas-men and their ilk—know the importance of cortical supervision for muscular development and achieve surprising results by making their clients stand in front of a mirror closely watching the contraction and relaxation of the muscles they are 'building'—which means that the training is carefully directed by the cortex. Skeletal muscles waste away when they are not cortically stimulated into contraction.

In lower animals that do not have a highly developed cortex, muscular movement is managed by the hind-brain—that part of the brain-stem which is known as the cerebellum. It is only in higher animals such as birds and mammals that the cortex has become superimposed upon the cerebellum to the extent that the cerebellum can co-ordinate but no longer initiate voluntary movement.

Muscles have two forms of contraction. One is directed by the cortex and results in voluntary movement; it is quick acting, shortens the muscle and consumes considerable energy. The other—called muscular tone—is involuntary and does not produce movement, but it puts up a strong resistance to relaxation.

The degree of muscular tone is probably controlled by the diencephalon, and an abnormally high tone expresses itself as tension. In a physical emergency the muscular tension or tone is increased. Increasing the tone of the muscles is basically an energy-saving device, because a muscle with a high tone can perform a faster and more powerful voluntary contraction than a flaccid one.

In animals there is thus a perfect co-operation between

muscular tone and voluntary contraction, but in modern man this collaboration has ceased to serve its purpose. Modern man still reacts to fear by raising the tone of his muscles, but his cortex no longer makes use of this in the physical exertion of escape because the artificial environment with which he has surrounded himself makes escape unnecessary. Modern man, therefore, is left with a useless tension which he registers as pain or discomfort. When an animal reaches safety after running away from a threat it immediately calls off the emergency-reaction and the muscles relax their tone, but modern man continues his emergency-reaction as long as the fear persists.

Rheumatic conditions are much more common in modern urban man than among primitive races. This appears to be due to the growing gap between urban man's diencephalic reactions and his artificial cortical behaviour.

Apart from injuries and infections with which this study is not concerned, there are thus evolutionary factors which have a bearing upon rheumatic disease. Man's bones and muscles have had neither the time nor the benefit of natural selection to make a complete adaptation to his recent up-ending; they are just able to support the body; but whenever additional pressure is brought to bear on joints that have undergone recent changes, the joints suffer damage. Additional joint-pressure may be due to obesity, continuous, increased muscular effort or prolonged high muscular tone. Obesity, hard manual labour and abnormal muscular tension are all post-Neolithic phenomena almost unknown to Stone-Age Man.

In obesity excess fat is slowly accumulated, and this gives the muscles and the skeleton time to adjust themselves to the new situation. Moerover, the obese patient takes the weight off his joints when he sits or lies down. At night the strained joint-surfaces are given a chance to recover from the wear and tear of the day. It is because the abnormal strain develops slowly and intermittently that the rheumatic disorders of the obese are not so severe as might be expected, though they are very common.

Just as obesity is almost certainly a post-Neolithic disease, continued hard manual labour did not exist before man learned to work in his fields, to build houses and to use metals on a large scale. Animals in flight and primitive man also put a heavy strain on their joints when the muscles contract against a resistance and thereby squeeze the joint-surfaces together, but such exertions are occasional and of short duration. Exertions of the kind performed by primitive man, even when extreme, never lead to the abnormal tissue reactions which are the cause of most joint-disorders.

It is the continually repeated strain from adolescence into old age that eventually causes damage. Yet here again the effects of heavy manual labour, for which man's body was not built and to which it has never had a chance to adapt itself, causes far less joint-destruction than one might expect on purely mechanical grounds. Again the reason is that a night's sleep brings regular relaxation, enabling repair-mechanisms to go to work. Finally, hard manual work is usually preceded by a long period of training.

If obesity came on suddenly, if hard labour were performed without previous training and if in both cases the pressure on the joint-surfaces were not interrupted in sleep, the articular disorders so commonly associated with obesity and heavy manual labour would be far more severe than they are.

The third way in which an abnormal strain can be put on joint-surfaces is by a sudden rise in the tone of the muscles which surround and move the joint. This type of abnormal pressure coming from tense muscles is much more dangerous than the other two forms, because muscular tone can be raised very suddenly in response to fear. The increased tone appears to be produced by the diencephalon and is beyond cortical control; therefore, a diencephalically clenched muscle cannot be relaxed by an effort of will. Most serious of all is the fact that an abnormal tone is not relaxed during sleep; there is thus no let-up in pressure on the joint-surfaces.

This type of strain may therefore produce particularly severe joint damage and is possibly the most important factor in crippling arthritis. The excessive muscular tone starts a vicious cycle in which fear causes the initial rise in tone; this leads to painful damage, while the pain in turn leads to increased tone as a normal reaction to the need for immobilization, causing still further damage to the joint. It is in this sense that so many diseases of the joints may be said to be psychosomatically initiated.

The crippling caused by a diseased joint is to a great extent due to muscular tone and not to the bony or cartilaginous destruction only. This is shown by the fact that hormones (which will be discussed in the next section) greatly increase the mobility of damaged joints by their action on diencephalic regulations and not by repairing structural damage.

These mechanisms can be well illustrated by discussing some disorders of the spinal column. The spine consists of a row of vertebrae separated by springy cushions known as discs, and it is held together by ligaments and large muscle-masses that run down the length of the back. These muscles are particularly powerful in the lumbar region, and an increase of tension in the muscles of the small of the back causes a pain known as lumbago, of which there are several forms.

Some people feel a slight back-ache when they have been standing or bending for a long time. An X-ray examination often shows a widening of the edges of the vertebrae—called lipping. Lipping is a bone-reaction to increased pressure in the intervertebral joints caused by obesity, the habitual carrying of heavy weights or nervous tension which has increased the tone of the back-muscles.

The lipping of the vertebrae does not in itself cause pain. It is often found by chance when a patient who has never had lumbago is X-rayed for other reasons. Even patients who suffer from this type of back-ache have long periods in which they are free of pain, though no change in the bone has taken place.

When a patient suffers from a lumbar pain after bending, it is usually because he is unused to this posture. His back-muscles tire rapidly; yet the erect human body is so accustomed to the use of muscular tone rather than voluntary contraction to maintain the vertical position that in this case too it replaces contraction by increasing tone as the muscles tire.

A voluntary contraction can be released instantly, but not so muscular tone. It is for this reason that when a bending person begins to feel pain in his back, he finds that as soon as he stretches the pain gets much worse. If he laughs off the pain and works the crick out of his back by moving the spine the pain disappears in a few seconds, because his cortical attitude allows the now no longer necessary reaction to be called off. If, on the other hand, the patient becomes alarmed, the clenching changes from a postural reaction into a normal reaction to fear, which means that the muscle cannot let go. The pain then persists; this increases the apprehensiveness, which in turn increases the tone, and once again a vicious cycle is established. Having had such an attack, the anxious patient grows fearful of bending; he avoids it as much as possible, and when bending is unavoidable the movement is performed by muscles which are already in a state of abnormal tension.

A different type of lumbago comes on as a sudden violent attack, making movement almost impossible and often occurring for no apparent reason. Yet there must be a sound reason for such a sudden violent pain, and it may be the following.

The arms of the higher primates have undergone little change during several million years. In them tone and voluntary contraction are well co-ordinated, but in the recently enlarged lumbar muscles tone and voluntary movement are not so well adjusted to each other. It is thus possible for the cortex to order a movement which is too brusque for a tone which has been abnormally increased in response to fear or anxiety. The result is that a voluntary movement made under such conditions can tear a few muscle fibres that are unable to yield to the bending of the spine. As long as there is no abnormally increased tone the movement can be performed without damage, but in an involuntarily tightened muscle the same movement may lead to damage, because the muscle is unable to relax sufficiently.

If the damage is fairly extensive the pain will be felt immediately, but if the lesion is microscopic it may not be noticed until the next morning when, upon awakening, the patient finds that he can hardly get out of bed. During the night repair of the damage has begun; there is a local inflammation and a further involuntary clenching of the affected area in order to ensure the immobility in which healing can proceed most rapidly, and so every time the patient tries to stretch his back-muscle by bending the pain is excruciating.

A small tear in a large muscle will heal rapidly—within three to four days—and if there is no anxiety connected with the condition the muscle relaxes and the pain is gone. But all too often there is a build-up of anxiety around such an 'attack' of lumbago. A cortically induced voluntary contraction is gradually added to the tone, which cannot give way owing to persisting fear, and the patient continues to hold his back rigid.

When a joint has been immobilized for a number of days it becomes stiff and the first movements are painful. In many cases of lumbago the patient is frightened of this initial pain, because he fears that it may precipitate a recurrence of the severe pain he has just suffered. The result is that the back stays rigid and becomes more painful when movement is attempted.

This never happens to the hand. An injury to the fingers may make it necessary to keep them immobilized for a certain period. When then the injury has healed and the dressings have been removed, the patient is told to exercise his fingers until normal mobility is re-established. At first, every time the finger-joints are moved there is considerable pain, but the patient persists in performing such exercises, as he is fully conscious of the fact that stiffened fingers would be useless to him. In this way he soon gets back the normal use of his hand.

With his back-muscles man is not always ready to do this— he is too frightened. The intervertebral discs, already carrying a weight which is close to their limit of endurance, are thus subjected to an additional and prolonged muscular squeeze and may in rare cases eventually slip or rupture. A disc that protrudes into the narrow bony channel in which the soft spinal cord lies compresses the nerves of the spinal cord, and this gives rise to serious disturbances in the lower part of the body.

That a slipped or herniated disc may be due only to a clenching of the back-muscles is suggested by the fact that in about 60 per cent of such cases, operated after X-ray and other investigations have shown a compression of the spinal cord to exist, no abnormality is found when the spinal canal is opened. The explanation is that the general anaesthesia in which the operation is performed eliminates all the tone and all voluntary contraction. This complete, artificially induced relaxation of the back-muscles allows the disc to slip back into its normal position.

The reason general anaesthesia alone is usually unable to cure a slipped disc is that as soon as the patient regains consciousness the old tension re-establishes itself. However, it would certainly be worth trying a short but deep general anaesthesia before surgery of the spinal column is resorted to in those very rare cases in which *all* other methods have failed.

Patients suffering from lumbago are usually advised immobility. They are asked to sleep on a wooden board, they are given corsets and forbidden physical exertion, and they are thereby alarmed instead of being calmed. The results of this approach to a basically psychosomatic problem are, of course, not encouraging, and it is at this point that the much maligned bone-setter, osteopath or manipulative surgeon triumphantly enters.

The manipulative surgeon makes an authoritative, clear mechanical diagnosis by stating that two vertebrae are out of alignment and that all pain will cease as soon as they are put back into place. A bone-setter would require the strength of a gorilla if he were to 're-set' vertebrae with his bare hands, but what he does do is psychosomatically unimpeachable and therefore often yields brilliant results. The manipulator at once allays all the vague fears and terrors engendered by the hemming and hawing of orthodox physicians and surgeons, and this positive clarity has immediate diencephalic repercussions—a sigh of relief and relaxation. He then frankly informs his patient that he is going to manipulate his bones. That, too, is appreciated. The patient's attitude is: 'I'm prepared for anything if only it will relieve my misery', and this is the perfect psychological attitude for the forceful stretching of over-tense muscles.

The manipulation of the spine consists essentially in stretching muscles by using the arms and legs as a lever. The manipulator therefore does to the back-muscles just what patients will themselves do to fingers stiffened by prolonged immobility, though they are usually unable to do this to their back. When the stiffened back is carefully, yet forcefully, mobilized in the right psychological atmosphere, the manipulation brings immediate relief. The patient is then told to move freely, and the diencephalon can call off its emergency reaction because the cortex has now been given an interpretation about which it can reason.

A good manipulator knows from experience, from the feel of muscular resistance and from the way the patient behaves whether he has been able to produce the right psychological atmosphere between himself and the patient. If he has any doubts in this direction he desists from forceful manipulation, for were he to persist before a diencephalic relaxation has taken place he could do more harm than good. His competence is to induce a cortical and diencephalic relaxation by his words, his personality and his manner and then to overcome the stiffness of prolonged immobilization by manipulation—a process which may be slightly painful, but perfectly harmless when the muscles are already relaxing. It is not his duty to break up an abnormally high tone by force, as an abnormal tone should be reduced by psychological methods such as allaying fear and inspiring confidence.

Many orthopaedic surgeons are frank enough to admit the surprising results often achieved by osteopaths; some try to use a similar technique, but they usually make the error of doing this in deep general anaesthesia. They think that all that is necessary is to widen the gap between two vertebrae and entirely neglect the psychic factor which is, usually, at the root of the disorder. In general anaesthesia the enormous advantage of the patient's cortical and diencephalic participation is lost; the patient suffers the additional anguish which general anaesthesia always entails and cannot immediately thereafter take up his bed and walk as he should to get the best results.

In the foregoing the spinal column has been used to illustrate the psychosomatic factor in various forms of lumbago, but similar mechanisms play an important role in the causation of diseases in other joints. If treatment were from the outset primarily directed towards relieving the excessive tone of the muscles surrounding the afflicted joint, progress into a crippling articular disease might—to say the least—be delayed.

Skeletal abnormalities of the feet such as the inward turning of the big toe and the hammer-toe are seemingly due to unsuitable footwear. An inherited tendency to sunken arches or flat feet can become manifest through overweight (fat or pregnancy), the habitual carrying of heavy burdens or long hours of standing. That prolonged standing is more liable to produce undesirable effects than prolonged walking is possibly because

human feet were, by their evolution, formed for running and
not for standing. Pre-Neolithic Man had no reason to stand for
long hours and spent most of his life lying down, squatting on
his haunches, walking or running. There were no vocations that
called for standing still—such as that of the herdsman or the
guard against the inroads of neighbouring clans.

Man has the habit of not distributing his weight evenly on
both feet when he stands still, though this would seem to be the
most sensible way to spare his feet. When man stands still for a
long time, he shifts his weight alternately from one leg to the
other as if he were walking in slow-motion. This too suggests
that walking was an earlier evolutionary achievement than
standing still.

Hormones and Rheumatism

It is an old observation that when a women suffering from
arthritis becomes pregnant the rheumatic pain is greatly diminished as long as the pregnancy lasts. To some extent this is due
to the absence of diencephalic flight-reactions during pregnancy.
Fear and anxiety do not raise the tone of the muscles as they
do in the non-pregnant body. There is thus less pressure on the
deformed joint-surfaces. However, the relief from pain is so
dramatic and often so complete that the muscular mechanism
alone seems insufficient to account for the phenomenon.

Some years ago it was discovered that the hormone known
as ACTH is able to relieve rheumatic pain almost completely.
This hormone has already been mentioned in the chapter on
obesity, where it was explained that ACTH stands for Adreno-
Cortico-Tropic Hormone, that the hormone is produced in the
anterior lobe of the pituitary gland and that its function is to
stimulate the activity of the adrenal rind or cortex—the outer
covering of the adrenal or suprarenal gland.

The pituitary and the adrenals have in common the fact that
they both consist of two quite different structures that are also
functionally separate. The anterior pituitary lobe and the
adrenal rind develop in the embryo out of glandular tissue,
while the posterior pituitary lobe and the adrenal medulla
originate out of nervous tissue. There are direct nervous connections between the diencephalon and the posterior pituitary
lobe, while nervous impulses initiate the secretion of the hor-

mone adrenalin from the adrenal medulla in the emergency of fear. The bodily regulations which are managed by certain diencephalic nerve centres via the posterior pituitary lobe and the adrenal medulla are largely concerned with reactions to fear and the survival of the individual in an emergency. During pregnancy this whole system appears to be damped.

The other endocrine system consisting of diencephalic chemical stimulants acting on the anterior pituitary lobe via a small portal system and the secretion from the adrenal cortex is concerned with a large number of vital permanent functions particularly directed towards such biological manifestations as growth, sex and pregnancy. In pregnancy the activity of this system is stimulated, and one of the many effects of this stimulation is a reduction of skeletal pain. It is not until the onset of labour pains that the posterior pituitary hormonal system again comes to the fore.

There are definite reasons why the suppression of skeletal pain is important during pregnancy. Like all pain, skeletal pain is a warning device and leads to disuse and immobility of the joints involved, the immobility being achieved by an increase in the tone of the muscles surrounding the joint.

In a four-legged animal the resulting compression of the space between the bones forming the joint has no serious consequences, because the joints of quadrupeds carry comparatively far less weight than most human joints. There is thus in animals a wide margin between compression which merely immobilizes and compression so great that it causes damage to the surface of the joint. In upright man this margin is very small, so that additional weight combined with abnormal muscular pressure is very liable to cause damage.

During pregnancy there is a sharp increase in the weight which the lower joints have to carry. It would therefore be particularly dangerous if pain in these joints caused a clenching of the muscles and a reduced mobility as a reaction to this pain, as this would render such joints particularly liable to permanent damage. In pregnancy the absence of pain and of the usual diencephalic fear-reactions leaves the joints mobile even when they are under additional strain.

The female skeleton has to make many adjustments to the weight-problem of pregnancy and the mechanics of childbirth.

Human pregnancy requires a change in spinal posture; the ligaments which hold the front of the pelvis and the sacro-iliac joints together are loosened so as to make a little more room for the foetal head to pass; the hips, the knees and the arches of the feet are under an additional strain to which they must respond. One would expect such adjustments to be excruciatingly painful, yet the pregnant woman feels little or nothing of them; she does not clench the muscles concerned and thereby avoids the danger of damage to her joints. She is protected from developing pain or arthritis in her joints by the stimulation of anterior pituitary-adrenocortical interaction.

The exact mechanism whereby the pituitary hormone ACTH eliminates skeletal pain is still unknown, but it does seem likely that in pregnancy it is the placental chorionic gonadotrophin which, acting on the diencephalon, produces an increased secretion of ACTH from the anterior pituitary lobe.

When the HCG+D method discussed in previous chapters is used in overweight patients suffering from rheumatic disease, a pregnancy-like condition is produced and rheumatic pains are relieved, in much the same way as in real pregnancy. This phenomenon is theoretically very interesting, though it does not furnish a practical approach to the problem of arthritis, as the pain returns as soon as the HCG+D treatment is stopped. Nevertheless, overweight arthritic patients are extremely grateful for the relief obtained during the weeks in which this treatment can be continued.

A further advantage of HCG+D is that treatment with ACTH or its synthetic and safer substitutes—cortisone and its modern derivatives—can be stopped during the treatment. As cortisone and particularly ACTH are hormones that are dangerous in excessive doses, the possibility of being able temporarily to suspend their administration without causing the patient to suffer pain is very welcome. Moreover, after treatment with HCG+D it is often possible to obtain the same relief with much smaller doses of cortisone than were previously necessary to keep the patient comfortable.

The relief of arthritic pain achieved by the HCG+D method is evidently not due to the mechanical effect of losing weight, as it occurs long before a significant weight reduction has taken place; nor is it due to the simple administration of chorionic gonadotrophin, as merely injecting this hormone has no such effect. Arthritic pain is only relieved dramatically when small daily doses of chorionic gonadotrophin are combined with a calorically deficient diet in the HCG+D method. There is some reason to suppose that the mechanism which causes the relief in the pregnancy-like condition evoked by HCG+D is identical with the hormonal mechanism responsible for the same phenomenon in real pregnancy.

Whenever overweight makes it possible to apply the HCG+D method for the relief of arthritic pain, there is the further advantage over the use of cortisone and its derivatives that there is no danger of adrenocortical degeneration, water retention, etc.

One reason why the administration of ACTH may have untoward side effects is possibly that the body has no means of storing this hormone. ACTH goes into action as soon as it is produced in the anterior pituitary or is injected, and it is very rapidly broken down in the blood into inactive components. The pregnant or non-pregnant body produces ACTH as required, and while the production is constant it at no time exceeds the requirements of a moment.

Such a fine adjustment cannot be achieved when the hormone is injected or, as in the case of cortisone, given by mouth. To obtain a therapeutic result the dose administered must always be in excess of what is needed at the time of administration. Otherwise, the effect does not last until the next dose. This 'shock treatment' must be extremely upsetting to the finely-tuned hormonal and nervous interplay in the body. In pregnancy and in the pregnancy-like condition evoked by HCG+D there are no staccato, unilateral hormonal impulses, and this probably accounts for the fact that the anterior pituitary stimulation thus achieved has no undesirable side effects.

When all pain is removed from an arthritic joint by the use of a local anaesthetic and if the patient is then told to use the diseased joint freely, the inflammatory process may rapidly get worse, owing to the increased mechanical stress which painlessness permits. This, however, does not happen when the joint-pain is hormonally controlled in pregnancy or by hormone therapy. Evidently the hormonal action is not merely one of reducing pain but also diminishes abnormal tissue-reactions to mechanical pressure. In pregnancy this protection of the joint-surfaces is obviously of utmost biological importance.

Gout

The many forms of rheumatic disease which plague modern man require continual re-classification as our understanding of their various causes grows. Among rheumatologists classification is argued with asperity, because in a field in which so many fundamental facts are still unknown views are apt to vary widely. Gout is not generally included in these disputations, because it is caused by a clearly definable—though not fully explained—disorder of protein metabolism. In gout damage to the joints is caused by uric acid being deposited in the cartilage which covers the joint surfaces. Uric acid is a halfway product in the breakdown of aminoacids, the chemical bricks out of which protein molecules are built.

The abnormal tendency to deposit uric acid in the cartilage of joints—but also elsewhere; for instance, in the rim of the outer ear—is almost certainly inherited; but as in the case of obesity, diabetes and many other diseases, the inherited disposition need not become clinically manifest unless other factors bring it out in overt disease.

Among such provocative factors modern nutrition seems to be of great importance in the causation of gout. The omnivorous human body can utilize proteins, carbohydrates and fats as fuel to maintain body temperature and to supply the muscular motor; but for those purposes it prefers to use fats and carbohydrates, as these have a higher caloric value, are more readily broken down into chemically useful compounds and are more easily stored as reserves than proteins. Thus when nutrition offers the body a superabundance of carbohydrates, fats and proteins, the carbohydrates and fats are consumed, leaving a useless surplus of protein after the needs of protein replacement in the structures of the body have been fulfilled.

In persons having a latent inherited disposition to gout the proteins are normally digested and absorbed as aminoacids, but the further breakdown of superfluous aminoacids is not completed in the usual way. Instead of being burned up, half-way products continue to circulate in the blood as an excess of uric acid, which may then become deposited in hard crystalline lumps known as a tophus in the joints. As long as the body is amply stocked with starches, sugars and fats it does not need the small deposits of chemical energy stored in the tophi.

There would thus seem to be two ways of preventing the clinical symptoms of gout arising in a person predisposed to the disease by heredity. One would be to cut the protein-intake down to the barest minimum compatible with health and the other to give a diet so low in fats and carbohydrates that the body is forced to use all its surplus protein as a source of energy.

The Neolithic institution of regular meals may also play a role in making an abnormal disposition to gout become manifest in disease of the joints. The sudden influx of mixed nourishment from the intestinal tract, usually far in excess of the requirements at the moment of feeding, enables the body to cover all its nutritional wants and to store fat and sugar as reserves, but this leaves it with a protein surplus which it cannot accommodate so quickly. Finally, modern man's habit of cooking his meat enables his digestive processes to break it down into assimilable aminoacids much faster than if the meat were eaten raw. This puts an extra burden on modern human protein metabolism for which the body has had no evolutionary preparation.

During the First World War the severe lack of food spread over a number of years in Germany led to the almost complete disappearance of gout. Similarly, food restrictions imposed in the United Kingdom during the Second World War considerably lowered the incidence of clinical gout. This shows that though there appears to be an inherited factor, the clinical disease can still be cured. As will be explained further on, the combination of fear and hunger, as may occur during war, is more likely to cure gout than hunger alone.

The joint most commonly affected by gout is the base of the big toe in the ball of the foot. It is difficult to understand why this should be so. One might be tempted to connect this favoured localization with the enormous mechanical strain to which these joints are exposed when, in walking or running, they alternately carry the whole weight of the body. But that would not explain the other favoured localization in the rim of the ear where there is no mechanical problem. It seems more likely that circulatory difficulties are involved in the problem of localization.

Gout is far more common in men than in women, in whom the disease never becomes manifest until after the menopause, while in men it often begins at a much earlier age. In patients suffering from gout the amount of uric acid found in the blood when they are fasting is raised higher than normal, but there is no direct relationship between the fasting uric-acid level and the severity of clinical symptoms. Patients with an abnormally raised blood uric-acid level may never suffer from uric acid deposits in their joints, while others may be severely ill with less circulating uric acid—evidently an inherited trait to form tophi is necessary.

The disease which we call gout consists of two clinically distinct phenomena. One is the steady and continuous process of laying down deposits of uric acid as long as nutritional habits make this necessary. The other clinical entity is a sudden violent and extremely painful reaction of the tissues surrounding the uric acid deposits—usually in the form of a very tender reddening and swelling around the base of the big toe.

Why the slow continuous process of depositing uric acid in a tophus should suddenly flare up is not immediately comprehensible. In the acute attack the body seems to be treating the tophus as if it were a foreign body of which it is trying to rid itself by surrounding it with an inflammatory reaction.

Patients suffering from gout are inclined to attribute an acute attack to something they have eaten; yet there is little evidence to support these notions. One usually finds that on other occasions the same food or drink had no such repercussions. It has never been scientifically proved that foods high in nucleic acids, such as sweetbreads, liver, kidneys, etc., or port wine and untold other dietary items, are really of importance in causing gout. This is merely assumed to be the case. As in common indigestion, it is probably *post hoc* and not *propter hoc* that an attack occurs. The only sure fact is that all-round over-eating and obesity are dangerous to persons genetically predisposed to gout.

On the other hand, observant patients can often tell a few days before that they are about to have an attack. They feel generally unwell, irritable and very short-tempered; they lose their appetite and have minor digestive and circulatory disorders. These symptoms strongly suggest a diencephalic mechanism and are reminiscent of the normal reactions to fear or anxiety.

In the chapter on obesity it was mentioned that in a state of emergency the body is better able to use abnormal reserves than when there is no danger and that this is why during war or famine excess weight is shed more easily than by dietary restrictions voluntarily imposed under otherwise normal conditions. As fear abolishes hunger and appetite, it is important that the body should be able to draw freely upon its reserves in an emergency; that is why prolonged terror opens up deposits of energy that are otherwise locked away, be they in the form of fat or of uric acid.

The complete chemical breakdown of uric acid yields a small amount of energy, and a tophus is therefore also an energy reserve, albeit an abnormal one. The only way the body can mobilize this reserve is by surrounding it with an inflammatory reaction, and this it proceeds to do after a few days of emotional stress.

Modern man often continues to eat in spite of a lack of appetite, because his presumptuous cortex thinks it knows better and must ignore diencephalic promptings. The cortex thinks it must force down more food into an already over-stuffed body to 'keep up strength'. Of such cortical antics the diencephalon is unaware and goes about its ancient emergency regulations as it has been doing for millions of years, paying no attention to cortical misunderstanding.

As long as excessive food is being eaten it is only an emergency reaction to fear which can cause the mobilization of a uric acid deposit. The only other mechanism which can bring about this mobilization is a deficient intake of protein or a deficient intake of fats and carbohydrates, which forces the body to use protein as fuel just as it does during famine.

If the view that the acute inflammation of a gouty joint is basically a healing process is correct, it would mean that these attacks could eventually cure the disease, provided the cortex took the diencephalic hint and stopped stuffing down more food than is demanded by real hunger. Such a view might satisfactorily explain a further observation: when an overweight patient who is suffering from gout is treated with the HCG+D method, it usually happens that he suffers a severe acute attack after about ten days' treatment and from then on remains free of attacks as long as he does not regain weight, regardless of what he eats after the HCG+D treatment.

In gout, as in obesity, abnormal deposits of fuel are locked away and there are only three ways in which they can be physiologically tapped. One is by the emergency reaction of terror, another is pregnancy or its artificially induced counterpart—the HCG+D treatment—and the third is starvation. In gout the pregnancy-like condition and the associated nutritional deficiency of the 500-calorie diet produce favourable results which are greatly superior to those achieved by dieting alone.

Gout may occur in patients who are neither heavy eaters nor overweight. As in diabetes, there seem to be a fat-type and a lean-type of gout, the latter usually being far more severe than the former though less subject to acute attacks. In the lean-type the tophi can grow to enormous size, break through the skin and cause permanent crippling. It would seem that in them the genetic factor dominates, while in the fat-type diencephalic mechanisms play a greater role.

The overweight patient who suffers from frequent acute attacks of gout is more often than not above average intelligence and usually has some deep-seated emotional problem. When a searching inquiry is made into the emotional status of such patients to find out what happened some days prior to the onset of an attack, the possibility of a connection between attack and emotions is brusquely and often blusteringly rejected. Yet the very bluntness with which the suggestion is brushed aside raises suspicion in the mind of the psychiatrically trained interrogator; if he then tactfully persists, it is extraordinary how much emotional material is usually produced. The expert interviewer frequently finds so much more than he hoped for that there may be some difficulty in distinguishing the basic emotional structure from the emotional incident responsible for an acute attack which occurred as a fear-reaction, in which the diencephalon orders a mobilization of reserves.

It seems as if the generally high intelligence of patients suffering from gout enables them to cover an incredible amount of emotional turbulence under a deceptively placid exterior. They are also experts at shunting an unwary psychiatrist off the mainline on to a dead-end track.

There are so many analogies between diabetes, obesity and gout that the latter condition could well have been discussed in the chapters dealing with metabolic disorders. The fact that gout manifests itself chiefly in the skeleton made its inclusion in the present chapter seem preferable.

With but few exceptions all the diseases loosely grouped together as rheumatic have their roots in the brain. Modern cortical activity has completely lost touch with the much older diencephalic mechanisms which the cortex disdainfully ignores. When the artifacts of human culture began to make the survival of the unfit—unfit, that is, for wild life—possible, the cortex eliminated the natural selection which would have better adjusted man's skeleton to the upright posture.

As the muscularly weak, those of short stature and poor runners are now no longer weeded out, and as strength, height and speed no longer determine sexual selection, there seems to be little hope that the adjustment of man's skeleton to the upright posture will ever be completed. The margin between healthy and diseased joints will therefore remain small.

Man's only hope of ridding himself of many of his joint-disorders lies in his ability to keep his weight down to normal, to replace hard physical labour by machinery and above all to acquire a better understanding of how his body reacts to fears which his cortical censorship forces him to bottle up instead of eliminate by admitting them and reasoning about them.

10

Disorders of Sex

IN TIMID wild animals danger as reported by the senses renders copulation impossible, because the process of natural selection has weeded out individuals that continued to copulate in the presence of a mortal threat. Only those who instinctively avoid or interrupt sexual activity and flee at the slightest sign of danger survive and pass on the incompatibility of sex and fear to their progeny. The importance of this trait for the survival of a defenceless species is obvious, and it is still fully preserved in modern man and woman.

In timid mammals it is the female who decides the moment at which she will permit the male to mount, and she is responsible for the safety of the couple until she submits to the male, thus leaving him free to proceed with his fighting or wooing. The moment the female is covered her responsibility ceases, and the male raised on her back takes over the duty of the sentinel. In wild life this arrangement precludes anything akin to rape or coercion, which exist only in man.

Female responsibility for safety and freedom from disturbance before the act expresses itself in the modern human female as shame, bashfulness, modesty, etc. These emotions are a cortical elaboration of the instinctive fear that the security in which alone the human sexual act is safely and satisfactorily accomplished has not been attained. Only the genuine emotion of shame is an expression of fear; coyness is a form of courting.

Apart from man, few mammals copulate face to face as do aquatic forms such as whales, manatees, etc., who use their buoyancy as support. Man's ancestors were forced to copulate in the prone position only after they had forfeited the support furnished by their forelimbs. In the prone, face-to-face position the male lost his ability to keep a watchful eye on his environment and was thus obliged to depend for safety only on hearing.

Even in civilized man the ear remains alert, and a sound unaccounted for is felt to be grossly disturbing during coitus.

It is strange that eminently diurnal man has relegated a function as important as sex to the darkness of the night and that his sex-life has become cortically associated with sleep. Possibly the stretching of the human body, the need for support, the uselessness of the eyes in man's coital posture and perhaps the regular post-Neolithic chores which he imposed upon himself during the day contributed to this biological peculiarity.

It is highly improbable that Paleolithic Man connected the sex act with pregnancy and childbirth, just as he was almost certainly unaware of the inevitability of death. These facts he only learned when the Neolithic revolution gave him the knowledge that drove him out of the Paleolithic Garden of Eden where he knew nothing to be ashamed of. The Biblical legend that the Neolithic female gained this awful knowledge from an animal is probably true, though she may have learned it from the domestic animals she tended rather than from that embodiment of evil, the tree-serpent, which was the most dangerous foe of man's arboreal ancestors.

Man has thus only recently discovered that Nature uses the sex-instinct to propagate the species, and of this discovery his diencephalon is completely unaware. It would be well if those who believe that man must confine his sexual activities to propagation would remember that to do this is not a law of nature. In wild life the male has no lust to propagate; there is only the sex-urge, which is satisfied regardless of whether this leads to conception or not.

In the broad sense that the sex-instinct is one which desires intimate contact with another living creature, it exists from birth in a vague, attenuated and generalized form. At puberty it concentrates on the sex organs, grows into a drive which rapidly reaches its maximum in a few years and then very gradually declines during the decades that follow.

At some stage in his evolution man freed himself of the seasonal rise and fall of his sex-instinct and was then able to cohabit daily for many decades, while the female became able to conceive all the year round. If man limited his sex-life to the purposes of propagation he could in many cases confine himself to two or three cohabitations every year, which would be entirely contrary to the physiology of his genital apparatus. It would also be against all biological laws if the propagation of the species were left to the discretion of the individual, and it is just for this reason that the sex-instinct is far more powerful than is necessary for the continuation of the species.

We do not know, but it seems reasonable to assume that early Paleolithic Man imposed few limitations on his sex and that only as his culture and the cortical censorship of his instincts developed did he start to raise a large diversity of sex taboos— most important among them the taboo on incest. This taboo probably did not become strict until Neolithic times after the connection between sex and pregnancy was understood, as it may then have been realized that incest would tend to limit the growth and health of the clan. Modern psychiatry has clearly shown that the aversion to incest is a cortical phenomenon and not innate in man's animal nature. Indeed, man's first sexual desires are usually incestuous.

There are thus three evolutionary factors which underlie many of modern man's sexual disorders. They are the complete domination of fear over sex, the enormous force of the sex-urge far in excess of the requirements of procreation and the strict cortical censoring of the sex-instinct.

In modern man the ancient dangers that threatened the copulation of his forefathers have largely disappeared. They have been replaced by new fears which are cortical and no longer physical. When the Neolithic cortex laid the heavy hand of its reasoning upon the genital sphere, it did not shrewdly try to learn from man's animal nature. In its presumptuous and high-handed manner it worked only with concepts which it drew from the inorganic, artificial world it was in the process of creating. It conceived such utterly false notions as, for instance, 'a man must preserve his strength; he must not waste his substance —as if man were given a pot of semen capable of being emptied.

If such a belief were true, the same would have to apply to the use of a muscle, whereas it is well known that disuse is detrimental to all muscles and weakens them. By the same reasoning, it would have to be concluded that conserving gastric juice by eating pap improves digestive capacity, whereas the contrary is true. There is no limit to the amount of sperm that can be produced by normally-functioning glandular tissues of the testicles, just as the female ovary has tens of thousands of potential egg-cells, of which only about five hundred mature during a lifetime—one a month for about forty years. Again there is this enormous margin of safety.

It has long been suspected but only recently proved statistically by Kinsey that sexual inactivity leads to the early cessation of potency, while increased sexual activity never does. Where this seems to be the case, premature impotence is invariably due to fear or cortical censorship and not to the exhaustion of the genital apparatus. False notions such as those mentioned above are a common source of fear in civilized man. They play a great role in the problem of masturbation and in the impotence of middle-age.

The usual mechanism that leads to premature impotence is the perfectly normal phenomenon that fear, worry or anxiety of any kind may on a given occasion interfere with erection. Unfortunately, the cortex is not necessarily aware of such fear and does not connect cause and effect, jumping to the wrong conclusion that the failing erection was due to genital exhaustion. This notion evokes new anxiety, fear and remorse, quite sufficient to turn every future 'attempt' into disaster. Due to this misunderstanding, sexual activity becomes more and more restricted and then prematurely ceases altogether, owing to prolonged disuse of the genital apparatus.

In the female the corresponding disorder expresses itself as an inability to achieve orgasm. The fear that prevents orgasm in an otherwise normal female may be the possibility of being disturbed. The female continues to be alert and cannot give herself up entirely as she is meant to do after she has surrendered to the male. Moreover, the male is often excited by the risk of disturbance, the female hardly ever. The difficulty is that in the modern sex-relationship the female often considers it her duty to give in to the male's courting before she feels safe, this being contrary to her primitive nature. She may be frightened of disturbance, of pregnancy, of pain or discomfort, the latter often because she is not fully prepared.

Premature ejaculation is another disorder which has a psychosomatic and hence an evolutionary aspect. Animals and primitive man do not curb their sex-instinct: that is the prerogative of modern civilised man, who has, by devious ways, come to look upon sex as a base and undignified urge—like tippling, smoking or indolence—to which he often reluctantly gives way. He thus rarely yields to the sex-instinct to the extent of which he is capable, and it is his cortex which applies the brake.

Semen, produced continuously in the testicles, is stored in two little sacks that lie beside the prostate gland—the seminal vesicles. There is a close relationship between the pressure of the stored semen against the walls of these seminal vesicles and the amount of sexual stimulation required to set the ejaculatory mechanism in motion. The fuller the seminal vesicles are, the less hormonal, psychological and tactile stimulation they require to set off contractions and thereby cause the emission of semen. Of this the 'wet dream', or 'pollution'—as it is revealingly called—is a clear example.

A premature ejaculation takes place when, at the time of coitus, the seminal vesicles are filled to capacity, and in this case it is both normal and inevitable. A disorder only starts when the phenomenon is incorrectly interpreted as a sign of weakness, than which it is nothing less. Labouring under this erroneous notion the disappointed male, often encouraged by his equally disappointed partner, still further restricts his sexual activity, with the result that the disorder unfailingly recurs. It is typical of modern man's attitude to sex—tainting even those who should know better—that in premature ejaculation the only logical advice, greatly to increase sexual activity, is so seldom given.

As fear is at the root of most functional sexual deficiencies, it is obviously wrong to treat them with stimulants such as aphrodisiacs and sex-hormones, which merely force the cortex to increase its block. Sedatives, physiological instruction and psychotherapy directed towards making a subconscious fear conscious are much more likely to produce results. In these cases the old tranquillizers—the bromides—are still the most suitable, and it is to be hoped that they will not be swept into oblivion by a deluge of quick-acting, less toxic, but also less lastingly effective, modern synthetic substitutes.

Marriage

Many of modern urban man's sexual deficiencies stem from an ever increasing cortical censorship over the diencephalic sex-instinct. Sex is the last instinct to have come under cortical control; therefore the cortex is still terrified of its getting out of hand, and a psychological crisis may follow when sex does crash through abnormally strong cortical barriers. To understand why this should be so, it is necessary to make a clear distinction between the instinct of sex and its cortical elaboration, which here will be called love or eros in the Greek sense.

The sex-instinct consists of the urge towards release in physical intimacy and the preliminaries of courting when these are purposefully directed towards coitus. Love in the sense here used is the wide emotional periphery with which the cortex surrounds the sex-instinct. Romance, friendship, companionship, the appreciation of the physical beauty or intellectual accomplishment of the beloved, the non-physical intimacy of an engaged couple, mutual confidence, respect and the planning of a married future all belong to this emotional periphery. The love which holds a family with grown-up children together and the mutual attraction which overcomes sexual incompatibilities and which persists after the cessation of all sexual activity in old age are also part of a cortical build-up around the instinct of sex.

This build-up is a cortical construction involving all the senses, memories and associations and particularly the censorship of the sex-instinct below the level of consciousness. The nature of this erotic structure depends on whether it has been built around a free and legitimate sexual activity in which the diencephalic sex-instinct can find an uninhibited outlet through the cortical barriers or whether the cortical build-up proceeds without physical consummation. An erotic construction erected before diencephalic release in cohabitation with the person concerned often ignores the enormous force of the diencephalic break-through in coitus when this finally takes place.

In the course of a long, platonic engagement the cortex builds up a complicated network of erotic associations of romance, admiration, getting to know each other, parental approval or otherwise, financial and career considerations, future life together, the question of children, religion, etc. The one thing this network often ignores, except for vague longings, is coitus. After exhausting ceremonies, such a couple suddenly and un-romantically finds itself faced on the first night of the honey-moon with the need to release the sex-instinct and to let sex run its course in a cold, new and unfamiliar environment of a hotel. This sudden unleashing may often have one of two results. Either the previous cortical build-up is so strong that the raw instinct can no longer break through, or the break-through destroys the build-up.

When the erotic cortical build-up is too rigid to allow the sex-instinct free passage, the female feels only shame, horror, dis-gust or fear; she may suffer an attack of vaginism, not achieve an orgasm or be frigid. The male may find himself impotent and disappointed, particularly if he has a premature ejaculation. From then on both partners generate a growing resentment to-wards each other, instead of blaming their own pre-coital emotional build-up for the failure of the wedding night.

Now one might think that this difficulty could be overcome by pre-marital sex; yet this is not so. Whenever sex is indulged in during betrothal, this may have the advantage that gross physical incompatibilities are discovered before it is too late; but the great disadvantage is that such sex is illegitimate and calls for secrecy and contraception. The need for secrecy deter-mines the nature of the erotic cortical build-up. When then after marriage sex suddenly becomes legitimate, the whole pattern changes and that fundamental change may block the normal sexual outlet. That is why a sexually very satisfactory illegiti-mate relationship so often becomes disastrous as soon as it is legalized in marriage.

Partners who blame each other for their deficiencies sometimes wish to reassure themselves of their own sexual validity. To do this they yield to an adulterous temptation, enter into a casual relationship without any previous erotic build-up and find that they are able to cohabit satisfactorily. Thereby their cortex, not understanding the real reason for this, becomes more than ever convinced that the marriage partner is at fault. The cortex reasons that when adulterous coitus is satisfactory, matrimonial failure must be due to the husband or wife, as the case may be. Obviously, in some cases this may be true, but it is not neces-sarily so. Many marriages go wrong because the failing partner cannot understand the reason for his or her failure. If an intellectually satisfying explanation based on the peculiar functioning of the human brain were forthcoming, many such marriages could be saved. To these unhappy couples the marriage counsellor must talk physiology and not heavily-loaded psychoanalytical jargon. They need instruction, not analysis, because they are 'in endless error hurled' and not neurotic. By its own reasoning the cortex never admits its mistakes, and such marriages are doomed to be wrecked on the rocks of cortical presumption, unless instruction is given.

The other unfortunate consequence of a long, romantic and chaste engagement can be that on the wedding night crude diencephalic sex is able to break through the cortical build-up and in doing so tears it to shreds, shattering all the enchantment of the days of betrothal. These are the couples who cannot stand each other all day but can have satisfying intercourse all night. Cortical eros broken by sex is not nearly so serious as the cortical blocking of sex, because a sexually satisfied, intelligent couple can often build up a new and different erotic structure around the diencephalic sex-chimney which, being legitimate and approved, now passes through the cortical censorship. Such a new, post-nuptial cortical structure is particularly normal, natural and strong if it includes the desire to have children, and the fulfilment of that desire further enforces the new erotic attachment. If children are not desired, post-nuptial love is usually more precarious because a normal woman can find no emotional fulfilment as long as she represses the biological sequence of bearing a child after she is sexually satisfied.

It would therefore seem that whichever way a long engagement is handled it is fraught with dangers for conjugal happiness. Only those who are constantly in touch with modern urban married life, such as Roman Catholic priests, doctors, psychiatrists and lawyers, know the rarity of a really happy and satisfactory modern marriage; they see what goes on behind the pretty facade of conventional marital propriety and are horrified, rarely realizing that a long engagement—be it chaste or otherwise—is often to blame.

Man's evolution and the twenty years or so his offspring require before they can dispense with parental support forcefully suggest that he is by nature monogamous. This does not mean that he will not occasionally and casually cohabit with another woman, but that he discard the mother of his children merely to obtain sexual relief with another woman is certainly contrary to his basic nature. Modern man's polygamous inclinations—in the sense that he is often ready to divorce his fertile wife and re-marry—are the result of three factors. One is that Western civilization fiercely condemns prostitution, concubinage and casual adultery. The second is that sex does not usually become legitimatized until many years after the instinct has passed its peak, which it does a few years beyond puberty, forcing man to look upon untold women as desirable sex-partners before he can gratify his sex-instinct with conventional, social and religious approval. The third reason is that modern man eventually chooses a wife for himself on grounds that are often purely sexual and not primarily conjugal. If then during a long en-gagement his sex is suppressed, he keeps a roving eye on the seductive charms of other women, and this pattern he carries with him into matrimony.

In a society which confines legitimate sex to wedlock, it is inevitable that matrimony often be entered into primarily for the purpose of sex gratification free from social stigma. Concep-tion becomes a *cura posterior* rather than a *primum movens* in making the decision. When then a child does arrive, it may dis-rupt the erotic relationship of its parents, because the wish to raise a family has not been the centrepiece of their cortical build-up from the outset.

Western man is surrounded by civilizations more ancient than his own. Their matrimonial customs are older, and in these civilizations conjugal felicity seems to be a less important prob-lem. In his self-righteous way Western man explains this by alleging that the 'poor' womenfolk of other civilizations or races are less 'emancipated' than his own, though many anthropo-logists admit that Western man and woman are perhaps the most inept of all races in matters of sex.

Though innumerable examples could be quoted, orthodox Hindu customs—with which the author happens to be familiar —will be used as an illustration of marriage-usages that lead to a greater happiness and stability of wedlock. It is not suggested that any of these customs be adopted by Western man as a solu-tion to his matrimonial difficulties. They are here described merely as a way of showing the origins of some of our marriage problems. We cannot fall back on earlier solutions; our troubles can be avoided only by finding new ways of dealing with them.

According to ancient Hindu custom, marriages are arranged exclusively by the respective parents. The choice is made meticulously, consideration being given to financial and familial background, genealogy, caste, health, intelligence and—not least important—beauty. What is rigorously excluded from consideration is love; in fact, every precaution is taken to prevent bride and bridegroom from seeing each other even at a distance, though if the parents already have Western leanings the prospective couple may be shown photographs of each other. In any case, the whole matter is often sealed and settled before puberty.

During the marriage ceremony bride and bridegroom are veiled, and only when the rites are over do they catch a first glimpse of each other's face, beautified with sophisticated Eastern cosmetics and framed in the finery of gorgeous silks and extravagant jewellery bought at great sacrifice by even the humblest. Symbolically the bride gives the groom his first ceremonial meal by placing a morsel of food in his mouth, and then they are again whisked apart and fêted separately.

Though they have only recently reached sexual maturity, the sex act has been explained to them without prudery or circumlocution. It has been presented as a wonderful, almost sacramental, initiation into man- or womanhood, and so when at last they find themselves alone they are like two excited children thirsting for those things to happen about which they have heard and for which they have been adequately prepared. Thus they are almost playfully initiated into sex. There has been no cortical build-up whatever, and of such a couple the diencephalon blissfully takes care without cortical encumbrance. For them their parents have provided a rapturous feast of the senses, and they know nothing of the burden which choice and decision load upon our youth, nor of the blight of parental disapproval with all its dire consequences for future happiness. The young bride enters her father-in-law's house, where she is received with warmth and tenderness, and as soon as she becomes pregnant she is treated with admiration and even respect by the whole large family. Some months before her term is up she leaves her husband and returns to her own family, where she is confined free of all interference from husband or in-laws. Only as a proud young mother does she return to her husband.

In such a marriage post-nuptial love can grow healthily and luxuriantly, and every student of orthodox Hindu marriage very soon comes to the conclusion that it does. Long after early ageing and many pregnancies have played havoc with the physical charms of his wife, the average Hindu male preserves for her a love, a tenderness, an esteem and a faithfulness that rarely find a match in Western urban society. At the early adolescent age at which Hindus marry, no sexual patterns have been formed; no cortical love obstructs the sex-urge, which at that time is so forceful that any blemish the well-tutored young wife may have is easily smothered in the joys of sexual fulfilment.

Young Indian newly-weds often indulge in sex to a degree that seems fantastic to Westerners. This is not because they are 'over-sexed', but simply because they are cortically less inhibited. Notions that over-indulgence may be harmful at their youthful age do not enter their heads, as such ideas have never been suggested to them. In eighteen years spent among them, the author has never seen any deleterious effects of sex carried to the point of exhaustion followed by a few brief hours of profound sleep and a full day's work continued day after day. This is because sex is self-limiting long before harmful indulgence is reached, and that could hardly be otherwise, as it would be contrary to biological laws if exceeding the margin of safety were left to the discretion of the individual.

There are very good reasons why a match made by the parents without regard to the sexual tastes of the marriage partners is apt to result in a more successful union than when the choice— and hence the responsibility—is the concern of the couple themselves. One reason is a law discovered by Zondy—the great Hungarian psychiatrist. Zondy found that attraction between two persons depends on their genetic structure. Inherited traits may be dominant or recessive. The sum of the dominant traits determines the appearance of an individual and is called the phenotype. Though the recessive traits do not appear in the phenotype, they are nonetheless present and may be inherited by the next generation. The sum of the dominant and the recessive traits makes up a person's genotype. Zondy's discovery is that a person having hidden recessive traits which correspond to the phenotype of another person will be strongly attracted to that person. Thus mutual attraction will be strongest if A's recessive traits correspond to B's phenotype and B's recessive traits to A's phenotype.

Cortical considerations do not enter into this genetic type of attraction. It is mutual 'love at first sight' and completely over-powering. If such a couple marries, they can almost certainly be assured of physical happiness and compatibility. Unfortu-nately, however, a person's genetic make-up is not necessarily all good. Hidden among the recessive traits of one and overt in the phenotype of the other there may be highly undesirable qualities of disease, insanity and characterological weaknesses, and these will be strongly accentuated in the offspring, causing untold misery to the parents. Yet the elementary force of this type of attraction renders the partners deaf and blind to all such considerations. When the choice is left to four parents with an entirely different genetic make-up—their marriages having also been arranged without spontaneous mutual attraction—the chances of genetic factors determining the choice they make for their children are remote. When two persons fall violently in love with each other, it is because they are genetically akin. The children of such a love are therefore to some extent exposed to the same genetic dangers as the offspring of an incestuous union.

It was probably to avoid the dangers of genetic attraction that older civilizations found it wiser to eliminate pre-marital love from marriage altogether, and there can be no doubt that this procedure is extremely effective. The compensation offered to the young for not being permitted to fall in love is the institution —rather foolishly called 'child-marriage'—which spares them all the many sexual problems of Western adolescents.

It might be argued that the still existent custom of concubin-age draws an ugly smudge across Oriental conjugal happiness, though it is confined to an utterly insignificant minority. Yet concubines do not affect an Eastern marriage to anything like the extent that the Western woman imagines, because to the Eastern mind sex and love are two entirely separate things, while in the West this is no longer so.

Through the centuries of Western civilization the sex-instinct has become more and more cortically repressed; it has, there-fore, also grown increasingly insistent and troublesome. At the same time the cortex has had to continue tightening the mesh of its censorship, and in doing so it hit upon the ingenious device of scrambling sex and eros and pretending that they are the same thing. This cortical trick is an extremely successful way of smothering the sex-instinct and keeping it under cortical control. The process has now gone so far that sex without love is frowned upon, while love without sex is ridiculed. Neither of these attitudes exists in other races, where diencephalic sex and cortical eros are much more clearly distinguished.

Once initiated, the sex-act is entirely under diencephalic control, and it is the more satisfactory the less the cortex interferes with its accomplishment. The muddling of love and sex is a source of endless conflict in modern Western sex relationships, yet there is no hope of a return to the earlier separation of the two. In evolution, be it biological or cultural, there is never a way back. Problems that arise can be overcome only by new solutions, never by old ones.

Though we cannot yet clearly see a way out, young men and women seem to be treading new paths which look promising. They are in open rebellion against the older maxim that, unmarried, they must regard themselves as sexless until they are already on the declining side of their sex-urge—say, twenty-five years of age. The modern young have, in dead earnest, developed an almost 'monogamous' society of their own, in which everybody seems to know who belongs to whom. They indulge in presexual dances and stirring musical rhythms, which seem to provide them with an outlet to which their physiology entitles them. The alarm with which the older generation is watching this development is probably unfounded. There is nothing morbid about these gregarious festivities, nor is there any evidence to suggest that they foster juvenile sex any more than the older ways. Sex-experienced adults are inclined to think that adolescent sex is similar to their own, in which coitus is the natural consequence of any sort of stimulation. With adolescents this is not so, as in them stimulation in dance and being together is not necessarily a means to an end but an end in itself.

As in modern Western society the sex-instinct cannot be legitimately channelled at an early age, it needs voluntary cortical control. This control must be inculcated as a conventional necessity of civilization, like the table manners that control the

instinct of hunger or the polite abstinence from violence under
the influence of rage. It is thus the conformity to a civilized
moral code which must be taught and for which voluntary
co-operation must be sought. This does not lead to the cortical
block by fear of physical retribution, which later causes so much
trouble. Sex must not be made to appear sinful or abnormal any
more than hunger is, nor must it be ignored or presented as
despicable.

Modern middle-class urban parents no longer make it a rule
that a suitor must be financially able to support their daughter
on the standard of living to which she has been accustomed.
They allow a young couple to marry on the security of career
prospects and are becoming increasingly prepared to guarantee
minimum support when necessary, just as in the old Hindu
joint-family system or among our simple peasants. It is at last
being realized that in modern Western civilization the best sons-
in-law cannot hope to support a family before they are thirty.
If, with insufficient means of their own, men marry early, they
may spoil their careers; and if they wait until they are sufficiently well off to support a wife in the luxury she is used to, the
pattern of a bachelor's promiscuous sex-life will certainly not
have prepared them to become more faithful husbands.

Modern urban man will have to extend his parental support
not only to adolescent education, but also to the sex-life of his
post-adolescent children. The notion that a beloved daughter
must have all the luxury of her home is a figment of middle-
class imagination. Most normal girls will delightedly exchange
a father's generosity for a home of their own, a man of their own,
a child of their own and a normal sex-life, even if this means a
few years of penny-pinching. In the same way a young husband,
free from sexual turbulence, can better devote himself to his
studies and his career in the security of economic support.

Marriage before a young couple is able to support itself has
the further immeasurable advantage that in such a union the
parents on both sides must be heard. Unless the parents approve,
the marriage cannot take place—at least among sons and daughters who have been brought up in a happy, balanced home
against which they feel no need to rebel with wild adventures.
It is extraordinary how careful the young are to take parental
approval into consideration once they know that there is, in

principle, no objection to giving financial assistance when the choice is fully approved. They realize that this will open the gate to legitimate sex without the need for secrecy and contraception.

In most countries parents are not rich enough to take the risk of having to support another family, or indeed several other families. For one thing, they are burdened with taxes for social services. In such countries it is the social services which should help to carry the load of happier young families by furnishing generous maternal benefits, free medical services, free education, lighter taxation and cheap housing for young couples, even if they are not earning wages. Some countries are already far advanced in these directions, but they are motivated by the desire to be fair to all, not necessarily by the realization of how important it is to encourage youth to marry early and to remove the financial burden of propagation.

In matters such as these, the younger generation is always biologically wiser than the older one. Fighting a hopeless rearguard action from the crumbling battlements of a past generation causes painful wounds on both sides. A little mock skirmishing may be good and educational as long as the older generation is aware that it is doomed to be the loser or to destroy the happiness of its sons and daughters. A previous generation can no more turn back the clock of cultural evolution than poor, outmoded Don Quixote could ever have become Sir Galahad or a valiant Crusader. The best the older generation can do is to watch the behaviour of the young, anxiously looking for signs and symptoms which indicate new ways of coping with the older problems.

Divorce

Just as modern Western man confuses diencephalic sex and cortical love, he no longer distinguishes between biological and cortical morality. Murder, manslaughter, robbery, thieving, giving the life of the mother priority over that of the offspring and the voluntary breaking-up of a fertile monogamous union are all things that do not exist in wild life. They are contrary to the best interests of the species and also contrary to the natural course of evolution. Their condemnation as unethical arises out of deep-seated, ancient biological instincts, and that is why

Western man's oldest moral preceptor—the Roman Catholic Church—clings to them so tenaciously.

But there are other moral precepts which have no deep biological roots; they are purely cortical and have arisen out of the cultural environment which man has created. Examples of this type of morality are claims that sex must be repressed, particularly in the adolescent; that divorce is preferable to adultery; that planned parenthood is an inalienable right and a duty to human society; that capital punishment is a just retribution; that the lame, the blind, the sick and the poor must be helped; that man must love his enemies, yet that the warrior should be regarded as a hero. It would be helpful if opposing schools of thought would clarify whether they are talking about biological or cortical morality, as this would narrow down their argument to the question of whether the biological or the cortical morality should be given precedence.

Cortical ethics are not laws of nature but artifacts, like the rest of human culture, which have no parallel in the animal world. Yet laws of nature cannot be applied to all aspects of modern man's behaviour, because he has placed himself outside of nature, which he already dominates to the extent of having freed himself from the basic evolutionary process of natural selection. Man will never return to those biological ethics which he has abandoned or is in the process of giving up, but he should understand clearly what he is doing. He must, know that when his cortex creates new ethical standards his bodily reactions, controlled by his diencephalon and his evolutionary patrimony, completely ignore the new morality. Unless he knows this, man cannot rid himself of the bodily and subconscious emotional responses to new cortical dictates, because this ignorance debars him from reasoning correctly about them. His presumptuous brain will expect the body to accept cortical fabrications unhesitatingly, and when it fails to do so the cortex wrongly concludes that the body must be out of order.

When conjugal disharmony is blamed on the partner, the often incorrect allocation of blame rapidly widens the rift and creates the illusion that with another partner all will be well. While the sex-life of the unhappy couple fizzles out, there arises a greatly increased temptation to find the ideal sex-partner. As this urge is consciously sex-directed, yielding to it is apt to be highly successful, first on account of the preceding period of abstinence, and second because there has been no previous cortical build-up. Such a relationship will, however, not necessarily continue to be successful after prolonged divorce proceedings have made marriage to the illegitimate partner possible, because the eros built around a clandestine affair cannot suddenly be transmuted into the legitimate pattern. The partners do not foresee nor do they understand this problem; they are therefore unable to reason about it, and to them subsequent disappointment appears a mystery. Another difficulty is that after a second marriage has failed it is often realized darkly that not all the fault lay with the first partner and that had this been understood earlier the first marriage might have been saved. Such a situation engenders a feeling of guilt not fully admitted, with the usual bodily repercussions of which a peptic ulcer is the most common. In some cases this realization leads to a second divorce and re-marriage to the first partner, it having finally been understood that 'it was all a ghastly mistake'.

Wherever divorce is made subject only to legal action and accepted as ethically unobjectionable, it is a concession to civilisation and contrary to the natural behaviour of an essentially monogamous species such as man. There are many strictly monogamous animals just as there are many polygamous ones; monogamy is thus nothing unusual in nature, and there are very important reasons for human monogamy. One is that the human child is not mature by the time the next one arrives, and the last born may need its parents for fifteen years after the mother's menopause. Moreover, parents can never be fully replaced by strangers.

Evolution is not in the least concerned whether parents like or dislike their duty to their offspring; all it requires is that the family hold together for the welfare of the children. It is therefore patently wrong to apply the same law to an infertile couple as to a fertile one. A childless marriage has no biological significance, and what the partners of such a marriage do is entirely their own business. But the moment a child is born to them this situation changes completely. The union then becomes a biological and social obligation and not merely a form of legitimatized sex. A childless marriage should therefore have an entirely different status and be governed by entirely different laws from a fertile one.

Biologically wise, the Roman Catholic Church recognizes this to the extent that it will more readily grant an annulment to a childless marriage than to a fertile one. By refusing to grant divorce it preserves, at least in principle, human monogamy. It seems wrong that a couple who have no intention of raising a family and practise contraception to that end should have the same legal and social standing as one serving the species. It also seems unfair that where divorce is ethically objected to, a person desirous of having children should be tied to an infertile partner by the same status and the same eternal vows as apply to fertile matrimony. There is no biological—and should be no ethical—objection to divorcing, at their request, a childless couple that is unwilling, unable or unfit to raise a family, and there should be no stigma attached to such a divorce. On granting a divorce to a fertile couple, on the other hand, the physical and psychological welfare of their offspring should be determining, and not the wishes of the parents. This would also emphasize the fact that marriage is primarily an instution for propagation and not for sex.

The death of a parent is a tragedy for the child, but a far greater tragedy is divorce, because the child interprets the separation of its parents as being cruelly deprived of one of its most elementary biological rights. It sees in divorce a deliberate, egoistic decision brutally and guiltily to forsake it for the prospect of a happiness in which it takes no part. Divorce shatters children's biologically well-founded belief that they represent the very core of their parents' bliss and makes them feel excruciatingly lonely in a world they no longer understand, a world which is treacherously and venomously hostile to their natural demands.

Modern psychiatry is making it increasingly clear that divorce is highly destructive to the emotional maturing of children and that when it is brilliantly and glibly explained to them that Mummy and Daddy are no longer going to be together or that Uncle So-and-So is coming to stay with them like a new papa, they silently treat the performance with a devastating biological cynicism of which their parents do not dream them capable.

In those countries in which quick-fire divorce is rapidly replacing clandestine adultery and is becoming a way of life among the upper classes, sexual immaturity is increasing; while where clandestine adultery is looked upon with less horror than the destruction of a family and where children have the benefit of domestic emotional security, they turn out later to be more emotionally mature. Yet as it is highly improbable that a society once having taken the step to easy divorce will ever revert to stable wedlock, new ways of saving the children have got to be found.

One way would be to remove them from their parents at an early age so that they are less exposed to parental incompatibility. As long as the parents are able to keep the hatchet buried during the holidays, the boarding-school works reasonably well. But perhaps a better insight into the difference between sex and love and the role of the cortical build-up, a clearer realization of what breaking up a home means to the children and a legal, social and ethical distinction between childless and fertile marriage might provide an even better solution for some of modern man's matrimonial problems.

Masturbation

Masturbation is a normal sexual outlet in the absence or unapproachability of a partner, and under such circumstances it is practised by all members of the higher reaches of the animal kingdom. Its danger is the cortical guilt evoked by moral condemnation and, worse still, the threat of dire physical consequences voiced by persons who are lacking in qualifications permitting them to express an opinion. The heaping of so much anguish upon the adolescent youth whom we deprive of a normal sex-life long after he has reached maturity may cruelly blight his adult sex-life.

Though these views have now been constantly reiterated for several decades by those in a position to judge, the same old nonsense is still being dished out to our boys, while girls are inexplicably much less victimized by this sort of persecution. The hoary notion that a man can 'waste his substance' still seems to linger on, though it has long been known that those who have an early and active sex-life retain their full powers longer than those who are abstemious. Moreover, it would be contrary to biological experience if such an important function

as sex could exhaust itself by over-indulgence. Sex is absolutely
self-limiting and cannot be indulged in to excess as far as the
organic function is concerned, nor is there a shred of clinical
evidence to suggest that its indulgence to the limits of capability
is in any way harmful to the body or the mind. Perhaps the idea
that excessive sex-gratification is harmful has arisen out of a
cortical short-circuit, in which the observation that mentally-
defective persons are uninhibited in their sex is taken to mean
that their lack of restraint has caused their idiocy. Only the
feeling of guilt and the fear of entirely fictitious consequences
are dangerous. They link sex and fear at an early age, and as
fear is the one thing that inhibits human sex, an ugly pattern,
which cannot later be changed when sex finally becomes legitimatized, is thus established.

To contend that masturbation can have disastrous physiological consequences which cohabitation evidently does not is
patently absurd. The condemnation of a normal bodily manifestation may evoke psychological, though never bodily disaster.
Well over 90 per cent of boys masturbate; it has therefore become a normal pattern of behaviour, and the blame for this
lies squarely upon our attitude to sex. Unless that is radically
changed, we should really cease to inveigh against this last
resort open to sexually mature youngsters.

Surely there must be some ghastly mistake when sex, that
should be a joyous heralding of man- or womanhood, is turned
into a drab and lurid conflict in which proud exhilaration is
often dragged down into the mire of youthful tragedy. It is
certainly contradictory that marriage at a very early age is
legitimate and ethically sanctioned, while a youth who is debarred from such legitimate sex is fiercely condemned for
resorting to a harmless outlet, and that this poor substitute which
he is forced to adopt is alleged to be sinful and harmful. It can
be said without scientific hesitation that a youth who has so far
repressed his sex-instinct as never to have masturbated is either
abnormally under-sexed or so cortex-ridden that he will never
achieve a smooth diencephalic break-through when he marries.
The preaching of absolute continence to those who have decided
to give up sex for ever, as in the case of Roman Catholic priests,
is certainly the best way to avoid sex interfering with their
vocation, particularly as it is voluntary; but to apply similar

maxims to the general population is liable to create matrimonial havoc.

Homosexuality

Homosexuality has nothing to do with human depravity or perversion, and it exists throughout the animal kingdom. A strict separation of the sexes in individuals is almost a vertebrate peculiarity, as the majority of the living inhabitants of the earth are bisexual and even in man the evolutionary process of separating wholly male from wholly female individuals is by no means complete.

In civilizations whose conventions do not fiercely outlaw homosexual practices these are indulged in by persons who are both capable and willing to love heterosexually, to raise a family and to perform and enjoy all the pleasures and responsibilities of parenthood. The idea of having to make up their minds whether they are homo- or heterosexual never occurs to them.

Among such peoples there will, of course, always be a few who practice homosexuality to the exclusion of heterosexuality, but their number is not nearly so great as it is among us, who insist on one or the other exclusively. There will also be some who confine themselves to heterosexual practices, but many will be found to have retained into adult life the bisexuality which we must consider normal in the early teens.

In these sex-wise civilizations, of which the Moslem world is an example, there still exists that intimate type of friendship between persons of the same sex. Such friendships have a faint, usually latent, erotic aspect which in no way interferes with the conjugal felicity of the participants of such a union. There is as little odium attached to two men embracing, kissing or holding hands in public as there is to two women doing the same thing in our civilization.

Among us this intimate type of friendship in which each feels ready to give his life for the other, while still existing in adolescent youth, is gradually disappearing from adult behaviour, because an erotic binding has become almost synonymous with a sexual binding, owing to the cortical scrambling of the two. The opprobrium which even a suspicion of eroticism among two of the same sex entails leaves few willing to face the risk of being suspected of homosexual tendencies.

Thus in our civilization an early decision between homo- and heterosexuality has to be made, because bisexual indulgence is regarded as even more depraved than homosexuality. Western cortical morality forces our youth to make a choice between what is presented to them as alternatives just at the time when they are emerging out of an age in which homosexuality is physiological. In modern Western society it is almost impossible to integrate homosexuality into heterosexual and familial life. One or the other has to be sacrificed. If heterosexuality is the loser a pattern is determinedly set, and then, with greater emotional maturity, a return to a heterosexual mode of living cannot be achieved.

When in the late teens the sex-urge is more powerful than it will ever be again, it imperiously demands an outlet. At that age a youth is only very exceptionally, and then only with the help of his parents, able to support a family. Yet over an illegitimate heterosexual affair there always hangs the threat of pregnancy.

Except for their sex organs, men and women are growing more and more alike in mental outlook and behaviour; the romantic, as apart from the sexual, allure of womanhood is waning fast, because we are doing all we can to minimize the inequality of the sexes. Boys and girls have become comrades in work and play. To the modern boy girls are no longer incomprehensible, mysterious beings with whom one day they will have to establish the relationship of love. Girls are increasingly being looked upon as a sex-partner, but one with whom the risks are very great.

Homosexual practices among consenting friends, on the other hand, are free of the perils of an illegitimate heterosexual relationship, and this applies equally to men and women. They are thus often preferred by the intelligent, the ambitious, the scrupulous and the timid. If these had been free to consider marriage at an early age without economic hardship, their youthful homosexual exploits would in many cases have merged easily into perfectly satisfactory heterosexuality.

Within the lifetime of the older generation sexual practices between two boys or girls were not popularly earmarked with a ponderous Greek word. No girl who had a 'crush' on a friend ever thought that this might debar her from intercourse with men. No boy who adored a school-fellow came to the conclusion that he must be abnormal or queer. To-day this is exactly what happens.

If the laws with which sexually regimented countries hunt down homosexuals were repealed, it would perhaps not reduce the number of those indulging in such practices; but it would certainly eliminate the need for emotionally immature youths, deprived of a normal sex outlet, to have to make up their minds one way or the other much too soon. There would then be a good chance of making them realize that a homosexual relationship does not necessarily slam the door on a perfectly normal heterosexual partnership.

Biologically, homosexuality is a normal outlet for the sex-instinct in the absence of the other sex, as is masturbation in the absence of any attainable partner. In man it is therefore common in Eastern harems, at sea, in warfare, in prisons and asylums. It is in such circumstances often practised by persons who would have heterosexual relations if they could. On the other hand, one frequently encounters persons who, by their appearance and demeanour, strongly suggest homosexuality to the experienced observer and yet perfectly manage a hetero-sexual relationship in marriage. There is thus no sharp line dividing homosexuality from heterosexuality; in fact, most people's sex seems to spread to a greater or lesser extent over both sides of such a hypothetical line.

In our civilization—and almost exclusively in ours—bisexual tendencies are categorically denied tacit acceptance, with the result that bisexuality must inevitably be shunted into one direction to the exclusion of the other. All too often our youth decides for the homosexual gratification it knows, rather than the unknown heterosexual outlet from which it is debarred because it is fraught with all the dangers of social and religious ostracism, economic complications and possibly a ruined career if practised out of wedlock.

The only alternative is prostitution, hardly a satisfactory solution. It would be ideal if youthful sex could be sublimated in such profound emotional attachments as, for instance, 'hero-worship', but the over-burdened curriculum of day-schools and the pictorial boosting of film stars and champions who cannot be approached leave little room for this type of sublimation, which is spontaneous and not the result of cortical determination. Legislating upon such matters is bound to achieve just the opposite result of what it intended, as legislation artificially sets up clean-cut sexual alternatives which are biologically non-existent. It is characteristic of the profound sagacity of the Roman Catholic Church and of Islam that they do not advocate the legal persecution of homosexuality among consenting partners, however much they may disapprove of such practices.

Among modern Western homosexuals a large contingent is made up of those who are psychologically debarred from sexually approaching the opposite sex. They identify all members of the opposite sex with their corresponding parent and would thus, as a consequence of this identification, be committing what to them amounts to incest if they had heterosexual intercourse. This subconscious conflict they cannot face, and so for them there only remains homosexuality as a cortically permissible outlet for their sex-instinct, though women may sometimes take refuge in frigidity.

A man's subconscious identification of all women with his mother—and in the case of girls, all men with their father—is always the result of a sexually-tainted fixation upon the parent at or just after puberty. Abnormal parent-fixation has become increasingly common in modern man partly on account of our complex civilization, which requires an ever longer period of parental surveillance before the young are ready to face life alone, and partly because open parental disunity is so frequent in the modern home. When its parents disagree violently, the child is forced to take sides in the domestic strife, and it usually attaches itself emotionally to the parent of the opposite sex. Such a close union between the child and the parent of the opposite sex, in which they become allies against the other parent, throws a balanced emotional maturing out of kilter.

The trouble with our enormously prolonged parental surveillance is that this must continue long after the child has reached sexual maturity. It then all too often happens that in the stormy upsurge of puberty the child gets its first sexually interested glimpse of adult nakedness from a careless parent of the opposite sex; and if during earlier childhood an excessive fixation to this parent has already become established, this glimpse assumes a subconscious, but nonetheless real, sexual character. To make matters worse, the unwitting parent is very apt to encourage and tighten the abnormally close binding, often as a substitute for a lack of conjugal felicity. If parents would realize how very dangerous such carelessness or egoism is for the emotional future of their children, they would in many cases save themselves the disappointment of having homosexual sons and lesbian or frigid daughters.

In wild life the progeny is brutally turned out to fend for itself the moment it is sufficiently mature to do so. But animals either reach physical and sexual maturity at the same time, or they become sexually mature after they can dispense with their parents. In modern man sexual maturity is acquired almost a decade before body and intellect can be sufficiently trained to face life alone. The only solution to this dilemma is to let the parents or social services carry the economic responsibility for early marriage. It certainly seems probable that with the widening of the gap between sexual and intellectual maturity the incidence of homosexuality will continue to increase. This tendency will be enhanced by a delay in repealing the laws against it; by the recklessness with which modern parents throw themselves into the emotional arms of their children; by failing to realize that the sight of a nude, adult body can do no harm to a teen-ager unless that body belongs to the parent of the opposite sex, and finally, by the popular misconception that a person must be downright homo- or heterosexual.

Seen from the evolutionary point of view with an eye on the survival of the species, and reason having been found for alarm at the speed with which our cerebral processes are burgeoning, an increase in homosexuality is not altogether a biological disaster. Among homosexuals the intelligence rating is high. If the propagation of outstanding intelligence is curbed it will be regrettable for the impatient ambitions of our civilization, but it will delay the extinction of Western man by slowing down his cultural advance, the pace of which is becoming biologically dangerous.

PART III

AN OUTLOOK

11

Survival and the Human Psyche

As RESEARCH into the finer working of diencephalic mechanisms and their relation to psychosomatic disease progresses, it may become possible to say exactly why anxiety will in one patient lead to spastic colitis, in another to arterial disease, in yet another to diabetes, and so forth. In many cases an inherited trait is responsible for the localization of the disorder, but in others those organs or systems which are already a source of anxiety are particularly liable to be involved, because the cortex is watching them with apprehension and is therefore prone to establish a cortico-diencephalic vicious cycle involving that particular organ or system.

For instance, a patient whose parents have both died of heart disease will be anxious about his own heart. When then a normal diencephalic response to an emotion causes his heart to beat faster or when gastric distension pushes his heart out of its usual position, he will be inclined to interpret what he feels as the beginning of the disease which killed his parents, thinking that he has inherited a weak heart. At once all his fears cluster like a swarm of angry bees on his heart, a vicious cycle is established and thus anxious cortical supervision may eventually lead to organic lesions. He and his family will then be convinced that he did indeed inherit a weak heart, yet this is not at all true.

However, it seems probable that the localization of psychosomatic disease also depends on the particular kind of anxiety, rage, guilt or frustration which is at the root of the disorder. In the chapters on disorders of the intestinal tract it was suggested that a repressed feeling of sexual guilt produces a peptic ulcer but that repressed religious or ethical guilt expresses itself as ulcerative colitis, though both diseases are caused by the same mechanism of extreme intestinal spasm. Many more such relationships between emotional variations of the same instinct and

269

the organ in which they find their clinical manifestation will almost certainly be discovered. But further progress along these lines can only be made after psychiatry and somatic medicine agree to adopt diencephalic physiology as the arena in which they will meet to settle their differences. Just as somatic physicians cannot hope to understand psychosomatic disease without reference to cerebral processes, so psychiatrists must realize that they can make little useful contribution to the clarification of these disorders as long as they confine themselves to the cortex.

In trying to cope with psychosomatic problems, somatic medicine sets its sights along the road which led it to spectacular success; but it would seem that the achievement of cortico-diencephalic peace does not lie on this road. This can be reached only after some high hedges have been cut down so as to allow research to go farther afield. The rigid experimental discipline that served man so well in the past is in danger of finding itself caught in a blind alley, in which the congestion of scientific data is blocking the main traffic—the alleviation of human suffering. It looks as if now that medicine must face subjective as well as objective facts, the continued adherence to the rules of factual observation is bringing a glorious era to a close.

In a brief span of one hundred years or so, the straight and narrow path of medical research developed surgery to limits beyond which there remains little room for further major conquests. Mechanical lungs, hearts and kidneys have been constructed and much of the working of the human cortex can be electronically reproduced. Every type of anaesthesia has been perfected and patients can be put in a condition which is almost identical with that of a hibernating animal. The great epidemics and innumerable infectious diseases, malnutrition and the dangers of infancy and childbirth have been very substantially reduced. The physics and the chemistry of the human body have been studied in their finest ramifications and man's anatomical structure is known in its minutest electronmicroscopic details.

Such stupendous results could be achieved only by following strict methods of research in which physical, chemical and animal experiments ruled supreme. This grand epoch raised the average life expectancy to almost double what it was and endless pain, suffering and tragedy have been abolished. Yet modern man's health and longevity are being increasingly threatened by a number of diseases for which no 'wonder-drug' has been found. In many cases research has discovered ways of alleviating suffering from these diseases and of prolonging the life of their victims. The removal of an ulcerous stomach, the introduction of insulin and the use of reserpin are a few outstanding examples of the therapeutic achievements of the passing era; but they differ from such discoveries as the antimalarial drugs, antibiotics, Salk's polio vaccine, etc., in that they are directed towards the suppression of a symptom and not to the elimination of the cause of the disease. They are therefore palliative and not curative.

A disorder can be prevented and cured only after every aspect of its causation is fully understood. The causation of all those diseases which are grouped together under the designation psychosomatic will never be understood so long as methods of a differently directed era of research are applied to them. By their very nature psychosomatic disorders cannot yield their secrets through physical examination, test-tubes, X-rays and laboratory animals. Further research conducted in this false hope may provide new and better palliatives but will not lead to the discovery of a single cure or method of prevention. Meanwhile, the public is growing alarmed. Its confidence in modern medicine's ability to deal with psychosomatic disorders is waning and the non-scientific fringe of 'healers' is thriving in its heyday.

Since the genius of Freud furnished it with entirely new tools of research, psychiatry has been busy polishing and sharpening them. It is offering these new weapons to the proud aristocracy of an era which is all but spent, but the offer is being haughtily rebuffed. Hesitatingly and with considerable misgivings, psychiatrists are beginning to be allowed to talk to somatically ill patients, but woe betide them if they dare suggest that prescribed diets, drugs or operations are in many cases a waste of time and money or that their own specialized knowledge might be usefully employed in the clinical management of a slipped disc, diabetes, gout or chronic diarrhoea.

Orthodox somatic medicine is still profoundly suspicious of psychiatric encroachment upon its field. This suspicion is justifiable. First, psychiatry concentrates on the cortex and does not include diencephalic physiology in its central sphere of interest. It has thereby isolated itself from the functions of the body. Second, psychiatry is trying to prove its worth in mental rather than bodily disorders. This is a pity, because the demonstration of its use in psychosomatic disorders would be most convincing to somatically orientated physicians who are not interested in mental derangements and do not consider themselves competent to deal with them. Somatic physicians have to be convinced in their own domain. Third, somatic medicine realizes that its very existence as an advancing branch of science is threatened if it adopts psychiatric methods—so different from its own—as wholeheartedly as it does the stethoscope, the blood-pressure apparatus, the laboratory and the surgeon's scalpel.

If in a new era man's animal instincts and reflexes were made a basis of study as an approach to disease, and if in psychosomatic pathology we would stop applying to man conclusions drawn from the behaviour of animals that have an entirely different evolutionary history, new ways of handling these disorders would soon be discovered. But such is the conceit of the human cortex that it refuses to see itself as a bodily organ, like the liver or the pituitary gland, with a physiologically interpretable function. Physiologists and anatomists may be awed by the tremendous complexities of a human kidney in health or disease, but this reverence for the miracles of evolution stimulates them to further studies; it does not make them shy away, as does the somatic physician when the brain and its functions threaten to intrude upon his neat and all too facile interpretation of psychosomatic disorders.

The majority of physicians of the somatic school readily admit that psychic factors play a role in many bodily disorders, but that is often as far as they get; they are loath to find out exactly what this role is. They will concede the usefulness of a sedative, but they rarely give the psychic factor a prominent place when they map out a therapeutic programme for a psychosomatic patient. Only as a last resort do they refer the patient to a psychiatrist, and this usually means that they are through with the case. In so doing they completely overshoot the mark, because in most cases the psychiatrist is just as helpless without the physician as is the physician without the psychiatrist. Psychosomatic disease cannot be cured by somatic therapy or by psychotherapy alone, for the same reasons that a surgeon cannot perform a major operation without an anaesthetist. No amount of sedatives, antispastic medication or dieting will cure a spastic colon, nor will years of psychoanalysis. It is only when both these approaches are combined in a clear understanding of the underlying diencephalic mechanism that quick and lasting results can be obtained.

If machines can be built to perform certain operations far better than the human cortex just as a microscope can reveal finer details than the naked eye, there is no more reason to postulate miraculous processes at work in the cortex than there is to consider them operating in the eye. To the cybernetic engineer cortical operations are no longer a mystery. What still baffles him is the working of the ancient brain-stem with its instincts, reflexes and regulations. These he cannot—as yet— reproduce electronically; in fact he has hardly tried, because he too is cortex-ridden. But the science of evolution now lies before us like an open book in which we need but read to understand from where the strange impulses that prompt our thinking come, and the progressive physician must soon start diligently thumbing this weighty tome.

It is cortical conceit which is holding modern man back from seeing and understanding himself as he really is and not as his cortex would have him be. Gross cortical presumption has led him to believe that the working of his body is influenced by the recent artificial environment which he has created and that hundreds of millions of years of evolution can be ignored because in a few thousand years his brain has built the gilded cage in which he lives.

In the story of evolution there are numerous examples of species that evolved very slowly, eventually became highly successful and then suddenly disappeared from the scene of life just when they seemed to be at the height of prosperity. Many theories have been advanced to explain this phenomenon. In some cases an abrupt change of climate and vegetation, in others the insurgence of new and better equipped animal forms and in yet others over-specialization have been held responsible for the sudden decline of apparently thriving species.

Of these theories over-specialization is believed to account for a particularly large number of cases. Some of the Ruling Reptiles became extinct because their bodies grew so large that their legs could no longer support them. They were forced to live half-submerged in deep water, where displacement kept them on their feet, and this severely restricted their normal diet of terrestrial plants. Their specialization in enormous size may thus have brought about their downfall.

The early carnivora may have died out because they at first very successfully specialized in preying upon their herbivorous cousins, which then learned to outwit them. Possibly the mammoth was hurried to extinction by the excessive growth of long, back-curving tusks which may have become an impediment rather than a useful adaptation for raking up the snow and ice of the frozen tundra. Of similar evolutionary processes innumerable examples could be cited.

Man's peculiar specialization is the freakish development of his cortex, which has a capacity far beyond the requirements of successful wild life. Paleontology suggests that when a particularly useful specialization continues to develop without regard to vital requirements, it becomes independent of a balanced evolution and can flourish far beyond the point of biological usefulness. Even a modern genius uses only a fraction of the potential capacity of his brain, and man's cortex probably still has vast resources of which we are totally unaware. A cortical development going beyond man's needs cannot be explained by natural selection, because a latent capacity serves no vital purpose. Excessive development of an originally useful specialization can only be understood as a process which continues under its own power and is independent of—or even opposed to—the best interests of survival. Perhaps the underlying evolutionary mechanism begins when the specialization becomes a dominating factor in sexual selection and therefore tends to go to extremes.

If the human brain has already entered into such an evolutionary phase we may look forward to a long and exciting intellectual future, but we must also be fully aware of the biological dangers inherent in the process and be prepared to meet the slightest threat to survival arising out of it. Modern man is better equipped than any of his predecessors to recognize such dangers in time because his knowledge of the working of the human brain is greater than ever before, but in the application of this knowledge to the wide range of bodily suffering which is threatening him Western man is as yet dangerously hesitant.

If psychosomatic disease can only be prevented and cured by a better understanding of cortical and diencephalic processes, one would expect races having no such understanding to succumb to psychosomatic disorders when among them there arose a fear quite different from those threats for which their evolution had prepared them. One would expect a cortically conceived hopelessness to have caused bodily symptoms from which they died and which may eventually have brought about their extinction.

Knowing that since the advent of Cro-Magnon Man—about 40,000 years ago—the human brain has hardly changed, it seems most unlikely that mankind has only recently started to suffer from psychosomatic diseases. In the case of modern Western man it is the tight censorial grip in which his conventionally harnessed cortex is holding his instincts and emotions that is causing him despair and frustration, but one can well imagine other events creating a feeling of utter futility and hopelessness and thus giving rise to a psychosomatic form of suicide. For instance, it is still a mystery why Neanderthal Man became extinct in an incredibly short time after a long and highly successful career and why his downfall occurred just when he seemed to be at the height of biological exuberance.

There is no reason to believe that a sudden change of climate or an epidemic was his undoing, because at the time when he faded out another human race—Cro-Magnon Man—was just beginning to thrive. At that time the world was still thinly populated and animal food was plentiful. It therefore seems most improbable that Cro-Magnon Man deliberately set about the extermination of his Neanderthal contemporaries, nor is it likely that he could have achieved this in so short a time, as the Neanderthalers were physically stronger and had weapons not significantly inferior to those of the Cro-Magnons; moreover, the older inhabitants must at first have vastly outnumbered the newcomers.

But the Cro-Magnon brain was superior to that of Neanderthal Man. It had developed articulate speech and the ability to

communicate abstract concepts. Though man for man the newcomers may have been no match for the older and more muscular race, they were much cleverer hunters. One can imagine
Neanderthalers watching from the edge of a cliff how the Cro-
Magnons hunted in the valley. To the brutish, fear-ridden
Neanderthaler these almost hairless giants with jutting chin and
towering forehead must have appeared to be superhuman
spirits. He saw them using a miraculous technique which was
utterly unfathomable and incomprehensible to him. He saw the
animal herds from which he had for thousands of years picked
what he wanted being ingeniously rounded up and driven into
traps, over a precipice or through a narrow gorge into the fires,
the clubs and the spears of hunters who jabbered excitedly and
made strange cries while they waited for the bag. As he gazed at
the elaborate preparations they made for the chase, Neanderthal Man must have felt an eerie terror and a sickening weari-
ness at the futility of his own poor efforts. He must have realized
that against these—what we would call God-like—beings he had
not the slightest chance to compete. More and more he must
have drawn away from such terrifying creatures, not because
they violently threatened his life, but simply because their
miraculous powers were too much for him to contemplate and
filled him with primeval panic.

Wherever the Cro-Magnons established themselves the Neanderthalers probably withdrew voluntarily, abandoning their
old hunting grounds to the newcomers. Gradually Neanderthal
Man lost his will to live a life in which the odds were hopelessly
stacked against him, and in this state of perpetual frustration
he may well have fallen a victim to some form of psychosomatic
disease which hurried him to his doom. Possibly also the cannibalism to which he had formerly resorted only in dire necessity
now became more common and hastened his downfall.

Once insuperable hopelessness destroys the will to live, suicide
is the last step. It is a typically human step, because only the
human brain can transmute the instinct of fear into the emotion
of hopelessness. Thus a possible explanation for the sudden disappearance of Neanderthal Man is that he committed racial
suicide out of fear—fear of the uncanny and seemingly supernatural beings that appeared in his midst. While it is probable
that through the ages Cro-Magnon Man might have ousted the

more primitive race, it is inconceivable that they could have achieved this as quickly and as completely as they did unless the Neanderthalers themselves contributed heavily to their own extinction.

Such a view is not entirely imaginary, as there are much more recent examples of similar processes. When Bechuanaland was first colonized by white settlers, the indigenous Hereros, a proud and warlike tribe, soon realized the utter hopelessness of resistance. They reacted by artificially aborting all their pregnant women in a form of racial suicide which brought them to the verge of extinction.

In the vast continent of Australia the aboriginals are not being pressed out of existence, and yet they are dying out rapidly for reasons which are by no means clear. Careful clinical research has been unable to explain this phenomenon on somatic grounds, and it seems that it is a psychosomatic expression of hopelessness—a form of suicide. Among the Papuans fatal despair seems to be brought on by the belief that the white man owes his superiority only to cultural achievements which really belong to them and which their ancestors had destined for them. By some trick of magic, they believe, the white man has intercepted the traffic of cultural goods on their way to earth from the heaven of the aboriginals' forefathers, the so-called Cargo Cult, thus depriving them of all possibility of cultural advance. Such a conviction is indeed a hopeless plight against which there is no remedy, and so again it may be essentially a figment of the aboriginal's own brain which is leading him down the road to extinction.

The Muruts of Northern Borneo are a primitive tribe of jungle-inhabiting hunters. Only recently in contact with civilization, their numbers are rapidly decreasing; very competent clinical and anthropological studies have not been able to furnish an explanation for this. Of married Murut women 40 per cent have never borne a child, and 37.7 per cent of live births die in infancy. Among the Muruts the usual tropical diseases are rampant; but the incidence is no higher than in other primitive peoples who are not declining in numbers, nor is the tribe in any way being forced out of existence. Thus here too, racially self-destructive processes are probably at work.

History suggests many other cases in which it is thinkable that psychic mechanisms played a greater role than sheer violence in the downfall of a race. It seems improbable that the proud and highly civilized Etruscans succumbed only to the Roman broad-swords; that the great empire of the Incas was physically des-troyed by a band of fanatical hooligans; that the primitive Veddahs of Ceylon, who have vast jungles in which they can live as they have done since time immemorial, are rapidly dying out only on account of pressure from more highly civilized races. Even the fact that primitive races have been known to disin-tegrate when distilled alcohol was brought to them can be in-terpreted as a form of self-destruction through an alcoholic oblivion from despair.

When the horrors of Nazism were at their height and when at one time it looked as if this insane doctrine might attain universal conquest, surviving Jews were often heard to say that in a world so horribly threatened with barbarity they would refrain from having children. If the Nazis had won the Second World War, the Jews who escaped the gas-chambers would surely have committed racial suicide, for which many of them were already planning out of hopeless despair.

Thus a tendency to self-destruction seems to be inherent in the over-developed human brain. It is a situation similar to that in which a parasite thrives so exuberantly that it destroys its host, thereby bringing about its own undoing. As the host can survive if the parasite's rapacity is kept within tolerable limits, so man will survive longer if he can release his body and his diencephalon from the cruel cortical grip to which civilization is increasingly subjecting him.

In psychosomatic disease urban man is already paying a heavy price for his civilization, but he now has the means sub-stantially to reduce the price if he will but make full use of them and realize to what extent his cortical presumption, deluding him that he has full control over his animal nature, prevents him from doing so. Western man will eventually go about the solution of his most pressing biological problem through a better understanding of psychosomatic mechanisms and will not adopt the only alternative, which is to give the cortex full rein; for if he did this, all his behaviour would become governed by rigidly conditioned reflexes. His mating and breeding, his drinking and feeding and all his many emotions would then have to conform to a fixed pattern applying to everybody; this would be entirely contrary to the way of life which he has so far followed.

We can to some extent foresee what happens when the human cortex is in full control of biological processes, as this is exactly the position in modern scientific agriculture and animal husbandry. In a prize bull all the natural instincts have been almost extinguished by careful breeding, and what is left of them is closely controlled and managed for him. He is fully protected from all the hazards of wild life, and, provided this suits his master, the bull runs no risk of his species becoming extinct; in his artificial environment he can survive long after his wild cousins have died out.

Similarly, the complete regimentation of human life to a point where there is no room for any sort of individuality or choice of behaviour can be considered an approach to the problem of human survival. From what one can gather, it looks as if the Communist world is experimenting with the latter approach by trying to apply to mankind the old principles which Neolithic Man used to domesticate animals. The ideology is based on the assumption that this is the only way to progress and welfare.

On biological grounds it seems unlikely that, in spite of great initial achievements, the Communist doctrine will succeed in cortically domesticating man or in taming his instincts. If Communists included selective breeding in their programme they might reach what seems to be their goal in a few thousand years, but without strictly controlled breeding it will take tens of thousands of years before the cortex can gain full control over the diencephalon, however fanatically cortical dominance is strived for. Again and again the diencephalon will find ways of circumventing the conditioned reflexes with which the cortex tries to contain it.

For a while the process of physically eliminating all those who do not or cannot conform may appear to solve the problem, but the use of terror induces a decline in the will to live and cannot therefore be continued indefinitely. When such methods bring about a marked rise in the standard of living, education and public health, the deleterious effects of cortical dominance will remain masked for some time, as there will be a rise in population, vitality and enthusiasm. In the early stages totalitarian terror is much less prone to produce the type of psycho-somatic disease from which Western man suffers, because it is consciously felt, accepted and not repressed. Only when, in successive generations, the mere thought of non-conformity becomes unacceptable for conscious contemplation and is therefore repressed, will an increase in psychosomatic disorders become alarming. If then the therapeutic procedure of making a guilt-laden emotion conscious continues to be fraught with the dangers of police reprisals, there would appear to be no way of coping with psychosomatic disease.

When other civilizations catch up with the highest economic standard of Western man, they will be forced to forego many of those cherished doctrines which enabled them to reach this standard. They will be forced to abandon their projects towards cortical domination and have to revert to the safer approach of cortico-diencephalic peace which Western man can envisage now. Only by the biological process of selective breeding has man been able to rear a lap-dog out of its wild ancestors, and it took him thousands of years. He has never succeeded in making a wolf behave like an Alsatian by mere training, and when he tries he ends his efforts by eventually shooting the poor creature, because he finds himself unable to control its instincts. Similarly, man can be trained up to a certain point, but once his dien-cephalic endurance is overstepped he either breaks away or becomes psychosomatically ill.

As Western man does not need ruthless cortical dominance to achieve prosperity, and as such cortical oppression as he has already imposed upon himself is endangering his health, his main biological problem is to tackle psychosomatic disease. This he can do by allowing the contending forces in his brain to come to terms. He can make peace between his animal nature and his cortical world by arranging for give and take on both sides. His cortex must renounce its presumptuous fiction that it already rules supreme and be prepared to make great conces-sions to the diencephalon, which it must accept as a partner seriously to be reckoned with in the management of human affairs. In return the cortex can be given a much better con-scious control of the animal instincts, because these will have been raised out of the obscurity to which they have been con-demned by the censorship at the level of consciousness. The diencephalon will readily accept such an arrangement, because it corresponds exactly to the pattern of man's pre-cultural evolution. The modern diencephalon is not rebelling against conscious cortical control. Only the repression which confines it to the subconscious and the utterly lacking cortical comprehension of diencephalic mechanisms force it to react by causing psychosomatic disease.

It is very unlikely that modern man will succumb to climatic changes, epidemics or destruction by his own technical achievements, which he has hitherto always proved himself capable of controlling. His almost complete domination of terrestrial fauna and flora in all parts of the globe makes it highly improbable that any new superhuman species can arise on the planet and bring about his downfall, though what space may eventually hold in store for him we do not know.

As far as one can now foresee the only enemy that seriously threatens man's continued existence is his own brain, with which he has so far been unable to come to biological terms. There seem to be ways of doing this, but it will be a hard struggle. Much of what he now cherishes will have to be dropped by the wayside, and it will be painful to tear himself away from many of those concepts to which he owes his spectacular rise. If he wants to free himself of the threat of psychosomatic suicide, he will sooner or later have to perform the painful operation of allowing new insights to criticize what he has hitherto considered the acme of his wisdom.

Ante Finem

The author is aware that he has been tramping on ground where angels fear to tread. He realizes that for this he must expect to be called severely to order.

It will be said that his approach is unscientific and his results undocumented, that his presumptuous cortex has jumped to too many conclusions and that his speculations go well beyond the scientifically permissible.

He can meet these justifiable criticisms only by stating it to be his belief that modern medicine is over-populated with pusillanimous angels who dare not use their tender feet.

INDEX